Informal Schools in Britain Today

This is one of three books prepared by the Anglo-American Primary Education Project, which contain descriptions of the way British primary schools work. The contents are also published as twenty-two individual paperbacks by the same publishers. The titles in the series have been cumulated in these hard cover volumes for the convenience of librarians and institutional users.

An additional title, THE PUPIL'S DAY by Ann Cook and Herb Mack, a series of photographic studies showing a typical school day for five young children, is available only in paperback form.

The paperback version of John Horton's MUSIC includes a 33⅓rpm 7 in. record.

Maurice Kogan, Project Co-ordinator
Anglo-American Primary Education Project

Informal Schools in Britain Today 1

Curriculum

Citation Press, New York 1972

ISBN 0-590-07277-3

Library of Congress Catalog Card Number 78-185539

This book is published simultaneously in Great Britain, Canada and other countries of the British Commonwealth by Macmillan Education Ltd and in the United States by Citation Press, Library and Trade Division, Scholastic Magazines, Inc.

Designer Richard Hollis

Printed in Great Britain

Preface

The purpose of the Anglo-American Primary Education Project is to provide descriptions of the way that British primary schools work. They are published in this series under the general title of *Informal Schools in Britain Today* and they have been written for American and British educators and teachers-in-training as well as for the general public.

The authors are either practitioners or expert observers of British primary education and, in most cases, they document the work of the schools through detailed case examples; where it is relevant, implications are stated and conclusions drawn. It is not the intention to provide theoretical discussions or prescriptive manuals to informal education, but rather to present accounts from which deductions and generalizations can be made. In so doing, these statements draw on the experience of that large minority of primary schools that have adopted informal methods.

It is hoped that these books will help educators who are looking for examples to substantiate change in particular schools and also those who are concerned, as teachers, educators or administrators, with the wider implications of the education of young children. For students who plan to become teachers these accounts of what happens in the classrooms of British primary schools provide ample material for discussion as well as helpful insights into the practice of teaching.

The series has been prepared under the aegis of the Schools Council in England with the support of the Ford Foundation in the United States. Planning was assisted by a small Anglo-American advisory group whose members are listed on page 6. The views expressed are however personal to each author.

British Directorate

Geoffrey Cockerill, Project Chairman/Joint Secretary, Schools Council for Curriculum and Examinations, London.

John Blackie/Formerly Chief Inspector, Primary Education, Department of Education and Science, London.

Molly Brearley/Formerly Principal, Froebel Institute College of Education, London.

Maurice Kogan, Project Co-ordinator/Professor of Government and Social Administration, School of Social Sciences, Brunel University, Uxbridge, Middlesex.

American Participants

J. Myron Atkin/Dean, School of Education, University of Illinois, Urbana, Illinois.

Ann Cook/Co-director, Community Resources Institute, 270 W. 96th Street, New York.

Joseph Featherstone/Writer; Lecturer, John Fitzgerald Kennedy School of Government, Institute of Politics, Harvard University, Cambridge, Massachusetts.

Professor David Hawkins/Director, Mountain View Center for Environmental Education, University of Colorado, Boulder, Colorado.

Herb Mack/Co-director, Community Resources Institute, 270 W. 96th Street, New York.

Marjorie Martus/Program Officer, The Ford Foundation, New York, N.Y.

Casey Murrow/Teacher, Wilmington Elementary School, Wilmington, Vermont.

Liza Murrow/Antioch-Putney Graduate School of Education, Putney, Vermont.

Mary Lela Sherburne/Director, Pilot Communities Project, Education Development Center, Newton, Mass.

Contents

Acknowledgements

The publishers wish to thank the following for permission to use photographs:

Fox Photos Ltd: pages 359, 360, 362, 364
Froebel Institute: page 372
Henry Grant: pages 313, 314, 315
G. W. Hale: pages 334, 336, 337, 338, 342, 343, 344, 345, 346, 347, 348, 349, 350, 351, 352, 353, 355, 363
John Howard: page 171
Vollans Photography: pages 423, 429, 430, 438

Mathematics for Younger Children

Edith Biggs

The Author

Edith Biggs, BSc, MA, has taught mathematics in grammar schools in various parts of England. She has also worked with teachers and children in many parts of the United States of America, and in other parts of the world. She was appointed His Majesty's Inspector in 1950, and in 1960 assumed special responsibility for meeting the demands of primary school teachers for in-service training in mathematics. In 1964 she was appointed Staff Inspector for mathematics. Her publications include: MATHEMATICS IN PRIMARY SCHOOLS, Schools Council Curriculum Bulletin No.1, HMSO 1965; FREEDOM TO LEARN (with J.R.MacLean), Addison Wesley 1969; MATHEMATICS TODAY (series of textbooks with Miss H.E. Vidal), Ginn, London 1947.

Introduction

So much has happened in the field of mathematics during the past fifteen years that it is not surprising to find some teachers in schools and some lecturers in colleges and universities, as well as the general public, confused about the issues involved.

There have been two major developments: first in the method of teaching the subject, and secondly in the content itself. The resulting changes sometimes reinforce each other—but in the initial stages they were quite separate, as I shall try to show here.

The change in teaching methods began more than thirty years ago in infant schools and was not extended to junior schools until ten years later. Despite large classes, teachers who realized the importance of a stimulating environment gave careful consideration to the quality and scope of the materials, stories and poetry they provided. The quality of children's art and craft, movement and creative writing became more individual and more imaginative. The narrow number syllabus was extended to include more purposeful counting and measuring.

There was a brief period (known as the 'free-activity' period) when some teachers thought that children could learn from a stimulating environment without the help of the teacher. (I remember one experience, in an infant school of nearly six hundred when the noise and confusion were more than I could stand. The teacher was unwilling to interfere except to prevent the children from doing physical harm to each other.) Happily this period was relatively brief, and its infection not widespread, but unfortunately it left a legacy of terms easily used in a derogatory sense, such as 'playway', 'free play' and 'free expression'.

How has the exploratory learning of today developed from such free activity methods of twenty years ago? First, teachers think carefully about the environment they provide, whatever the subject under consideration. Secondly, although the teacher should remain fully in control of the situation, this method of learning is different from class instruction. It is essential that the children work in small groups or even, on occasion, individually. The teacher needs to know when to ask a question of a group, either to start them off or to help their learning further, and when to observe what the children are doing and keep silent. She also needs to know when they are ready to practise skills, for practice is still essential. And at times a teacher needs to teach. There are some facts which children cannot discover for themselves, and these the teacher needs to tell them.

The strength of this method of learning is that it applies equally to aspects of the curriculum other than mathematics—for example, English, physical education, music, history and art. The teacher uses a wide variety of methods: class discussion at frequent intervals, group and individual investigation, group oral practice and individual written practice when the children are ready for this. The chief aims of this way of teaching are: first, to set children free to think for themselves; secondly, to give them opportunities to discover the order, pattern and relationships which are the essence of mathematics and which are to be found in the natural as well as in the man-made world; thirdly, to give children the skills. The third aim is just as important as the other two. But practice before children are ready (that is, before they have an adequate oral number knowledge of addition and subtraction facts) leads to inefficient methods (for example counting on in ones). Teachers are well advised not to begin written calculations (in isolation from experience) before the children know their number facts. But this does not mean that children should not record their findings at an earlier stage—for example, using three-dimensional materials, pictorially, by diagrams or in writing.

This way of working makes rigorous demands on the imagination and mathematical knowledge of a teacher. Many teachers, lecturers from colleges of education, advisers from local education authorities, and HMIs have been concerned with in-service courses for over twelve years. They can therefore appreciate the hard work which countless educators have contributed. They have watched some of this hard work and enthusiasm come to fruition in our schools, and have no doubt of the great benefits derived when pupils learn by this method, rightly applied. For the teachers it means relentless hard work on all fronts. For the children it can ensure success in a subject so abstract that it used to elude the majority.

Before continuing further, a brief description of the changes which have taken place in British infant schools, particularly during the past twenty years, may help American readers to understand expressions such as 'family grouping' and 'the integrated day'.

In Britain, children normally enter school at the beginning of term (semester) following their fifth birthday. This means that children are admitted three times a year. If all classes begin with the same number of children (more than forty when this experiment was initiated) children from each class have to be promoted each term to make room for the new entrants in the youngest class. So in one year a child might have three different teachers. In rural areas, however, all children from ages five to seven have long been successfully taught in one class.

Some teachers decided, therefore, to try the experiment of family grouping of the kind practised, by force of circumstance, in rural areas. The children in an infant school (age range five to seven-plus) were allocated to classes of equal size, each class comprising children from the entire age range. In this way new entrants could be allocated to a class which was already a settled 'family' unit. Of course, this arrangement has some problems, for example, older children may not be fully challenged (the headmistress of the school often makes herself responsible for taking the oldest children from each class at some time during the day). But most of the teachers at infant schools where family grouping is practised are convinced of its merits.

Another development arose as teachers became less timetable-conscious. When children were given more opportunity to choose what investigation they undertook, they often became completely absorbed in their task. Teachers were therefore reluctant to disturb them and divert their attention to another subject. In this way the programme has become more co-ordinated. Some teachers have developed this idea further and now attempt to integrate several aspects of the curriculum. For example, when a group of children are engaged on an investigation, the teacher tries to ensure that the use of reference books, a written account, a dramatic performance, the making of a model or picture, measurement or even a calculation are included.

These different ways of working have been accompanied by changes in classroom arrangement and equipment. In infant classrooms today—and in many junior classrooms, too, since the changes now affect many of these schools (age range, seven to eleven years)—it is usual to find the room divided into sections. In older classrooms this may be achieved by using bookcases, cupboards on their sides, or tables. A few schools are now purpose-built —but there is still much experiment to be done both in classroom method and in architecture. The sections often comprise a book corner (sometimes carpeted to ensure quietness), a section where water and materials for painting and representation of various kinds are available, a dressing-up and a home corner, a construction section where tools and waste containers are stored, a science section where children add their finds and questions from day to day, and a section where measuring materials of all types are kept. Some of the sections change emphasis as children's interests change.

How can a classroom be organized so that individual children have the varied opportunities they need when learning in this active way? How do we start? How can we prevent the classroom from becoming chaotic? How can we make a framework? How can we keep track of children's progress? Should a child be allowed to continue his investigations until he has found a solution or until he has lost interest? Should the timetable be flexible enough to allow this? How can a teacher ensure that she divides her time fairly among all the groups and individuals? What happens to the rest of the class while the teacher is attending to one group or even to one child? These are questions which concern teachers who are about to plan their work in this way. This is not the place to answer these questions in the detail they deserve. Other books do this more adequately.[1] A slow start may eventually be more rewarding. Teachers as well as children need to become accustomed to this way of working and to accept the responsibilities it demands.

A classroom in which discovery methods are well established is certainly not chaotic but it is usually busy, lively and exciting. Some children who become completely absorbed in a problem fall silent. Others want to talk out their ideas with their companions or with their teacher to help them over a difficulty. The teacher provides opportunities for learning in the form of real materials, environmental and structural, which are interesting or might be useful, and questions which will provoke thought. She observes the children, listens to their discussions and asks more questions when this is necessary.

The examples described here arose either spontaneously, as a result of the interests of specific children, or because the teacher, realizing the needs of certain children, planned the work herself. It is important to emphasize, therefore, that 'structure is in the mind of the teacher'. The teacher needs to be constantly aware of the framework within which she is working.

[1] MATHEMATICS IN PRIMARY SCHOOLS, Schools Council Curriculum Bulletin No 1, HMSO 1965. Also I DO AND I UNDERSTAND, Nuffield Mathematics Teaching Project, Chambers/Murray 1967

The examples following are not a blue-print for successful learning of mathematics. They may not appeal to children in different circumstances and in different surroundings. It is the teacher's own enthusiasm and interests which are often 'caught' by the children and transformed by them. The examples should not, therefore, be taken as they stand, although they may well be a source of ideas for teachers to apply to the children they teach.

It is important, too, to remember that children learn at very different rates. Some children will make automatic responses which lead their teacher to think that they have understood a concept when in fact they have not. Careful observations may well reveal that these children need more experience, perhaps in a different context.

To quote one simple example, children may well learn, through handling real objects, the relation: $5 + 2 = 2 + 5$. But this important concept cannot be said to be apprehended until it is put to good use. (Children find it much easier to add 2 to 5 than to add 5 to 2 in the early stages.)

In the accounts which follow, in Chapters 1 to 5, many of the experiences described support the experimental findings of Professor Jean Piaget. For example, the lengthy and varied experience required by some children before they acquire the idea of conservation of number. This is the concrete operational stage.

I should like to thank all children and teachers whose work in the classroom has given us so much pleasure.

1 Setting the Scene

The first narrative, written by a teacher of young deaf children, who had recently returned to teaching after bringing up a family, shows a very gifted teacher at work. She plans her day carefully in order to exploit the possibilities of the environment to the full. She is constantly on the watch for opportunities which will give the children mathematical experiences. She follows these up carefully to ensure that the children acquire basic knowledge in number, measurement and shape.

The class of four- to five-year-olds with which this work was carried out was an unusually oral and bright group of deaf children. The children came to me with plenty of free-play experience with all kinds of material, including simple sorting for colours, shape, size, etc. They could also count to ten fluently, but they could only use numbers up to five or six, as one would expect.

At first, I tried talking to the children in ones or twos as they played, but I found this was not very satisfactory. The children disliked having to stop for a long time in the middle of their play for me to try to get something across to them. I found I was having to repeat myself up to half-a-dozen times as I moved amongst the children. Gathering the class together in an informal group for talks—perhaps on the floor—worked much better. Then, next day, a short comment as the child played, helped the play to be more meaningful and purposeful. In these group talks, I frequently found I had to tell *them something basic at first, or demonstrate something new and then* let things develop.

I have grouped the work under specific headings, but of course, it was intermingled throughout the year. Certain topics followed each other in a logical sequence. We began by learning the words 'same' and 'different', as I felt these would be the most immediately useful. With these we could compare and comment on practically everything around us; and this really pleased the children. Then we tried the words 'a few', 'a lot', and 'nothing', learning them as a group, using all sorts of material. For example, I put my hands into a box of gravel, and scooped up as much as I could. Then I let it fall slowly on to a sheet of paper and said, 'This is a lot'. After they had all looked and repeated, I poured it back into the box and said, 'Now there is nothing'. Then all the children each had a turn. Similarly we tackled the word 'few', and I found they often 'played out' these group talks next day during free play. We went on to play with other materials—Smarties, other small sweets, sand, acorns, and so on. Then, instead of emptying the material back each time, I said, 'Can you make this few into a lot?' or 'Can you make this lot into a few?' One very young child, under four years old, at first did not know how to reduce a lot into a few, and kept adding more in the hope that the pile would disappear. All the children loved me to ask them to add or to leave nothing. They seemed fascinated by the empty table. Soon, the work became more individual, and we began to use specific numbers of soldiers, rabbits, cars, and other subjects. For example—'Nicola, put out four soldiers . . . Add two more . . . How many altogether? . . . Now take three away . . . How many are left? . . . Well, can you make that into five soldiers? . . . Now, can you leave only one soldier?' (and so on). In time the children became very competent and free with this work.

At the beginning of the morning, we 'marked the register', using a flannelgraph and felt figures. The blue figures were for the boys, and the red figures for the girls. At first we used a 'one to one' relationship. Picking up a blue one, I would say, 'Peter came to school'—and so on. Then—'But Paul stopped at home'—and so on. Then we counted how many girls and how many boys had come to school and wrote it on the blackboard. I linked the two numbers together. Then we counted how many children there were all together, and put up the correct felt number on the flannelgraph. At first I used the felt figures myself, and the children sat round and *watched. Then they asked to do it themselves, and took over. As time went by, they changed from using names, and, quite rapidly, counted how many boys and how many girls were present, and put up the appropriate numbers of felt figures—boys grouped together, and girls likewise. Then one day I put two of the red figures on one side of the blue ones, and two on the other side, and they were lost! They could only see two girls, and two girls—they could not see four any more! But not for long—the children grew so competent that, knowing there were nine in the class at the time, they knew that there must be three at home if six were in school. This work lasted from about January to May.*

We did a lot of number work at milk time—in a group. At first we counted the number of children and the number of bottles, having first checked—'one for Andrew', 'one for Peter', etc. We noted that the number was the same. Over the weeks they became aware that these numbers must be the same, or there would not be one each. Then I tried taking all the tops off, and hiding them in my hand, asked how many they thought there would be. They had no idea! They were quite intrigued with this relationship between the number of children, bottles, tops and straws—if we were having one each. Then, one day, one of the children separated the bottles of milk on the tray into those for the boys, and those for the girls. This opened the way for more opportunities of addition and subtraction. There was always much amusement if the child giving out the milk held up the last bottle and looked perplexed, wondering whose it was. The children also took turns in putting two straws into each bottle, and it was interesting to see how the quicker ones, if given five or seven straws, could quickly sort them out into two, two, and then an extra one to make up another two. The very slow child always put the straws in one at a time—he did not pick up two of anything until the week before the summer holidays.

At lunch time we all have lunch together in the classroom. Mac, my nursery assistant, and I sit at opposite ends, and the children sit on each side of the table. The length of the dining table depends on how many children are in the class—we simply join enough individual tables together. The children were surprised to find there was a reason why I asked them to pass the salt to Mac. It never occurred to them that it was because of the length of the table. They were interested to note how we could pass the salt to each other quite easily if the table was short. As the children were seated down each side, we counted the number of children down one side, and then I counted out the appropriate number of plates, and likewise for the other side. We wrote the two results on the blackboard sometimes, piled the plates together and counted the result; and wrote that on the blackboard. Sometimes—under my very close supervision—I let the children hold the pile of plates to feel how heavy they were. The children were encouraged to ask for specific amounts of food—'a lot', 'large', 'small', even 'very small', 'medium' and so on. We used numbers of spoonfuls for milk puddings—four or five spoonfuls. Those who loved milk pudding knew only too well that five was more than four, and that six was even greater!

One day I heard that Ruth had been going up a shallow flight of stairs in twos saying 'two, four, six'— so we all went over to the hostel to this shallow flight, with large number cards, one to ten, and laid them on the stairs, one on each stair, with the numbers turned inwards for easy reading and counting. First, we took turns walking up, counting as we went, and then back down again. This was their first introduction to counting from ten down to one. Then we walked up the stairs, two-at-a-time, first using the odd numbers, and then the even numbers. From then on the children really understood about alternate ones out. Back in class we had follow-up games—count-downs for rockets; a sort of 'musical chairs' in which they could only sit on chairs marked with even numbers—or, sometimes, odd numbers –when the drum beat stopped; we also threw numbers on the floor, putting a square around all the odd numbers, and a circle around all the even numbers, to show the pattern of alternation; then we hopped or jumped onto odd or even numbers, saying them as we went.

Before the year ended, I tried a piece of written work on the board. Peter was with me and was quite familiar—

from previous work—with the words 'Add one more'. I wrote this on the board and we started, using bricks. Half-way through, Peter suddenly realized what was happening, dropped the bricks, took the chalk out of my hand, and wrote up the rest himself.

Time

We have a large jig-saw clock; one piece holds the central hands, and there are twelve more pieces, one for each number. This was a particularly favourite toy—I think they were fascinated by the idea of the numbers going round—and playing with it taught them the clockwise direction of numbers. Using this, and the school clock, we would talk about 'nearly lunch time—we must wash' and then 'lunch time' and so on. From that they learnt approximate time. This was enough I thought. We also talked about the movement of the days of the week. I made a chart naming each day. Beside each name was a little picture illustrating something special we did on that day, for example, Monday—came to school; Thursday—dancing; Friday—go home; Saturday and Sunday—stop at home. We had a movable pointer which could be moved from Monday downward. Saturday and Sunday were grouped together, and then the pointer moved to the top again. It was a great help to the young boarders to see 'home' day coming nearer and nearer. We could work out—'three more days to going home' then 'two more' . . . and so on.

Weighing

Before we started weighing, I let the children play freely with the balance for a few days. I watched with some amusement as they put something on one side and then wondered why the balance became crooked. They often tried to correct this by straightening the top bar with their hands, and then looked puzzled when they took their hands away and the balance went back to a lopsided position!

[1]Heaviness and lightness are relative terms. It is perhaps less confusing to use the comparatives: 'heavier than' and 'lighter than' a chosen object

Then I gathered the group around me and produced the balance, and a carefully selected number of toys and materials, all of which were either very heavy or very light.[1] First, I picked out half a brick, weighed it in my hand, and said, 'This is heavy'. I passed it round the group for them to feel the weight. Then we put it on one side of the balance to watch the reaction to something heavy. Peter suddenly stood up and imitated the action of the balance. I was delighted! Then we all took turns, so that the children could really understand what was happening when we weighed something, and it was surprising how many children raised the heavy object on high, at first! I drew two circles on the floor and into one we put this heavy object. Thus, into the circles we sorted all the heavy and light objects, after testing. We finished up by counting how many of the things we had weighed were heavy, or light. The children themselves noted and imitated how a pan only moved downward slightly when the toy was light. Then we went on to compare two things—perhaps a small piece of metal and a large chunk of polystyrene. At first, I always made sure there was a definite difference. We hand-weighed first—no comment from me—and then I invited them to say which they thought was heavy, and which was light. When we had all offered an opinion, we tried weighing them in the balance to check. I found that this young age group did not like a lot of small objects—they preferred a single 'hand-sized' toy or familiar substance. At first, I was able to fool them with a large piece of sponge or polystyrene, but not for long. They became quite intrigued with these substances—so much size, and so little weight. After plenty of experience of differences of weight. I then offered them, one day, two like objects of similar weight. They did not know what to say about them, and looked quite startled when they balanced. Towards the end of the year we went on to small numbers of objects, such as cotton reels. If I put three cotton reels on one side, could they say how many would be needed on the other side to balance them? No, they couldn't! They all looked quite perplexed, and it took some time before they really understood. We only used numbers of reels or bricks up to five. I tried going further—comparing numbers of unlike objects—cotton reels with bricks, or large shells with 'conkers' (horse chestnuts), and entered the results like this; but only one six-year-old really understood this enough to want to do it on her own during free play. The others enjoyed doing it in the group with my help.

1	2
2	4
3	5
4	7

Money *The children bring sixpence for the school fund on Monday. First, we learned the names of the coins, and pointed out the appropriate number on the wall. After some time, I was delighted to note a quibble creeping in—that I should call the small one 6d, and a much larger one only 1d. Then Andrew arrived one day with two 3d pieces—and 'no sixpence!' I tried to show that this was just the same and we wrote it on the blackboard. Only the day before, there had been three boys and three girls in class, and Ruth looked quite startled as the connexion between the money sum and the number sum became apparent. Thereafter, each Monday we put out the money in a row, and noticed all the different ways of making 6d. They had to take my word for it, as their adding was not fluent enough; but they were most impressed and interested—and it did make a start. I also let them write the 6d in my little book each week. Before the year ended we also played a little 'shop' with pennies only, up to 6d, and at least they learned to give me the right number of pennies I asked for, and not just to hand them all over for me to take out what was necessary.*

Capacity *At first, I could find no meaningful lead-in, and then a set of standard-sized polythene milk bottles arrived. I realized that in their daily bottle of milk I had a set amount, with which they were all familiar. Just before milk time—so that the milk need not linger in any other container—I brought out the quart, pint, half-pint and one-third-pint bottles. I put them in a row, then produced their bottles of milk. We decided which polythene bottle was the same as their own. I poured a bottle of milk into this one-third-pint bottle, and we all agreed that it was indeed the same. We then looked at the half pint bottle—I asked where they thought the milk would come up to, and they said, 'the top', just as it had for the one-third-pint. They were all surprised when it did not! Immediately, they wanted me to try the pint and quart bottles—so we poured one bottle of milk into each and they were all most intrigued by the way the level of the milk dropped in each larger bottle. They asked if they could drink out of the new bottles; so I gave them straws,* *without comment, and we all had quite a bit of fun watching the child who had 'bagged' the quart bottle— his straw would not even reach the milk, and then dropped in! We continued this work until they had a good idea of where the known amount would 'come up to' in other vessels. Then we tried another idea—how many of our one-third-pints would fit into the pint bottle, and then into the quart bottle. When we came to try the half-pint bottle, we learned the word 'half', and I tried to show them how the half-pint bottle held one-and-a-half of their own bottles. Peter argued about this. He thought it ought to be two-and-a-half—he could see a half bottle of milk left, but I had opened two bottles! We learned the words 'full', 'half', and 'empty', and went on to use all sorts of shapes in water play. They particularly enjoyed making things half full. They wanted to go on to 'quarters' but I thought it was too soon. When discussing the amount of custard in the jug at lunch time we used 'a little bit', 'half', 'a lot' and 'full'. We also used a wide variety of containers for free play and experiment with sand.*

Length and shapes

We learned the words 'long' and 'short' first, and discussed how these were different from 'large' and 'small'. We examined all kinds of things around the classroom and in the cupboards. We played with lengths of ribbon, vinolay, string, cardboard, and so on. I would hold up two pieces, and the children decided which was long and which short. Then, I might move one piece up or down and ask again which was long and which short. One or two made mistakes at first, but it did not take long for them to realize that the length remained the same whichever way I moved the pieces. Then I tried the same method using strips of the same *length. Funnily enough the 'sameness' of length, regardless of position, took longer to acquire, but when they were sure that they were still the same length, I varied the positions of the two strips even further, and later used three and then four strips, all of the same length, and in all positions. We would start with them all in a row, so that the children could see that they* were *the same, and then they all took turns in moving them around. One day, without* comment, I moved the four 'same' strips into a square. They all looked quite interested, and we learned the word 'square', which I drew and wrote on the blackboard. Then I held up two long strips and two short strips, and we discussed how many of each there were. I handed them to a child, and asked her to make a shape. She immediately made a shape—and then looked amazed and puzzled. We left her alone for a few minutes, and it did not take her long to sort it out, and make an oblong. Before I could teach the word, Peter jumped up, very excited, and said 'Five, no, no, wait a minute'— and he counted round the oblong. 'One, two' (for the first long side) 'three' (for the short side) 'four, five', and 'six'. He knew a square had four sides, and this was his way of describing the new shape. I was thrilled by the spontaneous effort. I introduced the new shape as 'oblong'—not 'rectangle' as that sounded too much like 'triangle', which I wanted to use later. We discussed the fact that it had two long and two short sides. We examined objects around the room, and picked out the long and short sides.

Later, we learned the words 'round', 'triangle'—I simply handed three strips of paper to a child and asked her to make a shape, and then introduced the new word —and 'oval'—we used a hoop, slightly squashed by each child in turn. Then with all these new words, and this new knowledge, I brought out some boxes. We all examined these, and commented on the various shapes that go to make up a box, for example, a Typhoo tea box has oblong and square sides. To my surprise they described a Vim tin as having two 'rounds' and an 'oblong' shape.

Then I brought out a great pile of boxes and put them in the middle of the floor. I drew a large square on the floor and asked them what it was. Then I drew a large 'round' in another corner; then, as I started to draw a triangle they all shouted 'triangle', I realized that they must have some awareness of angles, for they knew it would not be an oblong. When I had drawn all the shapes, I let them sort the boxes into the various chalked shapes. They loved it. One child asked where a Typhoo tea box ought to go, as it had both square and oblong shapes. I asked her what she thought, and she decided 'oblong', which it was, predominantly. Another child, with a very flat, squarish cigar tin, looked amazed when it fell open, and 'changed' to an oblong. We let him put it in with the other oblongs. At the end we were left with the large egg carton which had contained all the other boxes. Peter looked around and saw almost nothing in the oval section, so he put the egg carton there. I looked surprised, but Peter pointed out the large egg printed on the side; so we left it there! They loved this kind of sorting, and I was sorry there was not time to sort the same pile of boxes for colour and size.

Afterwards, each child cut up a box and pasted the pieces on a sheet of paper. Then we counted the number of pieces on each child's paper. They were quite surprised to find everyone had six. They also played with large wooden mosaic shapes. They knew that two triangles made a square, and two squares an oblong. They had noticed spaces were left if they used circles, so they were not keen about using these! One day, Ruth thrilled us all by making a square with strips, and then, as she played with some cardboard shapes, a thought suddenly occurred to her, and she tried filling the large square with small square shapes. Then she counted out to us that she had used nine. She was really finding out for herself.

Stories, art, dancing, recipes

I found, as I went along, that the more I knew about the new trends in mathematics, the more I was able to use opportunities as they arose. For example, when I told the story of The Three Bears everything was drawn on the blackboard, and we discussed who would be likely to use the large bed, and so on, instead of me simply stating who had which. We also had models, and, to my delight, even my very slow child could match each to each correctly. We painted pictures, and all could paint the different sizes beautifully and freely. In free cut-out work all the children could cut out three different-sized bowls to put on the table. In dancing we found many ways of imitating the three bears. We could crouch low to walk as a baby, medium high for mother, and tall for father. We could take tiny running steps for baby, normal walking steps for mother, and long, slow strides

Baking corner for
six-year-olds

for father. After Jack and the Beanstalk *I gave them
long strips of paper, and we painted a long beanstalk.
We painted other long and short things—trousers,
socks, and so on; and we cut pictures out of magazines.
We made four large wall-charts with the cut-out pictures for 'large', 'small', 'long' and 'short'. We made
gingerbread from a recipe on the board, just using large
or small spoonfuls of things, for example, half a packet
of margarine. We rolled the gingerbread and cut out
shapes from templates to make a gingerbread house.
Peter pleased me by examining one of the templates and
showing me how it was made up of a triangle and a
square! This work was a little too long, but the children
were pleased with the result. The children mostly by
themselves, also made orange juice from a recipe on the
blackboard, and very competently, too.*

In the next account, another teacher describes
one aspect of her work with older, normal infants
(six and seven years old). She, too, emphasizes the
importance of questioning, the place of discussion,
and the need for the teacher to give guidance whenever this is required.

**Talking
mathematics**

*Some mathematics arises by discussion between the
teacher and a group of children. Children may be part
of such a group for up to twenty minutes or so several*

Child sorting—'What shall I make?'

times in a week. The work will usually be practical, and there will be plenty of communication in the group. The subject matter is usually controlled by the teacher although it may have arisen from either everyday situations, or from the materials the teacher provides. The work from week to week will normally show some progression.

This 'talking mathematics' group may be neglected by teachers who are afraid of not being able to ask the right question. Unfortunately you cannot tell beforehand whether it is the 'right' question—if there is such a thing. Sometimes you see afterwards that it was a useful question—sometimes there is no response. The 'group talk' may lead to follow-up activity with materials the teacher provides. This should provide the 'continuity' which seems to have disappeared from many schemes.

It is because I feel an inclination myself to neglect this way of working that I give, below, notes on some group discussions which seem to have been successful.

A seven-year-old using a hundred square to fill in multiples of three

Talking about a collection of household boxes. Containers in wide variety form an important part of the 'shape corner' and children often try to make similar boxes from card or sort them in various ways. Talking with a group may go something like this:

'Everyone choose a box...

'John do you know what was in your box?...

'Tell me about the shapes which make it...

'Who has a box which is like John's?'

(*This question is deliberately vague because I want to explore what arises from* their *ideas of what is like and what is unlike. No two boxes are* identical.)

'Yes, Linda, how is yours like John's?...

'Can you find any ways in which it is different?...

'What shapes would you have to cut out to make one like yours?...

'Are any other boxes like John's and Linda's?'

There are many variations on 'talking boxes'. Sets of building shapes lend themselves to this approach, but the household boxes seem more productive in the long run, as the children gradually add to the collection and

seem to become aware of the shape of things around them. The underlying ideas are 'sameness' and 'difference' and 'what makes it?' (for example, classifying and constructing).

Follow-up activities, apart from sorting and making could, for adequate readers, include a 'quiz' with questions like 'Can you find any boxes with triangular ends? Make a list . . . Can you find a box which has two different squares in it? What did it hold when it was full? . . . How are the Smartie box and the salt drum the same?'

Dienes logical blocks (blue, red and yellow shapes, circles, squares, rectangles and triangles—in two sizes and thicknesses). I purposely use an incomplete set for one activity. About eight children are round the table and the blocks are in a heap.

'Do you think that there is enough for two each? . . .
'Do you think there is enough for three each?'

One child shares them out.

'Can you think of a way we can sort the blocks into those which are in some way the same? . . .
'Yes, all the red ones. Put your red ones in the middle.
'How many are there? . . .
'What shapes are they? . . .
'How many squares? . . .
'How many triangles? . . .
'Are there any missing?'

(This last question sounds obvious—how are they to know that I left some out of the box to start with? Perhaps they've had plenty of free play anyway so they know all about them—but, even when I present them to children who have never seen the blocks before, they tell me about these mystical 'missing blocks'—the mental activity in this strikes me as pretty complex.[1])

[1]Those interested in theories of child development and learning are referred to Chapter Two of MATHEMATICS IN PRIMARY SCHOOLS. Schools Council Curriculum Bulletin No 1. HMSO Third Edition 1969

Then we might do the same—with the blue ones and yellow ones.

'Well, now, we've sorted them into colours, can you think of a different way to sort them?'

Gradually shape, thickness, overall size emerge—it gets harder and harder to think of different types of properties.

Next, invite two children to put a block each into the middle.

'How are they the same? . . .
'Yes, they are both thick . . .   Yes, they are both yellow too . . .
'How are they different? They are different shapes; one is large and one is small.   In how many ways are they the same? . . .
'In how many ways are they different? . . .
'Peter, you put a block in the middle . . .
'Can anyone find a block which is exactly two ways the same as Peter's and two ways different?'

Other activities involve one difference, three differences; and a variety of activities along these lines can be devised for follow-up, using work cards, worksheets, etc.

C

Finally, I try to make these doing *and* talking *groups—I think we ask children to write mathematical communications too soon, so that many are struggling with the idea* and *its written expression at the same time. After all we don't ask children to write directly they can speak—why do we sometimes ask them to record mathematics directly they have met it?*

2 Number

By the time children come to school the large majority have heard adults using numbers and have sometimes used and talked about the small numbers themselves. Numerals are among the many symbols (including letters) which they see around them on front doors, buses, cars and books, but usually do not understand. Here, narratives show how teachers introduce numbers in a natural way at very frequent intervals, and then associate the numerals with the situation and the spoken word as soon as the children are ready. There is no sense of pressure, but it is important not only to take advantage of every opportunity to use numbers in everyday classroom situations but also to use them in a more systematic way. Materials such as interlocking blocks or beads and coloured rods and, later, hundred squares and number strips made by the children themselves, give necessary practice in using numbers systematically. This is far more important than written recording but cannot be done satisfactorily with a whole class at once. It is important to realize that the environmental approach is *part* of the story, and not the whole story. A balance must be achieved. I hope that the following pieces of work, read in conjunction with the introductory narrative in Chapter One, will achieve such balance. Here are two accounts which show how teachers of young children organize this work.

1. Splitting up sticks

An often repeated activity, which seems a great favourite, is for everyone in the group to take a 'stick' of a certain number of Unifix cubes and for everyone to make up questions in turn like: 'Can you split your stick up into four bits all of different sizes?'; 'Can you split your stick into three bits all the same length?' This is very useful for analysis of numbers up to ten, and is a bridge between everyday activities involving numbers of things and recorded 'sums'. It focuses attention on 'how many ways' and on 'sameness and difference', and is an activity in which children produce the questions as well as the answers.

2. Using the hundred square[1]

This is useful with children who have had plenty of practical experience of handling quantities and bundling in tens. 'How many discs should I have in the box to fill the board?' 'How many do you think you'll have each if you share them out fairly?' (See page 31).

When this has been done—'Arrange your numbers in order from the smallest to the largest.' This is often a difficult task when each child has about ten numbers between one and a hundred. After this, we begin to fill up the board; sometimes filling up the numbers in numerical order; sometimes by saying 'Who has numbers which go in this row?'; sometimes child by child— which is hard for the first few. Follow-up activities for individuals include filling the number-square themselves; taking a random handful of discs, putting in numerical order and recording; using a hundred line in a similar way. (See page 33.)

The third narrative is by a teacher who introduced her young children to probability—an unusual experience for infants. It is interesting to notice not only the mathematical ideas but also the language which developed from this experience.

[1] A set of 100 numbered discs which fit onto a large nailed board

Probability with infants

Probability seemed a difficult theme for children of five to seven, until we realized that they were already using ideas associated with probability in many of the games they played: snakes and ladders, ludo, and so on. We heard them say such things as 'Bet I get six this time' or 'You always win'. We thought we might be able to extend these ideas and interests, help them to record the results, and come to understand a little about chance. We made large foam rubber dice—$2\frac{1}{2}'' \times 2\frac{1}{2}'' \times 2\frac{1}{2}''$—marked with a pattern of dots. These the children found exciting to use. Some dice were not exactly true, *and this led to interesting discussion about one which showed six more often than the others. The children enjoyed recording their throws on squared paper, first colouring a square for each throw, and, later translating the dot pattern to the number symbol. Often they filled a hundred squares with results of their dice throws and then commented on the total results and compared one's results with those of another. In this activity the combined use of language and number was most marked. Comments from the children were often like these:*

'I had sixty goes and four was the most. If I did it again, I think two would be the most, because it was nearly the most this time.'

'I played three games and number one came up most of all—if I play another game, one might still be most—I lost all the games but I might win next time.'

'If I had one more go, six might come up. It hasn't had a turn yet.'

The children showed often that they understood that there was a reasonable chance that numbers would occur with about the same frequency, given a large enough sample. This understanding also occurred when the children (with eyes closed) selected coloured squares from an equal number of each colour and stuck them on paper. Words such as 'possibly', 'perhaps', 'likely', 'probably', 'chance', 'most', became common in the classroom and were used by the youngest children.

From now on, the children will use dice with numerals and not dots for the games they have made themselves ('spacemen racing to the moon' is a favourite), so translating the symbol to the number of steps moved.

Also we shall introduce two-dice games where children can be encouraged to record the sum of the two dice throws and see how often different combinations of numbers come up. Why is seven the most frequent?

Some other mathematical activities which are associated with probability have been: (i) the children in a class each choosing a coloured disc to record each bottle of milk taken; then, each day, the totals of each colour were recorded and a guess was made about the probability of a certain colour being the favourite on any one day. Red was the colour chosen most frequently, but a child's comment was 'It could have been any of the four colours'; (ii) after keeping a record of favourite colours of sweaters, the five-year-olds predicted that ten children would be wearing blue sweaters on Monday; (iii) a traffic count, where the children compared the total number of vehicles at different times of day, and the types of vehicle. When talking about this latter, they said, 'Cars would be the most, because more people have cars', 'You always see more cars, and I bet I'll see more still when I go home', 'We should count them by my house. There are always more cars than lorries.'

In one class some seven-year-olds did, in fact, discover how many combinations could be obtained by turning over two dice on the table in front of them. This led to possible combinations of cards on the table and then to children sitting round the table and the number of ways in which they could be arranged. Six children moved themselves around until, after about ten variations, they began to realize that they could go on and on, and in fact, ended up by writing that there were so many different ways that 'If we go on, we shall have to work all afternoon and perhaps tomorrow as well.'

An approach to fractions
(patterns with squares of sticky paper)

Several children had been interested in patterns and puzzles which made squares from different shapes. They were given sticky paper to fold and cut as they wished, to see if they could make a few different shapes into a square. At first, four children worked together for a dozen or so squares, then two lost interest, two or three more appeared and helped, others showed interest and made helpful suggestions. But, however much their partners changed, two of the original group kept up their interest, and disappeared into the corridor for long intervals until they reached the stage where the red and

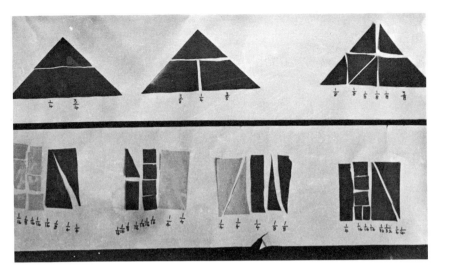

A seven-year-old made this pattern by paper folding and cutting, when investigating the various fractions into which a square of paper could be cut

blue paper was finished. Paula, the girl, then said she would like to 'name' the shapes. When she reached the first quarter, she asked how to write it, and was told she had one whole cut into four, that is $\frac{1}{4}$, and from then on had no difficulty in 'writing' much smaller fractions. The work was put aside until some days later when the boy Anthony said, 'I remembered in bed last night that we had not folded any rectangles into triangles'. Off they went again, using green and yellow paper. Now there was a crisis, as rectangles proved difficult to fold. Paula decided the best way was to draw from corner to corner with the aid of a ruler, and the problem was solved. After a time, Paula moved back to squares, and, when she reached a square cut into sixty-four pieces, she said, 'If I cut them again, they would be 128. The teacher asked, 'What shape would they be?' Paula said, 'Rectangles, but if I cut them again, they would be squares.' After much thought, she decided there would be 256, but though she wanted to, she could not go further. Another girl thought it would be 512, and then she was unable to go further. (This last child earlier, when counting rectangles in the ceiling, said, 'There are five rows of twelve. $12 + 12 = 24$; $24 + 24 = 48$, and another $12 = 60$.' She had also cut a piece of a drinking straw, measured it against the remainder, found it fitted ten times, and decided the short piece was an eleventh.) *Paula, still absorbed in her paper-cutting, said, 'I could go on cutting until there was nothing left.' The teacher asked, 'Then where would the paper be?' The reply was, 'It would be cut up until it was too small to see.'*

The children then wished to try what could be done with the triangle and circle. Paula took friends off to cut up the triangles, Anthony and his friends started on the circle. Paula had no difficulty in the 'naming', even when she met $\frac{3}{4}$ and then $\frac{3}{8}$. She said it must be $\frac{3}{8}$ because three $\frac{1}{8}$s fitted on. Later she wished very much to cut the triangle into very small pieces, but this became too much for her to fit back into the original triangular shape. It also proved too much for her helpers. (See page 39.)

3 Man must Measure

Measuring is an activity for which teachers find it relatively easy to provide first-hand experience. It is important for each teacher to keep careful records, not only of the experiences undertaken by each child, but also of the extent of the child's understanding. Planning ahead, and handing on records of each child's progress to the teacher next responsible for the children, should help to avoid unnecessary repetition of the same experience.

The first narrative in Chapter 1 showed how a teacher planned her work to include all types of measurement so that the experiences became successively more demanding. In this section, detailed accounts are included to cover some of the varied aspects of measuring of all types: length, weight, time, capacity and volume, area.

Time   An account, written by a headmistress, describes a project on Time, and is an excellent example of a co-operative effort by the staff of an infant school, and also of a headmistress's success in securing classroom experiment and staff-room discussion. Concentration on one topic at a time is a most helpful way of accumulating knowledge of how children learn, although care must be taken that mathematics is not divorced from the rest of the child's experience. The staff had been teaching children how to tell the time but had done little work on other aspects.

Objects used for Timing: *egg-timers, pulsimeters, clocks, second-timers, 10-second timer.*

Activities

Five to six years

1. *Comparing things which move slowly or quickly; pictures drawn or cut out—mapping (matching or one-one correspondence). Individual books made by each child, showing activities which he does quickly or slowly.*

2. *Times during the day—related to meal times, with collections of pictures of food to illustrate this. Collage pictures made to illustrate what children did during morning, afternoon, evening or night time.*

3. *Children were questioned to see if they knew 'yesterday', 'today', 'tomorrow'.*

Six to seven years (*whenever appropriate, recording included a picture and/or a graph*)

1. *Months of the year—birthdays.*

2. *Timing of sounds of musical instruments, such as triangle, cymbal.*

3. *Time taken to change for physical education.*

Time. These pictures were drawn by various children of ages five to seven years and show their ideas of growing old. This is not an easy concept for young children. A six-year-old, when asked to name the oldest living creature from three photographs comprising an old fisherman, a seagull and a dog, chose the seagull because she thought old meant nearest to death

One day I will be an adult like my mummy and ear wear rings

Then I will grow older like granny Jane.

John has a great granny she is 70 She is very very old.

4. *Time taken to drink milk.*
5. *One-minute interval—different things drawn in one minute.*
6. *Bus times—times taken to go to nearby towns and villages by bus.*
7. *Walking and running times compared.*
8. *Time taken to skip a certain distance.*
9. *Timing of songs—individual graphs made by the children.*
10. *Timing of night-light burning.*
11. *Timing of plastic bottle emptying:*
(a) *through stopper,*
(b) *through pin-prick.*
12. *Timing of routine actions, such as washing hands, combing hair, putting on shoes. Children worked in pairs and timed each other.*

Seven + years
1. *How time was spent during a school day.*

2. *Time taken to boil three kettles, all of two-pint capacity.*
3. *Use of* TV TIMES *to find longest and shortest programmes, and make comparisons.*
4. *Timing of clockwork toys and musical boxes.*
5. *Use of ramp—variety of things used to roll down ramp—all timed.*

Boiling Kettles

The school kettle							

The school kettle

Mrs Marlow's kettle

Mrs Tunnicliffe's kettle

1 2 3 4 5 6 7
minutes

Various children described this experiment in which they compared the time taken by three kettles to boil: There were two pints of water in each kettle. Two pints = 1 quart. Mrs T's kettle boiled the fastest of all kettles. Mrs M's kettle took the longest to boil. Mrs M's kettle took $4\frac{1}{2}$ minutes more than the school kettle because the school kettle took $2\frac{1}{2}$ minutes.

There were many other comments. The headmistress concluded:

There were exhibitions of children's work in the staff room where recording methods could be discussed. The staff have expressed a wish to choose another topic and develop it in a similar manner.

Weighing
Weighing is a sophisticated activity and children require considerable experience before they understand what they are doing, as shown by the first account in Chapter One. Older children on their first experience with 'balance' scales are also confused. An eight-year-old was asked to use balance scales to

divide a bowl of corn into two halves. She poured some in each pan until the bowl was empty. She pointed correctly to the heavier pan but when she was asked to make the pans hold equal amounts she took corn from the lighter pan and finally gave up. Later, when attempting a similar experiment with a cup of water, she again poured water from the lighter pan to try to achieve a balance.

By contrast, a five-year-old, with varied experience of comparing the masses of various objects, had no difficulty in finding which was heavier, a cup of beans or a cup of peas. What worried him was the—to him—contradictory result. He expected the cup of beans to weigh more than the cup of peas because 'beans are bigger than peas'. I watched him try the experiment three times. Discussion with an older child seemed, at last, to reassure him. 'Peas are smaller but you get more peas in the cup', he said.

Although most children have played with a see-saw (teeter-totter), and know intuitively whether the heavier child should sit nearer to or farther from the pivot, they do not associate this experience with balance scales—or even with a classroom see-saw made with a long ruler balanced on a wooden wedge, using identical cubes as models of children. The difficulty of the concept used in weighing is illustrated by the following story.

A visiting teacher to a seven-year-old class took with him a brick and a plank. He placed the plank over the brick, with the brick nearer one end, and stood on the end farther from the brick. 'Can anyone lift me?' he asked. 'Yes' chorused the class of more than forty children. Each in turn stood on the other end of the plank. When everyone had failed to lift the teacher the children suggested that they could lift him if they jumped on the other end. Once more each tried, without success. A boy who had been sitting where he could see the pivoting brick then asked if he could move the brick—which he did, in the right direction, and lifted the teacher with ease. This boy became so interested in weighing that he made his own balance scales with balsa wood, and maintained his interest for some time. However, this experience had little impact on the other children for when, one month later, I visited the class and carried out a similar experiment, the children responded exactly as before, jumping on the other end in their attempts to lift me. (The boy who had followed up the previous experiment was absent on that day.)

Extensive early experiences with balance scales (which normally precede the use of our complicated standard units of mass: ounce, pound, hundredweight, ton—or gramme, kilogramme, metric ton), used for comparing weights, are essential for the eventual understanding of certain scientific as well as mathematical principles. But there is difficulty here. The wide variety of dial scales we use to weigh letters and parcels, ourselves, the fish we catch, luggage for air travel, and truck loads, are complex instruments. These cannot be taken to pieces to find out how they work! A teacher of a six-year-old class tried to give the necessary understanding by providing, on her 'weight experience table', a variety of springs of all kinds, extension and compression, and, of course, elastic bands. She asked the children to experiment to see if they could find which springs were used in the different dial scales. This prompted the children, who enjoyed this experience, to make their own extension scales using elastic bands and a light plastic cup.

Capacity and volume Teachers today provide young children with carefully planned activities on 'water play' and capacity, long before they introduce standard units for measuring capacity and volume. By using a variety of containers, funnels, tubing and sieves, children discover the fascinating properties of water, and learn, at first hand, the meaning of such words as 'full', 'empty' and 'overflowing'. 'How many beakers can I fill from this jug?' and 'Share this glass of lemonade with your friend' are familiar situations which they can solve with ease. The following account describes a more usual experience for six-to seven-year-olds. Here are the children's accounts of their experiments. One child wrote:

We were each given cardboard. The cardboards were all the same size. We made some boxes but some of the boxes were big. And some were little. Some were wide. And some were narrow. The deepest was mine. I think Richard's will hold the most.

Another child wrote:

We put sand in all the boxes and then we weighed the sand. Pat's box holds two pounds one ounce. Irene's box holds two pounds nine ounces. Richard's box holds three pounds eight ounces and my box holds three pounds nine ounces.

A third child wrote:

We chose sand to fill our boxes because it filled them right to the top and filled them in the corner. We used some bricks they would not go right in the corner so we used sand and the bottle tops would not go in the corner. Janet's box holds the most and Pat's holds the least.

Length and area

Measurement of length often precedes the other measures. It is sometimes incidental to another activity. As with other measures, direct comparison usually comes first, and children's growing vocabulary reflects this. For example, 'longer', 'taller', 'shorter', 'narrower', 'wider', 'far', 'near' are learned through everyday experience. The use of units of the children's own choosing eventually leads to a realization of the need for standard units.

A collage giraffe was made by some six-year-olds whose teacher had told them of the habits and home of the animal. At the same time she introduced the children to standard units of length. As a result, they measured the giraffe and wrote:

The giraffe is very tall and from his horns to his feet it is fifty-two inches and his neck is twenty inches, his legs is thirteen inches and his nose to tail is fifty-six inches and his body is twenty-nine inches and that is the giraffe story.

Thirteen inches make one foot one inch.

The children did not, of course, realize that they had made a scale model of a giraffe. Another class of six-year-olds made life-size two-dimensional pictures of the shortest and tallest in the class. The teacher introduced them to tape measures for the first time and, fascinated, they measured arms, feet, legs, etc, on the pictures, and recorded their findings. When Hilary, the tallest, was taken to try new shoes, she surprised the shopkeeper by insisting that one of her feet was an inch longer that the other, since this was the result obtained from measuring her picture. The shopkeeper measured both feet on a gauge, and Hilary came back to school aware for the first time that the measurements of her 'portrait' were not true measurements of her three-dimensional self.

This discovery led to another: besides width and height, whole surfaces could be measured and compared. The children then began to compare the surfaces covered by hands and feet. A development of this work occurred after reading the story, A BEAR CALLED PADDINGTON. Three children brought their own teddy bears to school, and proceeded to do the work shown, entirely on their own. At this stage, some children ignored fractions and others counted a part of a square as a whole one. Here is some of the children's writing which accompanied the work. It is interesting to notice the care and precision with which the children described differences, and yet the difficulty they had with the words 'bigger' and 'smaller', often using these instead of 'taller' and 'shorter'. It is only after extensive and varied experiences that children, with their teacher's help, give precise meanings to the many words used in length, of which 'long', 'tall', 'short', 'wide', 'broad', 'narrow', 'thick', 'thin', 'high', 'low', are probably the most common.

Attractive patterns made when seven-year-olds rotated various shapes. All rotations led to a circle

We made this pattern by twisting a rectangle. We found the middle of a rectangle by ruling in diagonals. We put a nail in the middle of the rectangle and twisted it around it. Every time we rotated it and we got two circles.

49

The youngest
five-year-olds made
this chart to show
which group they
should join before
going home

A portrait gallery,
made by older
infants,
illustrating
hair-colour sets

Bedtime

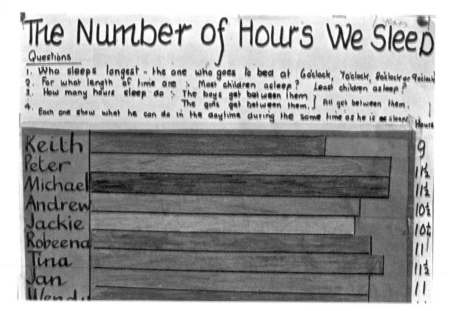

The Number of Hours We Sleep

There are eight people that are four feet in class one. Ruth is the smallest she is three feet eight inches. Lorraine Ball is the biggest. She is four feet six inches. One twin is taller than the other with an inch. The biggest wun in the class is four feet six inches, the smallest one is three feet eight inches. So the biggest one is ten inches bigger than the smallest is a girl. There is not a small boy smaller than anybody else because there are four the same and they are three foot eleven inches. Andrew Rumble is the biggest boy he is four foot three inches. Lorraine Ball is bigger than him by three inches.

Putting objects (or themselves) in order of height is not an easy activity for children since it involves successive matching. The idea of scale is another aspect of mathematics which children find difficult in the early stages. Here is one teacher's experiment in which she introduced both these ideas. She took the opportunity to work with a group of eleven six-year-olds when a student was teaching the remainder of the class.

First I asked the children, in groups of three or four, to put themselves in order of height. Then I asked the whole group to arrange themselves in order beginning with the shortest. This took some time and, when it was completed, the children were each asked to draw a picture showing the group arranged in order. I reminded them that they would need to mark in the floor on which they stood.

The results were interesting. One girl sensibly used the lower edge of the paper for the floor but, realizing that her 'children' were diminishing too rapidly, she started again in the middle. Some did not show all eleven in the group. Others added a wavering floor line afterwards. The only child to succeed in both tasks made a symbolic representation, drawing coloured rods to represent the children, and used the lower edge of the paper for the floor. (See page 54.)

I then asked the group to make a record of their actual heights. For this purpose the children decided to cut an outline of the tallest. The height of each child was

Records made by some six-year-olds after eleven children had arranged themselves in order of height. This figure shows a freehand drawing

then marked on this figure. In this way the children were able to see themselves set out in order of height. From this representation each child cut a length of string equal to his own height. I gave them a large sheet of paper and asked them to arrange their string heights, in order, on the paper. But of course the paper was not long enough so, after much discussion, (and abortive requests for more paper), the children decided that the fairest thing to do was to halve each 'string height'— and so had their first experience of scale drawing.

The final example on measurement was a surprising achievement for seven-year-olds, because the numbers concerned would normally be beyond the comprehension of such young children. There were 320 children aged from five to seven years at an overcrowded school. The older ones complained one day that they had no room to play games without bumping into other children. The teacher asked them if they could find out the actual playground space each child had when they were all out at play. They decided that they must cover the rectangular playground with newspaper to find out. Some children cut out foot squares and began to cover the ground, while others measured the length and width.

Different children wrote:

33
33
33
29
—
128 *feet long*
—

Me and Kerry mesured the width of the playground. We used the 33 foot tape measure once but the second time we only used 32 feet of it so the playground is 65 feet wide.

Kerry and Colin measured the playground. We used the long measure three times and the last time we only used 29 feet of it.

When the measuring was complete, the children realized that covering the ground with newspaper would take a long time. So the teacher gave them large sheets of centimetre square paper which they cut and joined together to represent the playground, 128 squares by 65 squares.

The children decided to take it in turns to number all the squares on the paper. They marked each hundred in red and started again at one, so that the top row was numbered one to a hundred, and one to twenty-eight and the second row began with twenty-nine. 'Lots of children counted in hundreds and I did too, wrote Susan. There was an exciting moment when the twenty-fifth row was complete. 'Stephen and Michael found out where to put the hundreds. They make a pattern.' From then on, there was no more numbering of consecutive squares; instead, successive hundreds were marked, following the pattern the boys had found. The red hundreds were then counted. 'There were 83 hundreds and 20 more, so the playground is 8320 square feet,' wrote Trevor and Peter.

The problem which next faced the children was to divide the 8320 square feet of playground among 320 children. It is interesting to see that they invented an ancient method of division for themselves. Each stage was recorded by a different child.

	8320 square feet for	**320** children
Colin	4160 square feet for	160 children
Trevor	2080 square feet for	80 children
Kerry	1040 square feet for	40 children
Robert	520 square feet for	20 children
Raymond	260 square feet for	10 children
	(note the opportunity missed here)	
Antony	130 square feet for	5 children

Raymond then used the number patterns and Julie and Theresa used interlocking blocks, to find that there were 26 square feet for each child. (As far as I know the children did not mark out 26 square feet in the playground, but they used rods to find as many patterns of 26 units as they could.)

I am not suggesting that children should be given a task of this magnitude. Normally such a problem would be quite outside the children's interest and experience. But this example shows the lengths to which children (and their teacher) will go to solve a problem, when it is one which fully engages their interest, and when they want to find the answer!

4 Shapes

The first two narratives in Chapter One emphasized the use of three-dimensional objects (cartons and containers) found in the environment. It is most important that children should be helped to abstract ideas of two-dimensional shapes from the wide variety of three-dimensional shapes which they see and handle every day of their lives. The names: cubes, cuboids (or rectangular prisms) and cylinders will precede squares, rectangles, circles and triangles if children are handling the everyday shapes of their environment as well as manufactured bricks.

Teachers do not always realize that the 'junk' box (with containers of every shape and size, pieces of wood, and so on) and the 'bit-box' (containing pieces of textiles, wallpaper, and so on) are rich in mathematical potential. Model making—for which boxes of different kinds are selected, measured and cut, covered with newspaper, and painted—is a highly mathematical activity and should be exploited to the full (for possibilities of introducing new vocabulary, too).

At first the feeling for scale is intuitive. There is no need to measure; the child searches until he finds the container he thinks is just right for his model. Later he cuts a piece off his cylinder to make the chimney the right height.[1]

In the film, MATHS ALIVE,[2] a seven-year-old boy, who has put together a 'cut out' model of Coventry Cathedral, has acquired such a firm grasp of the idea of scale that he is able to calculate the true dimensions of the Cathedral. A complete understanding of the important topic of scale follows extensive experience at a much later stage. Young children nevertheless appreciate scale models of all kinds

[1] For many examples see Chapter Five of MATHEMATICS IN PRIMARY SCHOOLS Schools Council Curriculum Bulletin No 1, HMSO 1965

[2] MATHS ALIVE— thirty-minute colour film of children at work on mathematics. NAVA, Paxton Place, Gipsy Road, London SE27

and the many stories concerned with 'scale'—THE
THREE BEARS, GULLIVER'S TRAVELS, ALICE'S ADVENTURES
IN WONDERLAND—have appealed to children through
the ages.

Children can often recognize and sort similar
shapes into one set before they can put into words
the likeness and differences of the shapes. For example, a five-year-old boy selected all the cubes (of
different colours and sizes) from a drawer but he
was unable to explain why these belonged together.
He required more extensive experience before, for
example, he was able to build larger cubes from unit
cubes. Margaret, a seven-year-old, faced with this
problem, succeeded in making a square base (2 by 2).
At first she was satisfied—until her friend pointed
out that the shape she had made was not a cube.
Margaret then added another layer. As she continued this activity, building larger and larger
'cubes', she was one layer short each time until she
built a cube of five unit edge, when she was immediately successful. Martin (aged nearly eight), with
little first-hand experience, found the problem
'make the largest square you can with this set of
square tiles' a difficult one (there were fifty identical
tiles!). After several attempts, his teacher gave him
a box of three-dimensional shapes and asked him to
sort out the cubes—he did this without hesitation.
'How did you know they were cubes?' she asked.
Martin replied, 'Because their faces are all squares,
so now I can make my square.' Even then, Martin
did not find this problem easy, because his method
was at first by 'trial and error'. (When at last he had
made a seven-by-seven square, Martin asked if he
could have more practice! His teacher suggested
that he should choose different (random) numbers of
tiles each time.) It is interesting to see that Martin
required experience with three-dimensional shapes
to help him to understand the concept of 'square-
ness'.

Symmetry is an important topic in mathematics, and recognition of 'mirror' symmetry can
come at as early an age as five. Stephen's first ex-

periment with a paint splash on his paper happened by accident when he folded the paper to throw it away. It fell open again, and the pattern Stephen saw excited him so much that he experimented with more than one colour. His teacher encouraged her children to make such patterns and to collect objects such as leaves and flowers 'like Stephen's pattern'. There was much discussion about sameness and difference as each object was studied.

Pat, a seven-year-old, had drawn round a cylindrical tin on a sheet of paper and, using a ruler, was trying, without success, to find the centre. I suggested she should cut the circle out and find another way—without success. I gave Pat a rectangular sheet of paper and asked her to find the middle without using a ruler. As she still hesitated, I held the paper on my palm with the ends curving slightly upwards. Immediately she took the paper and folded it twice to obtain the centre. Excitedly, she repeated the process with the circle. 'Could you find the centre of the circle in any other way?' I asked. This led to paper-folding experiments, in which the whole class joined, with a variety of shapes (squares, regular and irregular triangles), and also to a discussion of axes of symmetry.

A six-year-old boy who had struggled to replace the lid of a 'nearly square' rectangular biscuit tin, was asked by his teacher in how many ways the lid could fit on. After some thought, but without looking at the tin, the boy replied 'Two it will, two it won't'. He, too, was experimenting with symmetry. A collection of boxes of various shapes with fitting lids provides very useful experiences in rotational symmetry as well as in properties of basic shapes. 'This is a square box, 'said a seven-year-old, 'because its lid will fit on any way.' Her teacher gave her a cylindrical tin with a lid and asked her to find out in how many ways its lid would fit the tin. (See the examples of children's work on pages 49–50.)

Here is an account of a very attractive investigation undertaken by a class of seven-year-olds. Secondary-school teachers will be well aware of the mathematical significance of this particular investigation in laying foundations for translations and rotations, ideas of congruence, properties of shapes and paths of points.

Children's work on twisting shapes

The children (aged approximately seven-and-a-half years) who did this work had handled shapes for some time and used them to draw round to produce patterns. From mixed shapes, ordered shapes, shapes turned over and repeated, they progressed to patterns made from shapes pushed along. At this stage they started to measure the interval between each shape with straws, sticks or rulers to make their pattern regular. Next, one child found she could make an interesting circular pattern by holding down a square with one finger and twisting it. She was given a large sheet of paper. She found the centre of a square by drawing in the diagonals, and the shape was nailed on to the paper. Other children now requested large paper and different shapes, to see what patterns would appear, and were fascinated to find that, whatever shapes were used, the patterns (paths of points) were all circular. Some time later, another child found he could produce a pattern by holding down one corner of a shape and twisting it. There was new eagerness now to try this out with different shapes, and in each case the children found circles in their patterns. They also found that they must measure a regular distance and allow large spaces (between rotations) if they wished to paint their patterns. From their pencil drawings, they picked out the shapes they had used, with paint (once), and in each case noticed which lines were making the circular shapes in the patterns. Angela studied her pattern for a while and then went away to try to make a 'black square' by making very close lines (a very small angle of rotation). One boy then said, 'We don't need the shapes at all. In the rectangle, the short sides make one circle, the long sides make the next circle, and the diagonal makes the largest circle.' He then asked the teacher to help him to fasten a crayon onto a flat piece of wood, and to nail down the other end of the wood on paper. He twisted the wood, drawing an arc, but found his paper too small.

He then asked for the nail to be transferred to the middle *of the wood so that his circle would be smaller. Soon, he found the wood difficult to handle and asked for string. At first he used a simple piece of string, but later tied it into a loop, putting his finger into one end and his pencil into the other, to draw a circle. The children who had made the patterns then made 'spinners' by cutting out a shape in brilliant patterns and then threading it with a loop of string.*

Patterns in nature We cannot leave the absorbing topic of shapes without making reference to a field particularly attractive to young children: the wide variety of patterns which delights them in their everyday environment: leaf patterns, the branching patterns of trees, the patterns of cracked mud in drying puddles, the patterns of joins of paving stones or bricks, the symmetries of insects, animals or flowers, the curve of falling water and the varied tracks and trajectories of insects and animals.

A six-year-old, looking out of the classroom window at the snow on the roofs of nearby houses, said, 'Do you see that pattern on the tiles? I'm going to use that in the next picture I paint.'

5 Communication: Graphical Representation

Young children communicate the patterns and relations they have discovered, in a variety of ways. At first the emphasis is on talking—with the teacher and with other children. As a result of first-hand experience, children gradually build up a working mathematical vocabulary of shapes, number, length, weight, volume and capacity, area, and money. But they also communicate their findings in other ways: by models and diagrams, mappings and tabular forms, and by graphs using either three-dimensional materials such as beads and interlocking cubes, or squares and squared paper.

Graphs have an appeal to teachers as well as to children, but all too frequently it is the teacher who does the preparation of the framework of the graph, and the children are merely carefully guided 'square-stickers'. Often children do this without comprehending what they are doing. In the early stages, left to themselves, children do not choose equal units; they do not place the chosen unit on a base line, and they leave gaps between the units they use. It is only after varied first-hand experience and subsequent discussion that children understand the significance and value of these symbols and aids.

I had the interesting experience, in a country where child-centred education was being introduced for the first time, of comparing two similar pieces of work undertaken by six-year-olds and twelve-year-olds. Both were given unit squares to record their findings of favourite colours in the class. The twelve-year-olds had placed the squares at random—not on a base line, and with uneven gaps between each square. This surprised the teacher but when she discussed with them the possibility of rearrangement for ease of comparison, they immediately suggested using a base line and placing the units 'side by side without gaps.' By contrast, the squares of the six-year-olds were perfectly placed, edge to edge on the base line made by the teacher. On enquiry, this teacher revealed that she had placed the squares in position because she thought the children were incapable of doing this 'properly'. Children of all ages need to pass through certain stages of learning if their basic knowledge is to be sound. It is necessary to let them experiment, even though the results are untidy and lead to further problems. The 'mistakes' they make will help them to see the purpose of a base line. (I agree with Piaget that, in concept formation, children do not 'make mistakes' but give an honest account of a situation as they see it at any particular time.)

The photograph shows the results of an enquiry completed by twenty five-year-olds. The teacher wrote: 'Because we have several main roads intersecting at the school gates, the children put themselves into five sets in the hall at the end of each session. The work was done when twenty new five-year-olds came to the school. Each of the group drew and cut out a picture of himself. The pictures were of varying size but each one was put in the correct set by the child himself, to help him to remember where to go each day.'

Six-year-old children in the school, seeing this record, made a variety of similar records for themselves, using beads, squares, coloured rods and a block graph. (See page 51.)

The second illustration is the work of seven-year-olds. In this highly individual piece of work, which began with a small group, extended to the class and finally included all the girls in the school, the girls assigned themselves to four sets, according to the colour of their hair; fair, brown, black or ginger. Wool was used for hair which was styled according to the real and imaginary hair styles in the school. The teacher provided templates for the children to use in cutting the faces in order to ensure that the same sized unit was used by all children. When all the girls in the school were included in the survey, children and teacher decided that the graph would be too large to fix on the wall. After some discussion, the teacher suggested that they should use one head to represent four girls. (Afterwards she wondered how she might have helped the groups to suggest this scale for themselves.) Children were frequently to be found counting in fours to check the totals.

Sometimes the investigation suggested by a teacher proves too difficult for children. A teacher of seven-year-olds had asked them to record their bedtimes.[1] Each drew a picture of himself going to bed and another of himself getting up in the morning (the pieces of paper used for this purpose were of identical size) and arranged these in the appropriate sets. 'Who is in bed longest?' asked the teacher. 'Those who go to bed at 7p.m.' was the immediate and unanimous reply. In vain the teacher pointed out that one of the girls who went to bed at 7p.m. was up at 6a.m. The children were firmly convinced that those who went to bed first were in bed longest. So the teacher helped each child to work out how long he was in bed. Then *she* drew a graph in which she took one inch to represent one hour and made an entry for each child. (See the illustrations on page 52.) The teacher suggested that the graph would help the children to find out who was in bed longest. After examining the graph carefully, the children replied: 'But you've made a mistake—you've made us all go to bed at the same time!' Wisely the teacher abandoned any further attempt to press an idea which was too sophisticated for these young children. It is right that we should end with the story of an investigation which was unsuccessful because these are all too frequently unrecorded. Such occasions should not cause concern. All teachers find they have to adapt their plans and the experiences they provide;

[1]This account is to be found in THE ARITHMETIC TEACHER, May 1968, *Mathematics Laboratories and Teachers' Centres— the Mathematics Revolution in Britain*. For many further examples, see PICTORIAL REPRESENTATION (Nuffield Foundation Mathematics Teaching Project) Chambers/Murray 1969

even then, at times the children show us that they are not ready. Working in this way, with children actively learning from first-hand experience, makes constant demands on a teacher's resources and imagination. But it has its compensations: 'Teachers observe and plan. Children experiment and discover. This is what makes Maths alive!'

Appendix I

(Children between the ages of four and eight are given very wide experience in many fields by their teachers. The purpose of such experiences may sometimes be obscured. To help readers to see the links between experience and the 'structure' the teachers have in mind, this appendix has been compiled.)

1. Classification and sorting.

2. Matching two sets of objects (one-to-one correspondence). Cardinal number.

3. Comparison of two numbers or two quantities.
   (a) Qualitative, eg, greater than, less than, longer, shorter, heavier, lighter, etc.
   (b) Quantitative—by subtraction and by division. Ratio.

4. The measures (length, weight, capacity, time, area). Approximation (in-between-ness).

   Measuring follows a definite pattern throughout: Play-stage, after observing adults or older children. Comparison of two measures—longer or shorter than; heavier or lighter than; larger or smaller than. Measuring, using arbitrary units of own choice (once children have learnt that equal units are necessary). Understanding the need for standard units and use of standard units. Use of more than one unit.

5. Inequalities.
Putting objects in order, in a variety of ways. Ordinal numbers.

6. The operations of addition, subtraction, multiplication and division on quantities and on number.

7. Likeness and differences between various objects. Properties of familiar three- and two-dimensional shapes.

8. Patterns and relations in shapes and in numbers. Minimum number facts $(+ \ -)$ which should be our aim for immediate recall by about the age of seven.

(a) Number facts (addition and subtraction) up to 10. This is *half* the number shown once the commutative law has been discovered and *is used*.

(b) The diagonal numbers—doubles and halves—usually well in excess of 10.

(c) Adding and subtracting two from any number. Usually well in excess of 10.

(d) Adding 10 to a number (11–20). Multiplication (and division) tables 2, 10.

Appendix II

The normal environment possesses many possibilities for basic mathematical experiences which will be provided as part of a child's total experience. There are four groups which teachers need to keep in mind.

1. Materials to excite curiosity, interest and enquiry.

2. Reference materials: books, pictures, models, globe, maps.

3. Tools and measures to use. These should be reliable and of good quality.

4. Materials for recording:
   plain paper, coloured paper,
   squared paper, (squares of various sizes),
   coloured sticky paper,
   coloured beads and strings,
   identical coloured cubes,
   adhesive,
   powder paint and large brushes,
   felt pens.

Other materials for operations on numbers (Some of these may be brought by the children themselves)

Sorting trays or boxes and containers for counting, each with one numeral (1 to 10) fixed to the outside.

Interesting and varied objects for sorting and counting: beads, buttons, shells, small plastic tops, beans, pebbles, ribbon, straws.

Objects made by the children for playing shops. Real money.

Structural apparatus of all kinds Abacus with nails and beads. Square paper (1″ unit for children to make hundred squares and number lines and strips.) A hundred one-inch squares numbered 1 to 100. Interlocking cubes. Coloured rods of length 1 to 10 units.

Length: ribbon, lace, wool, string, drinking straws; yardsticks (in UK, substitute metre sticks, etc), and one-foot lengths from slatting, 1″ wide ¼″ thick, some unmarked, some marked in inches for children to label when they are ready. One-yard tape measures, made from a 1″ wide strip of 1″ squared paper and numbered by the children, are better than the commercial tape measures. A six-foot measure, marked in feet and inches, can be fixed vertically to the wall as a height scale. An unmarked map measurer (opisometer). A globe.

Weight: material for weighing: beans, rice, sand, marbles, nails, stone. Scales of all types: (a) balance type (suspended from above and not supported from below) and standard weights; (b) compression scales in wide variety from letter scales to personal scales. Assorted compression and extension springs. Elastic bands.

Capacity and volume: useful measures: empty milk and fruit juice cartons. Plastic containers and boxes, cups, jugs, basins and pails. Measuring jugs, funnels and tubing, sieves. Plasticine or clay. At least a hundred coloured 1″ cubes.

Area: scraps of textiles with repeating patterns. Square tiles. Coloured square inch and square feet. (In UK, use square centimetres and square decimetres.) Leaves and leaf prints.

Time: egg-timers, clock with sweep hand. Calendar.

Shapes: for constructional work and sorting: scissors, waste material of all kinds: eg, boxes and cartons, cardboard, and corrugated paper, newspaper and glossy magazines, silver paper, straw, twigs. Mosaic puzzles. Balls, hoops, wheels, wheeled toys. Assorted wooden shapes.

Booklist

Adams, L.D. A BACKGROUND TO PRIMARY SCHOOL MATHEMATICS OUP 1953

Association of Teachers of Mathematics NOTES ON THE TEACHING OF MATHEMATICS IN PRIMARY SCHOOLS Cambridge University Press 1967

Churchill, E.M. COUNTING AND MEASURING : AN APPROACH TO NUMBER EDUCATION IN THE INFANT SCHOOL Routledge & Kegan Paul 1961; University of Toronto Press, Toronto 1966

Goutard, M. MATHEMATICS AND CHILDREN Educational Explorers 1964

Ironside, Margaret and Roberts, Sheila MATHEMATICS IN THE PRIMARY SCHOOL National Froebel Foundation 1965

Mathematical Association A FURTHER REPORT ON PRIMARY MATHEMATICS Bell 1970

National Froebel Foundation SOME ASPECTS OF PIAGET'S WORKS National Froebel Foundation 1955

NUFFIELD MATHEMATICS TEACHING PROJECT (series) Chambers/Murray 1969; John Wiley, New York

Razzell, A.G. and Watts, K.G.O. MATHEMATICAL TOPICS BOOKS 1 to 6 Hart-Davis 1964; Doubleday, New York

Schools Council Curriculum Bulletin No. 1 MATHEMATICS IN PRIMARY SCHOOLS HMSO 1965

Sealey, L.G.W. THE CREATIVE USE OF MATHEMATICS IN THE JUNIOR SCHOOL Blackwell (revised edition 1965); Humanities Press, New York 1965

Whittaker, D.E. MATHEMATICS THROUGH DISCOVERY Books 1 to 3 and Teachers' Book Harrap 1965

Whittaker, D.E. PATHWAY TO MATHEMATICS Harrap 1967

Shapes   Ravielli, A. ADVENTURES WITH SHAPES Phoenix 1960

Weyl, P.K. MEN, ANTS AND ELEPHANTS Phoenix 1961; Viking Press, New York 1959

History   Smith, D.E. NUMBER STORIES OF LONG AGO Ginn 1948
Smith, T. THE STORY OF MEASUREMENT First and
   Second Series Blackwell 1959
Smith, T. THE STORY OF NUMBERS Blackwell 1959

See also AN INTRODUCTION, EDUCATING TEACHERS,
THE TEACHER'S ROLE, SCIENCE, MATHEMATICS FOR OLDER
CHILDREN in this series.

Suggested Audio-Visual Aids

1. *Dance Squared* and *Notes on a Triangle* are two 16 mm colour films, available from the Canadian National Film Board. The first runs for 3 minutes 30 seconds and the second for 4 minutes 56 seconds.

   These two films are available in the UK through the Canadian High Commissioner's Office, Canada House, Trafalgar Square, London SW1., and in the USA from the National Film Board of Canada, Suite 819, 650 5th Avenue, New York, NY 10019

2. Two films from the series
   CHILDREN AND MATHEMATICS

   Checking Up
   We still Need Arithmetic

   These are 16 mm black and white films, each 30 minutes long. Com/opt/sound.

   All foreign enquiries should be made direct to BBC Television Enterprises, Television Centre, London W. 12, though some films are obtainable in the USA from Time Life Films (non-theatrical division) 43 West 16th Street, New York, NY 10011.

3. *Maths Alive* is a 16 mm colour film, 30 minutes long, which is available from the National Audio and Visual Aid Library, Paxton Place, Gipsy Road, London SE 27.

4. *Donald Duck in Mathemagic Land* is a 16 mm colour film, 26 minutes long.

This is not available for purchase, but can be leased by local education authorities for a period of up to ten years, from Walt Disney Productions, 68 Pall Mall, London SW1., or in the United States from Walt Disney Productions, 500 South Buena Vista Street, Burbank, California.

5. A film from the series DISCOVERY AND EXPERIENCE

No. 2. *Maths is a Monster*

This is a 16 mm black and white film, 30 minutes long.

All foreign enquiries should be made direct to BBC Television Enterprises, Television Centre, London W.12, though some films are obtainable in the USA from Time Life Films (non-theatrical division) 43 West 16th Street, New York, NY 10011.

Mathematics for Older Children

Edith Biggs

The Author

Edith Biggs, BSc, MA, has taught mathematics in grammar schools in various parts of England. She has also worked with teachers and children in many parts of the United States of America, and in other parts of the world. She was appointed His Majesty's Inspector in 1950, and in 1960 assumed special responsibility for meeting the demands of primary school teachers for in-service training in mathematics. In 1964, she was appointed Staff Inspector for mathematics. Her publications include: MATHEMATICS IN PRIMARY SCHOOLS Schools Council Curriculum Bulletin No. 1 HMSO 1965 (4th ed. 1972); FREEDOM TO LEARN (with J. R. MacLean) Addison Wesley 1969; MATHEMATICS TODAY (Series of textbooks, with Miss H. E. Vidal) Ginn 1947.

Introduction

So much has happened in the field of mathematics during the past fifteen years that it is not surprising to find some teachers in schools and some lecturers in colleges and universities, as well as the general public, confused about the issues involved.

There have been two major developments: first in the method of teaching the subject and secondly in the content itself. The resulting changes sometimes reinforce each other—but in the initial stages they were quite separate. It has been interesting to notice how changes of method have resulted in a considerable extension in content at the primary stage, and yet the reverse is by no means true at the secondary stage. Many secondary schools have introduced new content without shifting the emphasis from instruction by the teacher to opportunities for more active learning by the pupil. New topics in mathematics have sometimes proved as distasteful as traditional topics, when taught unimaginatively and without giving the pupils opportunities for investigation.

A classroom in which discovery methods are well established is certainly not chaotic, but it is usually busy, lively and exciting. Some children who become completely absorbed in a problem, fall silent. Others want to talk out their ideas, with their companions or with their teacher, to help them over difficulties. The teacher provides opportunities for learning in the form of real materials, environmental and structural, which are interesting or might be useful, and questions which will provoke thought. She observes the children, listens to their discussions, and asks more questions when this is necessary.

The chief aims of teaching by discovery or, to use a less controversial term, learning through investigation, are: first, to give pupils opportunities to think for themselves; second, to provide experiences from the environment (natural and man-made) which will help them to discover the order, pattern and relations which form the basis of mathematics; third, to give them the necessary knowledge and subsequent skills.

There are three stages of active learning, each of which should form part of every investigation, although the relative time taken by each stage will vary with the age and capacity of individual pupils:

1. Exploratory stage. This may be initiated by the teacher herself—perhaps supplying materials and observing children using them, perhaps asking a provocative question. Alternatively, children may spark off an enquiry as a result of some object they have found. In either case, the teacher interferes as little as possible at this stage. She observes and asks questions only to help the enquiry further, and to prevent frustration.

2. At the second stage, the teacher focuses attention on certain salient points which she and the children—or she alone—have decided are of importance and interest. The question may still be open and challenging, but the teacher often controls the situation by her questions, making these more directed if she senses stalemate or frustration.

3. When the investigation is complete, a follow-up is necessary to ensure sound learning. This may take the form of a practice period, if the investigation has resulted in a child devising a method of calculation, or of a similar but more challenging problem, if a group of children are having their first experience of a concept.

There are certain points which must be emphasized about learning by this method, for there has been much misunderstanding about so-called 'discovery learning':

1. Practical work is time-consuming, and teachers must always have a clear mathematical aim in mind for each activity undertaken by the children. As wide a variety of mathematical ideas as possible should be abstracted from any one investigation.

2. Pupils do not normally learn from one discovery alone. It is therefore essential to plan progressive experiences in important topics. These topics should be reintroduced at intervals, each time at a more demanding level than before.

3. All pupils do not require the same kind of experience in order to learn a particular mathematical concept. Some need extensive and varied experiences with real materials, while others soon put materials aside and investigate in a more abstract way. Investigation does not necessarily require real materials. Sometimes a solution to a problem is a pattern or relation, and paper and pencil are required.

4. The work should be planned to encourage pupils to investigate and experiment for themselves. Their suggestions should be followed up, and they should not feel restricted by their teacher's programme.

5. It follows that teachers need to keep careful records of children's achievement and progress.

In 1968, one hundred teachers and lecturers met to follow up mathematics courses held in 1966. Teachers were invited to bring work from the classroom, and a large hall was set aside for the exhibition. The hall proved totally inadequate to house all that was brought, and, although four additional classrooms were used, it was not felt that the accommodation did justice to the exhibits. The children's work contained in the chapters which follow is derived partly from this source.

In some schools, the first attempt at investigational methods in mathematics had taken place after the course in 1966. For example, the headmistresses of neighbouring infant and junior schools brought a most varied collection of work. They explained that, of the twenty members of staff of the two schools, seventeen were now actively engaged in discovery methods in mathematics, the remaining three were 'on the brink'. These changes had occurred since 1966.

The selection of work was a difficult task, as the standard was uniformly high. Eventually it was decided to choose work which could be assigned to five major aspects of mathematics: *number, measurement, statistics and probability, shapes and their properties, relations*. The five chapters in this section have been arranged according to this selection.

Some of the examples described arose either spontaneously, as a result of the interests of specific children, or because the teacher, realizing the needs of certain children, planned the work herself. It is important to emphasize, therefore, that '*structure is in the mind of the teacher*'. The teacher needs to be constantly aware of the framework within which she is working.

Therefore, the examples quoted are not a blueprint for successful learning of mathematics. They may not appeal to children in different circumstances and in different surroundings. It is the teacher's own enthusiasms and interests which are often 'caught' by the children and transformed by them. The examples should not, therefore, be taken over as they stand, although they may well be a source of ideas for teachers to apply to the children they teach.

Mr John Howard (Senior Lecturer in Education at Bishop Grosseteste College of Education, Lincoln, England), who was present at the course, undertook to photograph as much of the work as possible. We hope that the results of our collection will be of interest to all teachers and prospective teachers who are trying to make the learning of mathematics more active for their pupils. We hope, too, that it will help parents to understand their children's work.

It has not been possible for all the material collected from the course to be reproduced. Material reproduced here has therefore been supplemented by numerous examples encountered during the past two years.

We thank the teachers and children whose work appears here—and all the others whose contributions made it so enjoyable.

Children at work

1 Number

This section was one of the smallest—perhaps because teachers find this a difficult topic to teach by discovery methods. It has therefore been augmented from various sources.

Estimating and counting

What is the purpose of including this activity? Does it interest children and is it a valuable exercise in itself?

When a child can describe a number such as 28 as two tens and eight units, it does not follow that he knows how to apply this knowledge when counting a collection of objects. Frequently young children (and sometimes adults also) have no idea how to organize a count of between 20 and 200 objects. And if a count is not efficiently organized, then we become bored and lose count, and we have to begin all over again.

Of course it is better if the counting has some purpose. For example, when children are collecting boxes to make models, are there enough for every pair to have, say, four each? Such a question might provide a sufficient motive for young children. Daily counts of everyday classroom occurrences such as how many boys and how many girls are present, what numbers are having milk and school meals, and making up the stock for the class shop, provide plenty of purposeful counting activities and give teachers opportunities to see which children require counting practice.

Estimating and counting which involve large numbers are, perhaps, harder to justify on grounds of motivation. Yet, when children have been asked to estimate, they are usually interested in the answer, especially if individual estimates show a wide variation. Mathematically, the activity is valuable because of the resulting appraisal of the different methods children use to obtain an approximate answer, and because of the experience it gives in the important idea of rounding off a number. The following example illustrates this.

1. I had the good fortune to be able to give children of various ages the same assignment: Estimate how many beans there are in this bag. Check without counting every bean.

(a) The first group to tackle this problem were seven-year-olds. Their estimates were as wild as my own! Janet suggested counting in twos or threes, and found it hard to accept that this was equivalent to counting every bean. Peter said: 'If we could find a way of halving the beans we could count half, then double.' Unfortunately he did not pursue this further. I held up a cup and asked if this would help. 'Fill the cup and count how many cups,' was the immediate reply. Later I was told that there were six-and-a-half cups, and that one cup contained 110 beans. Robert arranged the cups in pairs, and counted 220, 440, 660. 'Half of 100 is 50, and a half of 10 is 5, that's 55,' said Mervyn. 'That's 715,' said James, to our surprise. So these children, who would not have been able to multiply 110 by $6\frac{1}{2}$ were taking the first steps towards multiplication, and found a solution to their problem.

(b) Irving, a slow nine-year-old, organized his count carefully. He put each set of ten in a separate cup. Towards the end of the count (nearly 400), he ran out of cups so he poured each lot of five sets of ten into a larger cup. I was relieved at this for I anticipated difficulties with the final count, but Irving was able to count up in fifties.

(c) Earl and Mervyn, two boys of eleven, undertook to find out how many pieces of pastina (small uncooked pieces of Italian pasta made with wheat flour) there were in a large jar. They first counted out 100 pieces, and were as surprised as I was to see how little space these occupied. They then scooped samples of a hundred at a time, judging 'by eye' according to the volume. Later I thought their samples were increasing in volume, and asked them to take a count (it was 200). This made the boys decide to take a larger sample as a pattern: ten sets of a hundred. But even a thousand pieces of pastina occupied a small fraction of the smallest cup, so a sample of five thousand was finally taken as the unit and the level of this sample was marked on the cup. When the count reached 29,000 (including the early samples which the boys refused to put back), they compared the counted and uncounted pastina in two identical milk containers. They found, to their relief, that the two quantities were nearly equal and announced the total to be approximately 58,000. At this point, George joined us. George had a flair for approximation, so I asked the boys whether 58,000 seemed a reasonable answer in view of the methods they had used. George suggested 60,000, and Earl and Mervyn agreed to this when they remembered that their earlier samples of a hundred had increased in size.

I was very much aware of the increase in confidence these boys gained in dealing with large numbers as a result of this experience.

On another occasion, I was concerned in a count of a different kind.

2. Some ten-year-olds had been discussing large numbers. 'What does a million look like?' they asked. I suggested that we should start by looking at a thousand. 'Do you think there are a thousand tiles on this floor?' I asked. (I had no idea of the answer.) There were wild guesses. I suggested the children should find out. The room was rectangular, and there were 36 tiles one way and 37 tiles the other way. To my surprise the children began to count on, in ones. I suggested they should try to find a better method—with no result. 'What do you have to do to

the two numbers?' I asked. 'Multiply them,' was the immediate response, but still they did nothing. 'Do you know 30×30?' I asked. '900,' they chorused, 'and 6×7 is 42, so that's 942,' one said with relief. This was said with such confidence that for the moment I was convinced! It was only later that I realized the opportunity I had missed. A diagram not only shows immediately that 942 is too small, but also gives a quick method of finding the answer by partial products $(900+210+180+42)$.

	30	7
30		
6	30	7

It also leads to the normal method of long multiplication.

ie 30 (30+7)

  6 (30+7)

I asked the children to draw a diagram, suggesting that they divide the room into easy blocks of tiles. 'You know how to multiply by ten,' I said. As a result, most children produced this diagram, and wrote:

	10	10	10	7
36	360	360	360	7 × 36

360	10×36
360	10×36
360	10×36
252	$7 \times 30 + 7 \times 6$
1332	

This, too, can lead to the usual method once the children can take the next step:

$$36 \times 30$$

I was surprised that these children were unable to do the calculation. The teacher had left, so I could not find the reason for this. Perhaps the children had not been given enough practice to fix a method they had invented? It is admirable to encourage them to devise and refine their own methods, but children require some practice if they are to achieve efficiency in reasonable calculations.

It is not difficult to plan experiences for children which will help them to devise their own methods of division. The problem lies in giving them such activities *before* they have been taught the intricate tricks of long division. I have tried the following example, but more often with adults than with nine-year-olds.

3. An elevator sign read: 'Maximum load 2000 kilogrammes.' I weigh 53 kilogrammes. How many people of my weight could be carried in this elevator? Provided I have previously given oral practice in multiplication by ten (deliberate structuring!), I find children or adults calculate:

```
2000
 530    10 of you
────
1470
 530    10 of you
────
 940
 530    10 of you
────
 410
```

The conclusion varies. I have had the following solutions:

```
410              410
371   7 of you   106    2 of you
───              ───
 39  37 of you   304
                 212    4 of you
                 ───
                  92
                  53    1 of you
                 ───
                  39   37 of you
```

Some children (and adults) can be persuaded (by questioning) to subtract higher multiples of 10, eg, 1590 (30 of you), and so refine the method:

```
 20000
  1590      30 of you
  ─────
   410
   371       7 of you
  ─────
    39      37 of you
```

Others prefer the longer method. It is surely better for them to be able to perform such calculations correctly even if this takes a little longer!

What immediate number knowledge do pupils require to be able to calculate efficiently? I list below the *minimum* number facts which should be our aim for immediate or quick recall before children are given practice in written calculations.

Immediate recall

a. Number facts up to ten. This is almost half the number shown in the table on page 88 once the commutative law for addition (eg, $5+2=2+5$) has been discovered and is used.

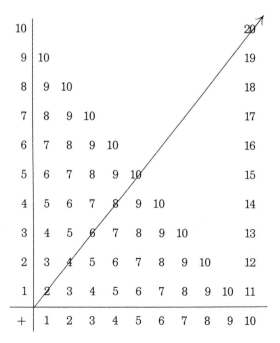

+	1	2	3	4	5	6	7	8	9	10
10										20
9	10									19
8	9	10								18
7	8	9	10							17
6	7	8	9	10						16
5	6	7	8	9	10					15
4	5	6	7	8	9	10				14
3	4	5	6	7	8	9	10			13
2	3	4	5	6	7	8	9	10		12
1	2	3	4	5	6	7	8	9	10	11

b. The diagonal numbers—doubles and halves—usually known well in excess of 10×2.

c. Adding two to, and subtracting two from any number—usually known well in excess of ten.

d. Adding ten, first to numbers one to ten, and then to the unending sequence of numbers. (A number line 100 units long, and number strips one to ten units long are invaluable at this stage.)

e. Multiplication of any whole number by ten.

f. Multiplication (and division) by three up to 10×3.

g. Squares of numbers up to 10^2.

Quick recall

a. Adding 9 to a number, eg, $9+7=16$ because $10+7=17$, and 9 is 1 less than 10.

b. Adding the near doubles, eg, $6+7$ as 2 sixes$+1$ and as 2 sevens-1.

c. Use of distributive law to build up tables, eg:
$1 \times 2 = 2$
$2 \times 2 = 4$
$3 \times 2 = 1 \times 2 + 2 \times 2$
$\quad = 2+4$
$\quad = 6$
(This is very important, too, for understanding, later on, the working of products such as:
$47 \times 58 = 40 \times 58 + 7 \times 58$)

d. With multiplication, as with addition, the number of facts to be memorized is almost halved, once the commutative law for multiplication (eg, $7 \times 2 = 2 \times 7$) has been discovered and is used. See opposite.

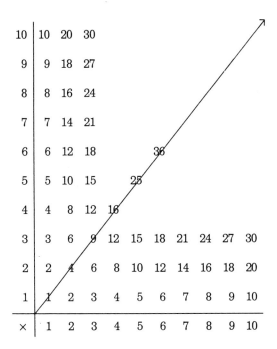

×	1	2	3	4	5	6	7	8	9	10
10	10	20	30							
9	9	18	27							
8	8	16	24							
7	7	14	21							
6	6	12	18			36				
5	5	10	15		25					
4	4	8	12	16						
3	3	6	9	12	15	18	21	24	27	30
2	2	4	6	8	10	12	14	16	18	20
1	1	2	3	4	5	6	7	8	9	10

e. Multiplication by 4 and 8 (once doubling is known), eg:
$7 \times 2 = 14$
$7 \times 4 = 28$
$7 \times 8 = 56$ by successful doubling (corresponding division facts)

f. Multiplication by 5
$9 \times 10 = 90$
$9 \times 5 = 45$ by halving

g. Multiplication by 6 and 9 (from the multiplication table of 3)
$8 \times 3 = 24$
$8 \times 6 = 48$
$8 \times 9 = 72$

Very slow pupils should not be deprived of the enjoyment of mathematics because they cannot remember multiplication facts. For them a self-made multiplication square can be kept readily available for reference, but all should be encouraged to memorize tables of two and ten.

4. An unusual piece of work involving a count was done by some twelve- to fifteen-year-olds. It concerned the Christmas carol: *The Twelve Days of Christmas:*

On the first day of Christmas my true love sent to me a partridge in a pear tree.

On the second day of Christmas my true love sent to me two turtle doves and a partridge in a pear tree.

At the end of the carol, on the twelfth day, the presents are: 12 drummers drumming, 11 pipers piping, 10 lords a-leaping, 9 ladies dancing, 8 maids a-milking, 7 swans a-swimming, 6 geese a-laying, 5 gold rings, 4 calling birds, 3 French hens, 2 turtle doves, and a partridge in a pear tree.

The teacher wrote:

This work was done by twelve-, fourteen- and fifteen-year-old girls in the selective forms of a comprehensive school.[1] It formed part of the miscellaneous mathematical activities which occupied girls after their examination. It is a summary of work which occupied mathematics lessons for several weeks at the New Year. The cumulative nature of the story, which was very humorously and dramatically portrayed in a film the girls saw, had a considerable effect on them. They were eager to discuss the film, and to find out just how the gross overpopulation of the house occurred. With delight they settled down to computation and tabulation, as a result of which the answers to various intriguing questions were revealed, for example:

[1]Comprehensive schools contain pupils from the whole ability range (in contrast to 'selective' schools). Pupils are, however, often placed in streams—or tracks —according to ability within these schools

How many French hens were there, in all, by the twelfth day?

Of which kind of gift was the greatest number received?

How many miscellaneous gifts arrived on any particular day?

Tabulation led to recognition of number patterns. Soon someone suggested graphical representation. The regularity and symmetry of the resulting graphs were anticipated, since the girls had had experience of similar number patterns resulting from calculations of areas of rectangles with a given perimeter, and of lengths of chords of a circle. The discovery that these new graphs were of the same shape as 'The areas of rectangles' and 'A number and its square' caused great excitement. The twelve-year-olds stopped at this point. The fourteen-year-olds generalized the result and related it to an algebraic graph. The fifteen-year-olds continued the investigation until they had explained the resemblances to their own satisfaction.

The work described here was prepared for an exhibition of work to go overseas. It was voluntary and was largely unaided. Advice was given if it was asked for. Some of the contributions were very considerably neater and more attractive than the usual standard achieved by their contributors, and in every case they were submitted with pride.

Mary wrote: Have you ever thought what would happen if you were in the position of the fair lady who was the recipient of the gifts? The same presents as you had received yesterday and the previous days will arrive again today as well as the gifts for today, so as you can imagine this would cause chaos by the end of the twelve days!

	Total
Jennifer wrote: 1 partridge on each of 12 days	12
2 turtle doves on each of 11 days	22

She then drew a column graph to illustrate the total of each gift.

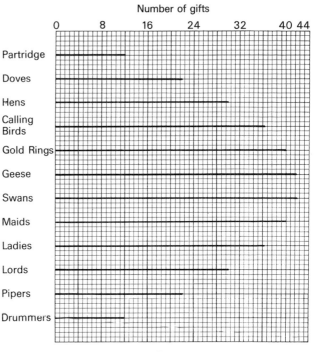

Number of gifts

| | 0 | 8 | 16 | 24 | 32 | 40 44 |

Partridge

Doves

Hens

Calling Birds

Gold Rings

Geese

Swans

Maids

Ladies

Lords

Pipers

Drummers

Graph to show the total number of each different gift

Julie made a table and then found the algebraic relationship, adding the zero values afterwards to complete the graph.

x	13−x	y
1	12−	12
2	11	22
3	10	30
4	9	36
5	8	40
6	7	42
7	6	42
8	5	40
9	4	36
10	3	30
11	2	22
12	1	12

Theresa drew the graph of $y=x^2$ *to the same scale and cut it out. She wrote:* When the graph of $y=x^2$ is turned upside down it fits the curve of $y=x$ $(13-x)$.

Elaine did her calculation a different way:

1st day	1	1
2nd day	1+2	3
3rd day	1+2+3	6
4th day	1+2+3+4	10

12th day 1+2+3+4+5+6+7+8+9+10+11+12 78

She too drew the graph (below). This curve resembles the graph of a number and its square.

Julie drew the graph of x $(x-1)$. *The table for this is identical with Elaine's table. Ann wrote:*

Number of gifts on each day

1st day	1
2nd day	1+2
3rd day	1+2+3

Generalized forms—

xth day $\quad$ 1+2+3 . . . . +x

$$S_n = \frac{n}{2} [2n+(n-1)\,d]$$

$$S_x = \frac{x}{2} (x+1)$$

Graph to show the number of gifts which were delivered each day

This is the complete curve which forms the boundary of the column graph.

This project is an admirable example of the close association between number patterns and relations, algebraic and graphical relations. In a later section we shall give further examples of this important aspect of arithmetic.

Number patterns

Patterns of all kinds have a strong appeal for young children, and number patterns are no exception (page 49). Discovery of pattern in number gives children confidence, and is especially valuable in helping them to understand that numbers do not behave in a wayward fashion, and that they can expect to discover patterns.

5. Even at the age of seven, some children become aware of patterns in number.

For example, a seven-year-old boy, John, watched his teacher as she worked with a group of eight-year-olds, helping them to build up the 'binary pattern of the kitchen weights'. The children arranged their results as a table:

32	16	8	4	2	1	oz
					1	1
				1	0	2
				1	1	3
			1	0	0	4
			1	0	1	5
						6

For example, to weigh a 3 oz parcel, the children set out one 2 oz weight and one 1 oz weight.

The teacher sent John away to read a book, because she thought he was too young to do this work, but he was soon back at the front, where he could see what the others were doing. Next morning, he brought a piece of wallpaper to school 'because an ordinary piece of paper was not big enough to show the pattern'. He had noticed the 1010 pattern of the unit column and the 1100 pattern of the second column, and expected a 111000 pattern in the third column. He was most excited when he discovered a different pattern. Of course John could not perform operations with binary numbers, but the pattern of the table made a strong appeal to him.

The second piece of work arose with eight-year-olds who had been working with a hundred square. A child suggested investigating less conventional arrangements of the set of natural numbers 1 to 100. From a group discussion, various methods of arranging the set were forthcoming: eg, numbers continuing like a snake to 100:

Vertical numbering in tens

1	11
2	12
3	13
4	14
.	.
.	.
10	20 etc

From discussion of the vertical method, it was eventually decided to build up to the hundred square by dealing with it in sections.

$$\begin{bmatrix} 1 \\ 2 \\ 3 \\ . \\ . \\ 10 \end{bmatrix} \begin{bmatrix} 1 & 2 \\ 3 & 4 \\ 5 & 6 \\ 7 & 8 \\ 9 & 10 \end{bmatrix} \begin{bmatrix} 1 & 2 & 3 \\ 4 & 5 & 6 \\ 7 & 8 & 9 \\ 10 & 11 & 12 \\ 13 & 14 & 15 \end{bmatrix} \begin{bmatrix} 1 & 2 & 3 & 4 \\ 5 & 6 & 7 & 8 \\ 9 & 10 & 11 & 12 \\ 13 & 14 & 15 & 16 \\ 17 & 18 & 19 & 20 \end{bmatrix} \text{to} \begin{bmatrix} 1, 2, & \dots & 10 \\ 11, & \dots & 20 \\ 21, 22, & \dots & 30 \end{bmatrix}$$

Some children decided to include 'the pattern of 12', and so in their vertical numbering they chose 1–12, ie:

$$\begin{bmatrix} 1 \\ 2 \\ 3 \\ . \\ . \\ 12 \end{bmatrix} \begin{bmatrix} 1 & 2 \\ 3 & 4 \\ 5 & 6 \\ . & . \\ . & . \\ 23 & 24 \end{bmatrix} \begin{bmatrix} 1 & 2 & 3 \\ 4 & 5 & 6 \\ . & . & . \\ . & . & . \\ 34 & 35 & 36 \end{bmatrix}$$

When the groups began making comparisons, they looked for repeating patterns and listed them. But they had some difficulty in expressing their findings precisely. After they had made a number of comparisons, they found that they did not need more than a glance, as each pattern showed a similar result: eg, when dealing with the pattern of seven, they found seven similar patterns of the end digit, and the difference within each pattern was seven.

(Look for the cycle of repetitions of the end digit in each column.)

1	2	3	4	5	6	7
8	9	10	11	12	13	14
15	16	17	18	19	20	21
22	23	24	25	26	27	28
29	30	31	32	33	34	35
36	37	38	39	40	41	42
43	44	45	46	47	48	49
50	51	52	53	54	55	56
57	58	59	60	61	62	63
64	65	66	67	68	69	70
71	72	73	74	75	76	77
78	79	80	81	82	83	84

Column 1: *185296307*418. What will the next eight digits be? Do you recognize the set of digits (italicized)? Compare this pattern with that in the second column, and so on.

To follow their investigations further, they decided to extend the setting-out of the numbers beyond 1–12, to find if the patterns continued— which of course they did.

This work led to many other table patterns in weight, money, length, etc, and to the comparison of these tables; eg, what patterns in weights and measures resemble the patterns of table 2, table 4, table 8, etc?

6. A lecturer from a college of education describes some work which he carried out with nine-year-olds.

These examples of number patterns were originally developed to help a class of forty nine-and-a-half-year-olds ('B' stream children), who were having difficulty in understanding the significance of place value, and particularly with the use of '0' as a place holder.

I first discovered this weakness by using a series of simple diagnostic tests. From these tests I also noticed that some of the boys were quite capable of coping with the examples, but were unsure about how to record what they were doing. I thought that it might help if we investigated number patterns, as a way of aiding the children to acquire a more relaxed attitude when handling numbers. I felt there was a need to do something which would liberate them from the grip of the basic formal operations, and give them a sense of fluency.

I took as my starting point the examples of number patterns and magic squares set out in JUNIORS LEARNING MATHEMATICS.[1] *For all this work, the children used quarter-inch squared paper. Magic squares led to a variety of multiplication squares. I then began thinking up various ways of playing with the series of natural numbers. For example, the natural numbers increase by one—what happens if we increase by two or three at each step?*

[1]By Barnett, Faithful and Theakston, Ward Lock 1962

The natural numbers:	1 2 3 4 5 6 7 8 9 10
adding two:	1 3 5 7 9 11 13 15 17 19
adding three:	1 4 7 10 13 16 19 22 25 28
adding four:	1 5 9 13 17 21 25 29 33 37

The least interested noticed the emergence of the sequence in the second column, the more advanced began picking out odd and even numbers and, with some prompting, found the pattern 'hidden' in the diagonal lines. Such simple exercises were completed by all the children, there was no rush, and each finished at his own speed. The quicker ones went on to another pattern and all had a sense of getting something done. No one could get things wrong!

I introduced the children to the distinction between 'number' and 'digit',[1] and from this we went on to examine what happens when you write out the multiplication tables and then go down the columns adding the digits of each product. They had little difficulty in seeing that this addition might have to be performed more than once. The digits of the number 48 add up to 12, which again adds up to 3. Thus, for the table of threes we got the following digit sums:

Compare this with the table of twos!

	digit sum		digit sum
1×3= 3	3	1×2= 2	2
2×3= 6	6	2×2= 4	4
3×3= 9	9	3×2= 6	6
4×3=12	3	4×2= 8	8
5×3=15	6	5×2=10	1
6×3=18	9	6×2=12	3
7×3=21	3	7×2=14	5
8×3=24	6	8×2=16	7
9×3=27	9	9×2=18	9
10×3=30	3	10×2=20	2
11×3=33	6	11×2=22	4
12×3=36	9	12×2=24	6

What happens when we do the same thing with the other tables?

[1] Eg: 25 is a number; 2 and 5 are digits

Other patterns were produced by simply staggering

rows of numbers and adding the results in vertical columns. Here the layout of the numbers makes a pattern in its own right, something which caught the imagination of one or two boys who went on to make elaborate patterns of their own on the same lines:

		1	2	3	4	5	6	7	8	9	10	
	1	2	3	4	5	6	7	8	9	10	11	
1	2	3	4	5	6	7	8	9	10	11	12	

Adding: 1 3 6 9 12 15 18 21 24 27 30 33
Difference: 2 3 3 3 3 3 3 3 3 3 3

and this figure always equals the number of rows except for the first figure. (Perhaps the reader would like to investigate this apparent inconsistency.) Similarly the rows can be moved in and out at will:

		1	2	3	4	5	6	7	8	9
	1	2	3	4	5	6	7	8	9	
1	2	3	4	5	6	7	8	9		
	1	2	3	4	5	6	7	8	9	
		1	2	3	4	5	6	7	8	9

Adding: 1 4 9 14 19 24 29 34 39
Difference: 3 5 5 5 5 5 5 5

Another arrangement we tried was to pair off the natural numbers and see what happened when they were multiplied together:

1×2 3×4 5×6 7×8 9×10

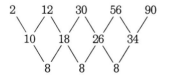

. . . writing the products underneath
. . . finding the differences
. . . taking further difference

What happens when we do the same thing, starting with the next pair in the series:
2×3 4×5 6×7 8×9 . . . ?

Again the pairs can be added:
1+2 3+4 5+6 7+8 9+10

3 7 11 15 19 . . writing the sum
underneath
4 4 4 4 . . taking the
differences

Numbers begin to show their inner consistency in this way.

The variety of simple number patterns which can be devised solely on the basis of the series of natural numbers[1] kept the intelligent ones in the class fully occupied. There are, of course, other possibilities with figurate numbers. When doing these, I used the small self-adhesive spots which can be bought in a variety of colours, and which have obvious advantages in the classroom. Using these, the children made up numbers based on triangles, squares and rectangles.

```
o      oo     ooo    oooo
       oo     ooo    oooo
              ooo    oooo
                     oooo
```

1 1+3=4 1+3+5=9 1+3+5+7=16 *the beginnings of square numbers, and the possible foundation of later work on indices.*

```
o      o      o      o
       oo     oo     oo
              ooo    ooo
                     oooo
```

1 1+2=3 1+2+3=6 1+2+3+4=10 *and so on with rectangular numbers.*

Prime numbers[2] were investigated through pattern. A column of the natural numbers was examined to see which numbers could be divided by any other number. The ones which cannot, stood out.

[1] 1, 2, 3, 4, etc are called natural or counting numbers

[2] Prime numbers are numbers whose only other factor is 1. So 2, 3, 5, 7 are prime numbers; 4, 6, 8, 9 are not prime

1	1
2	1
3	1
4	1, 2
5	1
6	1, 2, 3
7	1

8	1, 2, 4	
9	1, 3,	
10	1, 2, 5	
11	1	
12	1, 2, 3, 4, 6	
13	1	
14	1, 2, 7	
15		

From these examples it will, I hope, be apparent that such simple number patterns are easy enough to invent. Moreover, the children soon made up their own patterns. Several boys and girls worked out new patterns at home as well as during school hours. The use of coloured pencils and gummed paper also adds interest. Even the most unresponsive girls were finally won over when they saw the patterns of numbers involved in curve stitching. There are, of course, various possibilities in such number patterns. Without going into detail, I must point out that after five weeks or so the children were able to work out multiplication and division problems, using the principle of logarithms. Perhaps there are opportunities here which we might easily overlook if we confine ourselves to traditional number work in the four basic operations. I felt that the main gain in all this play with numbers was in the fresh enthusiasm it aroused among the children, and, in one or two cases, something like a research attitude. I hoped that the children had gained a feeling of release and had been made a little more aware of their own ability to make numbers work for them rather than the other way round.

7. A ten-year-old girl who was transferred from a school in which she learnt arithmetic only (and by traditional methods) delighted her new teacher when she produced the following piece of work, her first creative work in mathematics:

Strange numbers
One day I tried taking square numbers away from each other.

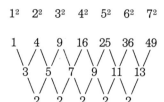

1^2 2^2 3^2 4^2 5^2 6^2 7^2

1   4   9   16   25   36   49

3   5   7   9   11   13

2   2   2   2   2

Then I tried it in power 3 like this:
1^3 2^3 3^3 4^3 5^3 6^3 7^3

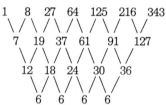

1   8   27   64   125   216   343

7   19   37   61   91   127

12   18   24   30   36

6   6   6   6

I thought there might be a pattern between these numbers so I did the same thing again only this time using power 4:

1^4 2^4 3^4 4^4 5^4 6^4

1   16   81   256   625   1296

15   65   175   369   671

50   110   194   302

60   84   108

24   24

I started to study these numbers and found what I thought was the pattern:

2   6   24 (the last number of each
                     pattern)

   ×3   ×4

If this was right, using power 5 we should get:
$5 \times 24 = 120$

I tried this out and this was my answer. (*Difference between 1^5 $2^5 \rightarrow 6^5$ worked out in detail.*)

102

Now can the reader work out what the answer would be if power 6 were used?

8. Factor patterns by an eleven-year-old.

Teacher's notes

As the class had been working on number patterns for some time, this gave me the opportunity to suggest that somebody might like to examine factors and construct a 'graph' to show factor patterns. Julie wanted to do this, so we talked about it and decided on the size of the graph to be produced. As the work proceeded, Julie pointed out certain obvious patterns, and we discussed the possibility of other patterns arising. She had little difficulty in constructing the graph, and fully understood what she was doing.

When the work was completed, we discussed the best ways of interpreting the graph and recording some of the information shown on it. The written work required a number of rough copies before the finished copy was to our mutual satisfaction. Julie is a bright, intelligent girl, and I am sure that in doing this type of work she has gained a greater understanding of mathematics. Apart from a little help in preparing the graph, and brief discussions now and again as the work proceeded, this is her own work.

Julie's own account

I started working on the factor graph when we were doing some work on number patterns. To do this I had to get a large piece of paper because I wanted to work with high numbers and find how many factors these high numbers had. As I began working I saw a number of patterns coming out. For example for number one, I filled in every square (vertically), for number two every second square, for number three every third square, and so on. As I got further I noticed that the tables were forming long diagonal lines. There are no diagonals above the table 'one' diagonal because one is the lowest table. (Author's note: Which multiplication tables would provide entries above the diagonal?)

An interesting pattern, of 3 squares, occurs at (8, 9), (15, 16), (24, 25), (35, 36), (48, 49), (63, 64), (80, 81).

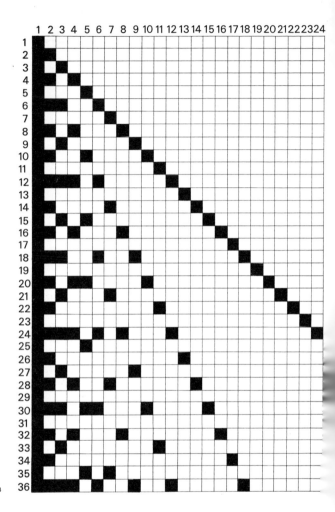

Factor patterns

I found this pattern was:

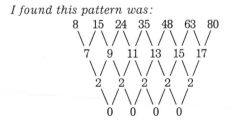

A further pattern occurs on the following numbers like this:

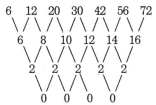

$$6 \quad 12 \quad 20 \quad 30 \quad 42 \quad 56 \quad 72$$
$$\diagdown \diagup \diagdown \diagup \diagdown \diagup \diagdown \diagup \diagdown \diagup \diagdown \diagup$$
$$6 \quad 8 \quad 10 \quad 12 \quad 14 \quad 16$$
$$\diagdown \diagup \diagdown \diagup \diagdown \diagup \diagdown \diagup \diagdown \diagup$$
$$2 \quad 2 \quad 2 \quad 2 \quad 2$$
$$\diagdown \diagup \diagdown \diagup \quad \diagdown \diagup$$
$$0 \quad 0 \quad 0 \quad 0$$

Another pattern like this occurs on the numbers (10, 9, 8), (22, 21, 20), (34, 33, 32), (46, 45, 44), (58, 57, 56), (70, 69, 68), (82, 81, 80):

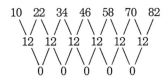

$$10 \quad 22 \quad 34 \quad 46 \quad 58 \quad 70 \quad 82$$
$$\diagdown \diagup \diagdown \diagup \diagdown \diagup \diagdown \diagup \diagdown \diagup \diagdown \diagup$$
$$12 \quad 12 \quad 12 \quad 12 \quad 12 \quad 12$$
$$\diagdown \diagup \diagdown \diagup \diagdown \diagup \diagdown \diagup \diagdown \diagup$$
$$0 \quad 0 \quad 0 \quad 0 \quad 0$$

I looked to see if, as the numbers got higher, they would have more factors, but it is not so. For instance, 24 has got 8 factors and 50 has only 6. The numbers with the most factors are numbers 60 and 84 with 12 factors each, and the ones with least factors are the prime numbers 1, 2, 3, 5, 7, 11, 13, 17, 19, 23, 29, 31, 37, 41, 43, 47, 53, 61, 67, 71, 73 and 83. (Author's note: As the above work suggests, factor patterns are a very rich topic. It is suggested that interested readers should make a table for themselves, and make a note of the variety of patterns which emerge. An alternative version of this table can be made by labelling all shaded squares in column 1, all squares in column 2 with numeral 2, and so on. Columns, rows and diagonals, as well as patterns of the type described in Julie's experiment, are worth investigating.)

9. Crazy animals by a twelve-year-old (See page 117.)
This was a topic which was inspired by toys given away with a particular brand of toffee.

As the class had seen combinations of sets before, it seemed a good idea to have a look at the combinations which could be obtained using these toys. Each toy depicted an animal and could be split into a head and a tail. There were four animals, each available in four colours, and any head could be joined to any tail. The animals were cockerel, elephant, camel, and fish, and each was obtainable in the colours red, blue, green, and yellow.

It would have cost too much to supply the proper plastic toys and so it was decided to make enlargements, using squared paper, and thus duplicate the required number.

The shapes were cut and painted, and finally cut into heads and tails. From this, charts could be made of combinations.

Two charts were made. The first was a simple chart, showing the range of possibilities for each animal made of one colour only ($4 \times 4 = 16$ combinations). The second chart was suggested by a first-year form to show all the possibilities for all the animals in four different colours each ($4 \times 4 \times 4 \times 4 = 256$ combinations).

The whole class was occupied for four mathematics periods, and some boys completed the work after school.

These examples show that number is a topic which can have a fascination for virtually all pupils, provided they are encouraged to discover, from the outset, that number patterns usually emerge when we operate on a number sequence (such as the counting numbers, 1 2 3 4 5 6 7 8 9). For example, the operations $+4$, -1, $\times 3$, $\div 2$, squaring, etc, would all lead to new number sequences (provided we do not make an arithmetical slip). Constructing and finding new number patterns lead to a gain in confidence in handling numbers as illustrated by a slow nine-year-old who said, after several sessions on such work, 'I love arithmetic now. You always get your answers right—or, if you do make a mistake, you can find it before the teacher does.' Such confidence motivates children to learn the useful number facts they require.

Moreover, since many number patterns arise through spatial patterns (such as patterns made with identical squares or triangles), this work can be reinforced in another field. No pupil, however slow, should be denied the opportunity of discovering and appreciating basic number patterns.

2 Man Must Measure

Measuring can be a very satisfying and demanding activity—or it can be a complete waste of time. Running around with a tape measure or trundle wheel is not necessarily a mathematical experience. Since practical work is time-consuming, we, as teachers, need to have a clear mathematical purpose in mind for each practical activity. In addition, measuring experiences need to be relevant to children's interests. Above all, the activities should be carefully planned, from term to term and year to year, so that they become successively more demanding. In fact, measuring experiences can be structured so that they give children opportunities for learning a wide variety of important interrelated mathematical ideas such as comparison, by subtraction and division; approximation; ordering (putting in order) operations of subtraction, division, addition and multiplication; ratio and proportion. Some examples of children's work will illustrate this.

Length 1. Teachers have found that many preliminary experiences are necessary before children are ready to appreciate the need for standard units of measurement. For example:

Some eight-year-olds who were having their first experience of measuring told me, with some excitement, that they had just measured the width of the classroom and found it to be six-and-a-half bodies. 'Whose body?' I asked. Three friends jumped up: one was at least a head taller than the other two. 'Would it have been different if you had used Roger (the tall boy) only?' 'Yes,' was the reply. 'Roger would have been tired.' 'But would the width have been six-and-a-half Rogers?' I persisted. 'Yes, was the immediate answer. 'It's the same room, isn't it?' So these children, at their first experience of measuring, had not yet realized the need for equal units and certainly not for standard units. But one child quickly pointed out that the answer would have been fewer Rogers, since he was taller than the others. It is important to stress that children and adults normally pass through certain stages in their learning, depending on previous experiments.

2. Here is an example showing how teachers plan experiences which lead children to appreciate the function of standard units:

A class of eight-year-olds read in the Bible that Goliath's height was six cubits and a span. Unable to visualize this, they decided to make a model of Goliath. They drew a large face and then experimented to find out what the height would be. First they marked out the height using a boy's cubit (length from elbow to middle finger tip) and span. They were disappointed to find that Goliath seemed to be only a mini-giant. This made them realize that people in Goliath's time would have used man-sized units, so they marked out the height using the cubit and span of the headmaster. This time they were satisfied, and completed their picture. But they found it very difficult to explain to children in another class how tall the giant was. This made them return to their model, and measure its height in feet, units already familiar to them. When they told their friends that Goliath was ten feet tall, they appreciated that he really was a giant. Later, the teacher tried to persuade the children to find Goliath's height in metric units. After some discussion they refused, pointing out that metric units were not suited to Goliath's day and age. 'It's like making Goliath travel in an aeroplane,' they said. These varied activities in measurement, first with arbitrary units (of the children's own choosing), and later with a wide range of standard units, appropriate to the work in hand, ensure an understanding not only of measurement of all types, but also of the fact that measurement can never be more than an approximation. For example, the degree of approximation appropriate for the diameter of a car cylinder is very different from that appropriate for the distance from Edinburgh to London!

3. The next piece of work was done by a group of eight-year-olds in a small rural school. Here is the teacher's description of how the work arose:

It began last term with a BBC Broadcast 'Time and Tune'. One of the songs was about a brontosaurus, and the children really enjoyed it. We contacted the local library, and the librarian was able to send us several simple books on dinosaurs. From these books, the art and English developed. Then the BBC broadcast a programme on fossils. The story of Mary Anning and her discovery of the skeleton of the Ichthyosaurus was told. The children were delighted because they had already found this story in their books. In the previous term, the children had measured each other and made a graph of their heights. They had made a plan of the classroom and the hall, and I think it was natural for them to compare the length of the dinosaurs with the lengths which they already knew. Here is the children's writing in which they make comparisons between the lengths with which they are already familiar: the school hall, and their own heights. (Once again, biggest and smallest are used in reference to height even though this is a sophisticated piece of work.) The children drew a graph showing the length of some of the dinosaurs they studied.

Length of our hall is 40 feet
The classroom is   25 feet
Mandy's height is   4 feet

Mandy wrote: 'The Diplodocus is twenty times as long as me. The Diplodocus is the biggest dinosaur on the graph. It is twice as long as the hall and five feet besides. The Diplodocus is seven times as long as the

Glyptodon and a foot more. The smallest dinosaur is Glyptodon. It is twelve feet long. It is three times the length of me so that it makes me four feet. I am just over, so we took it to the nearest foot. Although the Glyptodon is very big it is tiny beside the Diplodocus.'

4. Some nine-year-olds were asked whether their classroom was twice as long as it was wide.

The teacher had hidden the measuring sticks and tapes, so that the children were compelled to use arbitrary units. One counted the breeze blocks of which the walls were made. Others counted the square tiles on the floor or the larger squares on the ceiling. The remainder decided to pace the length and breadth. The variety of answers can be imagined, but all the children were able to check for themselves whether the smaller measure was half the larger and the larger twice the smaller. Next, the room was measured in imperial and in metric units and the results were compared. This enquiry was the starting point for an understanding of averages. How many centimetres long is your average pace? How many paces do you need to take in order to obtain a reasonable average? The children solved this by various methods: finding the average using 10, 20, 30 paces; walking until they were 'in their stride' and measuring a single pace. They compared results obtained by the different methods, and tried to find the best method. Finally, they used pacing to measure the playground, and checked using a long measuring tape. This activity was followed by a spirited discussion about approximation.

Weight and volume

1. It is sometimes difficult to separate experiences in these two aspects of measurement, more particularly with older children who are beginning to accumulate experience concerning the difficult concept of density. The examples given here illustrate the close inter-relationship between these two topics.

A class of eight-year-olds had weighed themselves in kilogrammes, to the nearest whole number—a novel experience for them. Now, my own weight of fifty kilogrammes is very convenient and I asked the children if any of them were half my weight? To the children's surprise and delight, six, of assorted heights, had recorded their weights as twenty-five kilogrammes. When these children ranged themselves in order of height, there was much discussion about the variations in size and shape. Finally, all the children in the class arranged themselves in three sets: those who weighed less than twenty-five kilogrammes, those who weighed more, and the set of children weighing twenty-five kilogrammes. So the initial experience of weighing had served to introduce ideas of approximation, of comparison and ordering, and of inequalities—ideas of major importance in mathematics.

2. Another group of eight-year-olds in the same class, had made a collection of containers, and were asked by their teacher to put these in order beginning with the smallest.

To the teacher's surprise, the children began by weighing the containers, and 'ordered' them from lightest to heaviest. Then they discussed trying to find out which container would hold most sand. (They rejected water because one container was a cardboard box.) Once more they weighed each container, this time filled with sand. 'We shall have to subtract the weight of each container because they are all different weights,' said Ann. Again the teacher was surprised that the children compared contents by weighing, and asked if they could compare quantities of sand in any other way. Eventually they poured the sand from each container into pound jam jars and compared the levels. 'But weighing is easier,' they commented. (And so it is, if dial scales, which can be easily read, are available.)

3. Nine-year-olds, Stephen and David, were asked to arrange in order, from lightest to heaviest, water, beans and marbles.

First, they weighed a cupful of each, but they were puzzled by the results they obtained; beans, water, marbles. Stephen's immediate reaction was to put first a marble and then some beans into the water. He was reassured to see them all sink to the bottom, as he expected. Both boys discussed the experiment with their teacher, commenting: 'But the cup of beans was not *full* of beans. There were air spaces between the beans.' The teacher then asked the boys if they could first estimate and then find the fraction of air space in a cup of marbles. They estimated the air space as one quarter. Their first method of finding the actual fraction was to fill the air spaces in a cup of marbles with water, then pour off the water into a scale pan and read its weight. They compared this with the weight of a cup filled with water and found the fraction to be nearly one half. They then wondered if any water had been left on the marbles so they checked by a second method. They first weighed the cup of marbles and then weighed the cup after the air spaces had been filled with water. By subtraction they found the weight of the water—which differed very little from that obtained by the first method! Of course they then repeated the experiment with the beans. They wrote: 'But we had to be very quick because beans soaked up water.'

4. Some ten-year-olds were asked to bring to school two large stones of different shapes but which they estimated to be of the same volume. They were asked to check their estimates in two ways.

At first they weighed the stones—no two weighed the same. 'But how can you be sure that they are made of the same material?' asked the teacher. Some children compared the volumes by immersing the two stones, one at a time, in a wide glass jar partly full of water and marking the levels as each stone was immersed. Others filled a jar to the brim with water; they stood this in a scale pan, and lowered each stone in turn into the water. In each case, the overflow was both weighed and measured in a homemade measuring jar. It was found that no one had found stones of identical volume although some were very nearly the same. These children were then asked to find how many times as heavy as water their stones were; so each weighed the stones and compared the weights with the corresponding overflow. 'The stones are nearly three times as heavy as water', they said. They then repeated this experiment, using marbles, a large iron weight, and other materials which interested them. Finally the children put the materials in order, from the lightest to the heaviest. They had no idea, of course, that they had been comparing 'specific gravities' and using ratios with confidence.

Area Examples of straightforward measurement of areas will be found in Chapter 4. Here is a more complex application of measurement of area.

Some ten-year-olds were asked to find the average pressure on each square inch of their feet (when standing on both feet). Here are some of the results, which were carefully arranged in order. Although each child calculated the area of his/her foot to the nearest half square inch, the pressure was given in pounds per square inch to two decimal places, in order that the results could be put in order according to pressure. Even so, some children were found to have the same pressure; results for girls and boys were entered in different colours to see if anything further could be discovered.

Name	lb/sq. inch	weight (lb)	Area of both feet (sq. inch)
Karen	2.79	84	34
Hazel	2.54	94	37
Jimmy	2.25	84	37
Heather	2.17	61	28
Colin	1.76	67	38
Robert	1.61	45	28

This table provoked considerable discussion about variation in weight and foot area. Finally, the children began to ask whether the pressure on the feet of various large animals would be very different from their recorded findings for the class. Hazel wrote: 'Our class wondered about the pressure of an elephant's foot, so before Christmas I wrote to Belle Vue Zoo asking them to draw round an elephant's foot. In about another week I received the elephant's foot.'

Hazel calculated:
Area of elephant's foot — 136 square inches
Weight of elephant — 3 tons 5 cwt

She calculated that the pressure would be 13.38 lb per square inch. (In the UK, 1 ton=2240 lb).

Time When children become confident in measuring they can be given more complex problems, as the following examples show.

1. A ten-year-old was using a ramp fitted with rails down which a truck could run freely. He was experimenting to see what he could do to alter the speed of the truck, taking the time with a stop watch. After first adding loads to the truck and later changing the gradient of the ramp, he asked his teacher: 'If I use two bricks to prop up the ramp instead of one, and if I time the truck from top to bottom of the ramp, will the second time be half the first?' The teacher answered this truthfully: 'I don't know. Why don't you experiment to see?' So Peter and his friend spent a morning on this problem and made a graph to show how the time changed with the number of bricks used to prop up the ramp. (This problem eventually led Peter to discover the calculus.)[2]

For simple problems on time the reader is referred to pp 42, 43 MATHEMATICS IN PRIMARY SCHOOLS Schools Council Curriculum Bulletin No. 1, HMSO (3rd ed. 1969)

[2]For details of Peter's work see *ibid* pp 80, 81, 82

2. The next account illustrates the importance of the questions teachers ask their children. Questions should be as challenging and undirected as possible.

They should give just enough help to interest a child and set him thinking. It is always possible to close an open question if children require more help and guidance. It is *never* possible to open a directed question. By the time such a question has been asked, the child already knows the answer! The following two contrasting examples illustrate the importance of asking questions which allow children to do the thinking and planning for themselves.

For several years I had given considerable direction to children and teachers in isolating the variables when working with a pendulum. For example, one assignment was: 'Time the pendulum for thirty swings for lengths 6 in., 12 in., 18 in., as far as 48 in. Draw a graph. Can you find from your graph the length of a pendulum which beats seconds?'

A group of ten-year-olds performed the experiment carefully and obtained a reasonable result. A month later, I discussed the pendulum with the same group. 'What did you discover?' I asked. Their recollections were so hazy and confused that we had to start at the beginning once more.

Page 117
Number patterns can be as attractive as patterns with shapes

Twelve-year-olds were intrigued by the number of combinations they could make with the separate heads and tails of four animals in four different colours

Page 118
Which is the most popular pet? (Eight-year-olds)

Bird watching. A sustained observation by ten-year-olds

Page 119
Chance and probability. Pin tossing by thirteen-year-olds

The Blue Whale. Is the model a true scale model? A sustained investigation by nine-year-olds

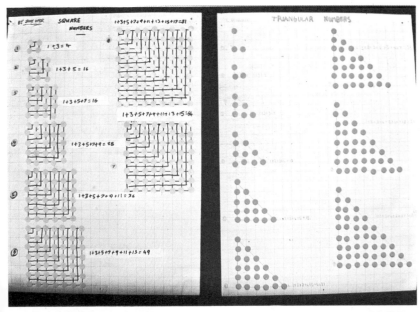

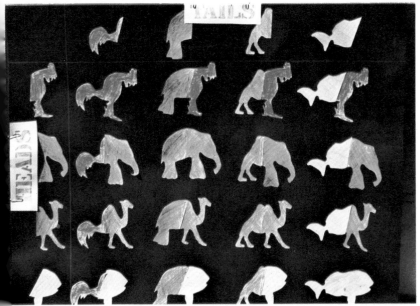

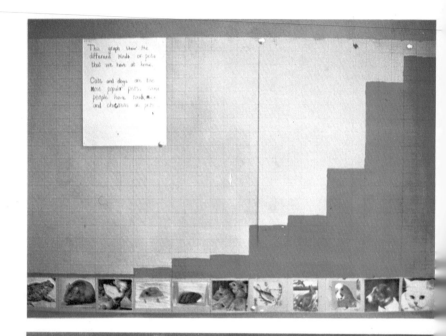

This graph show the
different kinds of pets
that we have at home.

Cats and dogs are the
most popular pets. Some
people have toads, mice
and chickens as pets.

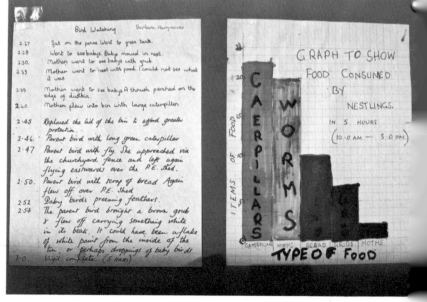

Bird Watching   Barbara Humphreys

2.27   Sat on the fence. Went to green tank.
2.28   Went to see babys. Baby moved in nest.
2.30   Mother went to see babys with grub.
2.35   Mother went to nest with food. I could not see what
        it was.
2.35   Mother went to see babys. A thrush perched on the
        edge of dustbin.
2.40   Mother flew into bin with large caterpillar.

2.45   Replaced the lid of the bin to afford greater
        protection.
2.46   Parent bird with long green caterpillar.
2.47   Parent bird with fly. She approached via
        the churchyard fence and left again
        flying eastwards over the P.E. shed.
2.50   Parent bird with scrap of bread. Again
        flew off over P.E. Shed.
2.52   Baby birds preening feathers.
2.54   The parent bird brought a brown grub
        & flew off carrying something white
        in its beak. It could have been a flake
        of white paint from the inside of the
        tin, or perhaps droppings of baby birds.
3.0   Vigil complete. (5 Hrs)

GRAPH TO SHOW
FOOD CONSUMED
BY
NESTLINGS.

IN 5 HOURS
(10.0 AM — 3.0 PM)

ITEMS OF FOOD

CAERPILLARS   WORMS   BREAD   GRUBS   MOTHS

TYPE OF FOOD

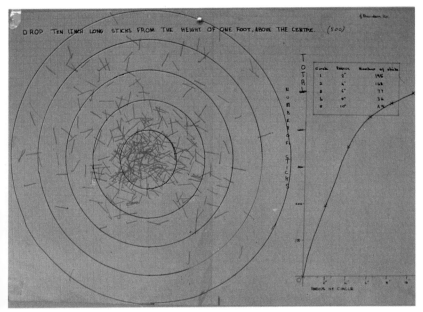

DROP TEN 1 INCH LONG STICKS FROM THE HEIGHT OF ONE FOOT, ABOVE THE CENTRE. (500)

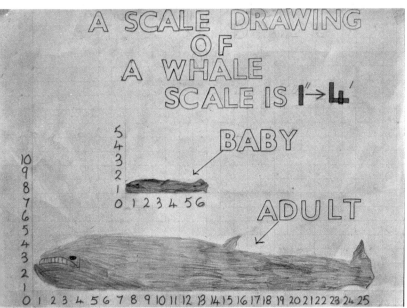

A SCALE DRAWING
OF
A WHALE
SCALE IS 1″→4′

BABY

ADULT

What is the best
shape for a package?
An enquiry by
thirteen-year-olds

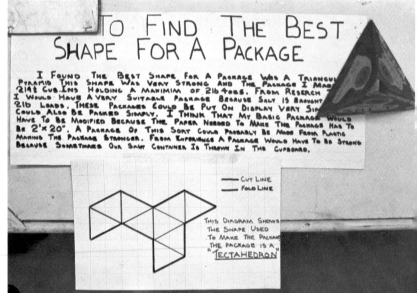

TO FIND THE BEST
SHAPE FOR A PACKAGE

I FOUND THE BEST SHAPE FOR A PACKAGE WAS A TRIANGU
PYRAMID THIS SHAPE WAS VERY STRONG AND THE PACKAGE I MAD
214½ CUB.INS HOLDING A MAXIMIM OF 2lb 4ozs. FROM RESEARCH
I WOULD HAVE A VERY SUITABLE PACKAGE BECAUSE SALT IS BROUGHT
2lb LOADS, THESE PACKAGES COULD BE PUT ON DISPLAY VERY SIM
COULD ALSO BE PACKED SIMPLY. I THINK THAT MY BASIC PACKAGE WOULD
HAVE TO BE MODIFIED BECAUSE THE PAPER NEEDED TO MAKE THE PACKAGE HAS TO
BE 2'x 20". A PACKAGE OF THIS SORT COULD PROBABLY BE MADE FROM PLASTIC
MAKING THE PACKAGE STRONGER. FROM EXPERIENCE A PACKAGE WOULD HAVE TO BE STRONG
BECAUSE SOMETIMES OUR SALT CONTAINER IS THROWN IN THE CUPBOARD.

— CUT LINE
— FOLD LINE

THIS DIAGRAM SHOWS
THE SHAPE USED
TO MAKE THE PACKAG
THE PACKAGE IS A
"TECTAHEDRON"

Last summer I was working with a group of nine- and ten-year-old boys in Lower Manhattan. We had decided to time various objects which the boys had chosen to roll down a long slope in the corridor. We had no stop watch, so I had added a length of fine string and a piece of plasticine to our collection. When the boys asked for a stop watch, I asked them if they could devise a means of timing from the materials I had provided. On seeing these, Richard immediately suggested making a pendulum. It so happened that there was a large hook fixed at a height of seven feet above the slope to which the boys attached the longest pendulum they could make. 'Where shall we start?' I asked. 'Up at the ceiling, straight out,' Earl replied. 'Does it matter where we start?' I questioned. They decided that it did matter, and we set the pendulum swinging. 'Does it beat regularly?' I asked. 'Let's count,' they replied. But the boys decided that the pendulum was swinging too slowly for effective timing. 'How shall we change the beat?' I asked. 'Shorten the string,' suggested Richard. 'Lengthen the string,' said Adrian. 'Add more plasticine,' said Robert. 'Give it a push,' John said. They experimented with different lengths until they were satisfied with the beat. 'How shall we count?' I asked. 'Number of swings in half a minute,' said Mervyn. I gave him my watch with a second hand, and he was soon timing confidently from any starting point of the second hand. 'It swings much faster when we shorten the string,' they commented as they continued their experiments with different lengths, 'but it doesn't change when we alter the weight.' These experiments were rough and ready, and needed a careful follow-up with a good point of suspension, but I want to stress that all *the thinking had been done by the boys themselves, and the suggestions came from them and not from me. 'The sense of personal discovery influenced the intensity of their experience and the vividness of their memory.'[1] We were so engrossed that we forgot all about the purpose of the timing.*

[1]CHILDREN AND THEIR PRIMARY SCHOOLS, he Plowden Report) HMSO 1967

3. Finally, here is an example of practical experience on 'time' undertaken by twelve-year-olds who

were unaccustomed to practical investigation of any kind.

Teacher's notes
This experiment, although not only concerned with rockets, was referred to as 'The Rocket Experiment'. The idea behind the experiment was to time various journeys over a fixed distance. The experiment was performed with boys walking, running and riding bicycles over 100 yards. To add interest, a rocket on a line was included.

It was originally intended that the experiment be used as a basis for the calculation of speed, but I found that the concept of speed, meaning distance covered in a given time, was non-existent. The experiment was therefore used solely as a method for comparing times which were later developed as speeds in miles per hour. Had these secondary pupils had previous experience, they would not have met with so much difficulty. The experiment was conducted as follows. A course of a hundred yards was measured prior to the experiment, and timekeepers, runners, walkers, and cyclists were selected. The time each participant took to cover a hundred yards was measured.

(A conversion graph from which the distance covered in each interval of time can be read (eg, 15 seconds, $\frac{1}{2}$ minute, 1 minute) obviates a good deal of tiresome calculation when pupils are still struggling to understand the ideas involved.)

3 Statistics, Choice and Chance

Many of the investigations carried out by pupils (from five-year-olds upwards) involve the collection of information, the subsequent ordering of data, and the interpretation of results. Usually a single investigation provides the starting point for others as the following examples illustrate. Normally a graphical representation can provoke many interesting questions (which are not always followed up in the examples quoted).

All representations included in this section (except the last one), are block graphs. A block graph is a *count* and the number (frequency) is normally represented on the 'vertical' axis. Further examples are given in Chapter 5.

1. With the help of their teacher, a class of eight-year-olds drew up a questionnaire, to obtain the information they required. Here is one of the completed questionnaires:

How old are you? Nine
When is your birthday? 14th June
What colour are your eyes? Green
What colour is your hair? Dark brown
What is your height? 4 feet 7 inches
How much do you weigh? 5 stone[1] 3 lb
Which school house are you in? St Michael
How many brothers have you? One
How many sisters have you? None
What kinds of pets do you have at home? Cat
Do you belong to any clubs? Brownies
What are your hobbies? Dancing and stamps
Can you swim? Yes

[1] 1 stone = 14 lb

Can you ride a bicycle?   Yes
What is your favourite food?   Apples
What is your favourite colour?   Yellow
What is your favourite lesson?   English
Which television programme do you like most?
  Monkees
Which size do you take in shoes?   2

This is what some of the children wrote about
the information they had collected.

2.   Our favourite colours.

*I have asked Class I, Class IV and Class VI about
their favourite colours. This is what I have found out,
there are twenty blues and twenty-seven reds and there
are six blacks and there are a dark brown and a light
brown and twelve oranges and fourteen pinks and
there are nine light yellows and thirteen purples and
there are two turquoises and there are seven greens.*

In the block graphs which showed the favourite
colours of each class included in the questionnaire,
the colour order was arbitrary. No attempt was
made either to keep the colours in the same order
for every class (eg, red, blue, green, yellow, etc) or
to put the colours in order according to preference.
These points might well have followed, after
discussion, as developments of the original investigation. (Adults, too, are sometimes more ready to
pass on to another topic than to develop one in
more detail!)
The next piece of work done by the same child
ren shows this development. (See page 118).
The children wrote:

*This graph shows the different kinds of pets that
we have at home. Cats and dogs are the most popular
pets. Some people have toads, mice and chickens as
pets.*

3. Bird watching.

The photograph shows the careful observation and recording of a class of nine- and ten-year-olds who observed the visits of parent birds to a nest from 10 a.m. to 3 p.m. (See page 118).

4. Investigating the juniors.

This piece of work undertaken by ten-year-olds arose in unusual circumstances.

There had been a serious fire at the school, and equipment had been destroyed. The headmaster therefore decided to discuss with the older children possibilities for interesting mathematical investigation which would not require equipment. Here are his notes on this experiment and on the information collected:

The scheme arose when it became obvious that the children were far more interested in facts and figures dealing with themselves than in any more remote number topic. Our aim was to involve as many children in the school as possible and to interest all the class teachers by demonstrating in a practical way the possibilities of this sort of work.

Twenty-two children, aged ten to eleven, undertook to obtain statistical information from all the children in the junior school (including those with reading difficulties—and non-readers!). They prepared their questionnaires and divided themselves up into seven investigating teams (one for each class).

Each team approached the class to which it had been appointed, with a request for twelve separate items of information about each child. The class teacher was left with a copy of the questionnaire, but the children in the teams wanted to obtain and record the information by themselves, through questioning the children in the class. They arranged with class teachers to call back in about a week's time, and meanwhile all the children in the junior school busied themselves obtaining their own vital statistics in readiness for the next visit of the investigators.

Information required *All junior children in the school were asked to answer these questions:*

(a)   *Name*
(b)   *Date of birth*
(c)   *Address and type of dwelling*
(d)   *School or home lunches*
(e)   *Height in feet and inches*
(f)   *Weight in stones and pounds*
(g)   *Size of shoes*
(h)   *Number of brothers and sisters*
(i)   *Weekly pocket money*
(j)   *Own pets (as distinct from family pets)*
(k)   *Spectacles*
(l)   *Number of teeth*

Ultimately, the investigating teams returned with their information complete on each class, the answers being written in small notebooks which they had prepared for this purpose. The teams then proceeded to collate all this information in chart form, one chart for each class. These class record sheets became the source of information for all future investigations, which we could now see would be almost endless. We therefore covered these sheets with polythene, after folding the individual names out of sight, giving each child a reference number to avoid embarrassing anyone.

Next, each of the teams thought of a particular investigation which it would like to carry out, using the information obtained, and including all the children in the junior school. The seven topics they chose reveal the keen interest which the children have in comparing each other in certain ways. Pocket money, food, pets, brothers and sisters, type of dwelling (this is a new housing estate) come well to the fore.

First, they wrote down the title of their particular investigation, and then guessed at the sort of conclusions which they thought it would reveal. (Nothing could persuade them not to do this, and they were all the more eager to see if the figures would prove them to be right!) Next, they extracted from the class record sheets the information relevant to their particular

126

investigation. They then tried to arrange the figures in such a way as to enable them to be able to draw conclusions from the information. Totals (by age, class, and sex), averages, and percentages were the commonest ways of doing this.

It was already beginning to be clear that in many ways the expected results were going to be contradicted by the figures. Some surprises were in store.

Here are the conclusions:

(a) *On the whole, boys seemed to have better teeth than girls.*

(b) *Children who had lunch at school were heavier than others and the longer they had been attending lunches the heavier they were likely to be.*

(c) *Children with brothers and sisters had* more *pocket money than* only *children (one boy suggested that it was because the parents had bigger family allowances).*

(d) *Children living in houses seemed to be heavier, and to keep more pets, than children living in flats or maisonettes. This information however proved difficult to manage and very hard to demonstrate, and mistakes were made.*

(e) *Children who had more pocket money than others did not necessarily have worse teeth.*

Next the teams tried to find ways of showing these findings graphically. Different investigations lent themselves to different methods of presentation. The simplest method was by block graph. Where more than two pieces of information had to be plotted, representation proved difficult and discussion followed. Sometimes a three-dimensional graph was used to represent three pieces of information. Scattergrams were also tried but children found them difficult to interpret. Occasional mistakes were traced by comparing two methods of presentation.

For example, in a scattergram showing height and reach, the range for the reach of the set of children taking part could be represented on the horizontal axis and the range for the corresponding heights on the vertical axis. The reach and height of each child would be represented by a point: ie, the number pair (reach, height). If there were more than one child with the same reach and height, interlocking cubes could be placed one on top of the other, to show the number of children with each particular reach and height. In this way, three dimensions are used to represent the three variables, reach, height and number of children.

Each team collected the results in a book of its own. Each team then visited all classes in the school, to explain the work and show the results.

It was also pointed out that there were very many more investigations possible, using the class record sheets, for any groups of children who wish to undertake the work.

5. 'What advice can we give the captain of our football team who always loses the toss?'

Teacher's notes

The opportunity was taken to investigate the simple probability of a coin landing 'heads' or 'tails'. This was developed as a class topic.

'Fifty, fifty,' was their own estimate and, after discussing what this meant, it seemed an opportune moment to allow those children who had some idea of percentages to record their results as percentages of possible success. This gave rise to a graph, symmetrical around the 50 per cent axis. They quickly realized that they did not need to compute two percentages for each toss. For example, if the percentage of heads was sixty, that of tails would be forty—to make 100 per cent in all. The remainder of the class recorded the results on the graph as the result of each successive toss was announced.

The graph was a cumulative graph. For example after the tenth toss, the percentage of heads from ten throws (in black) and the percentage of tails from ten throws (in red) were both recorded. The children discovered, after a few calculations, that the sum of the two percentages of heads and tails was always one hundred per cent. The graph showed that the percentage of heads and of tails approximates closer and closer to fifty as the number of tosses is increased.

6. This piece of work was followed by several investigations involving dice, counters and coins. After the children had recorded the scores of a single die for a total of over two hundred throws, and obtained a fairly even distribution, they decided to record the total score of two dice. These were thrown 720 times and the resulting block graph, of the frequency of occurrence of scores two to twelve, was called 'Lucky Seven'.

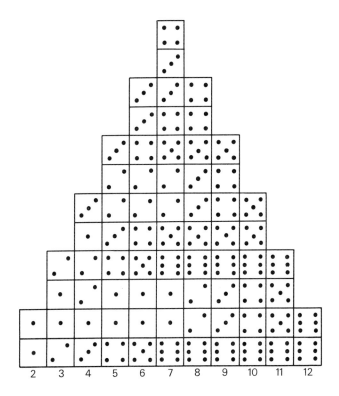

The children then set out to investigate why the score seven occurred most frequently. They did this first with the dice, recording each score as on each die: eg, for score four they recorded:

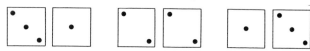

The children finished by making an addition table for the numbers one to six with the sevens triumphantly marked in black along the diagonal.

6	7	8	9	10	11	12
5	6	7	8	9	10	11
4	5	6	7	8	9	10
3	4	5	6	7	8	9
2	3	4	5	6	7	8
1	2	3	4	5	6	7
+	1	2	3	4	5	6

7. A 'fair' seven-faced device—twelve-year-olds.

As the teacher's notes indicate, this was part of a much larger piece of work which included throwing of one die, two dice, etc, many times, and comparing the actual and expected frequencies of numbers (or sum of numbers) thrown.

Teacher's notes
This was only part of a piece of work on 'fairness' and

*'unfairness' in the throwing of dice. By experiment and
graphical recording of results, it was seen that regular
solids were fair dice, in the sense that each face had an
equal chance of turning up. Then the class experimented with various devices to see how fair they were.
One of these devices was a seven-faced solid. On looking at the graph this die produced, it could be clearly
seen that the faces having a large area stood a better
chance than the faces having a small area.*

*The class then went on to 'discover' a fair device
for throwing seven so that each side had an equal
chance of turning up. This took the form of a regular
seven-sided spinning device. Although this should have
produced better results than the seven-faced solid, the
results were just as bad—as a consequence of poor-
centring of the spindle.*

8. Pin dropping—thirteen-year-olds.

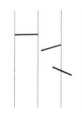

This class had undertaken an investigation into
the value of π, by dropping a stick onto a sheet of
paper ruled with equally spaced parallel lines. The
length of the stick was exactly equal to the distance
between the parallel lines. The number of times the
stick fell across the parallel lines was recorded. The
ratio of the total number of throws and the number
of times the sticks intersected the lines gives a fair
approximation to the value of $\pi/2$. It is very difficult
to explain this, even intuitively, as the result
depends on the sum of the series of probabilities
(expressed as fractions) that the stick will fall
across the lines. This requires an extensive knowledge of mathematics. However, the pupils were
undeterred by the lack of explanation, but continued to investigate a further problem. Would they
obtain a similar result if the stick (in this case a
pin) were dropped on a sheet of paper on which
equally spaced concentric circles were drawn?
Would the ratio of the number of times the pin fell
across the line and the total number of throws still
give an approximate to π? they asked. The result is
shown on page 119). The mistake made is an in-

teresting one. The pins were shorter than the distance between the concentric circles. A second variable was introduced also. Can you see what this is?

4 Various Shapes and Sizes

It is only comparatively recently that teachers have introduced young children to working with shapes. Perhaps for this reason, the work ranges over a wide variety of topics, and it is difficult to find a common trend. The examples which follow come from various sources. Although teachers are giving children more and more experience with three-dimensional shapes, I have not included many examples because, at exhibitions of children's work, three dimensional models are more difficult to transport.

1. I was working with a group of children, of ages seven and eight, from Lower Manhattan, who were unaccustomed to learning by investigation. I began by asking each child to choose a box from my large collection of containers and to tell me how he made the choice. The first response always referred to colour. When I asked each child to choose a second box which was like the first in some way, attention was gradually directed to the shapes of the boxes.

Earl, who had chosen two boxes of very different proportions, said that his were square. Since many of the boxes in the collection had square sections, I selected one of these and asked the children to put boxes with square 'ends' in one set. This caused considerable discussion during which the children developed their own vocabulary:

Long boxes with square
                   sections : long or tall squares
                              (according to position)

Short boxes with square

sections :	flat squares
cubes :	square squares
All other rectangular	
boxes (prisms) :	squares
cylinders :	round things

My attempt to teach the name 'cube' met with complete bewilderment. Later, in discussion with teachers, I was shown sugar 'cubes' and ice 'cubes' (both cuboids and not cubes), and understood the children's difficulty!

To focus attention on square shapes, I asked each child to check that the ends of the boxes we had put together in the square set (tall squares, flat squares, and square squares, in the children's vocabulary) really were square. I had provided no rulers, so Peter picked up a piece of string and stretched it across the end (position AB). I asked him whether the length at the edge was the same as his length (AB), and stretched the string in a 'slanting' position (CD). He hesitated, and then shifted his string to the edge, matched the length and cut it off. He next compared this length with the adjacent edge. We discovered that some of the boxes we had thought had square ends were not square.

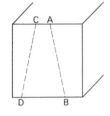

2. I then gave each child a sheet of plain paper (quarto size), and asked them to make me the largest possible squares. All but two folded the paper again and again, in a vain attempt to make a square shape of any size. Peter and Phyllis used pieces of string, as they had used these to test whether the boxes were square—cutting a length of string to match the width of the paper, and marking off this length from the longer edge. The excess was then carefully folded over and cut off. We talked about the square corners of a square, and I asked the children if they could fold a rough piece of paper to make a square corner. They made one fold —but it was some time before Robert thought how

to fold the paper a second time to make a firm square corner. We used this to find whether various angles were 'square corners', including the angle between the diagonals of squares on Phyllis's dress! The children were interested to discover that this *was* a 'square corner'.

I next asked the children to make, from sheets of paper, paper aeroplanes and darts, which we tested in flight. Then, once more, I asked them if they could make me the largest possible squares from rectangular sheets of paper, by folding. This time some of the children succeeded in doing this by matching adjacent edges.

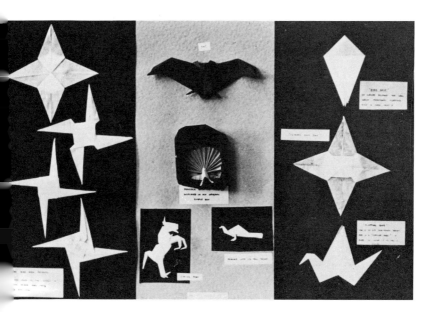

Origami by a nine-year-old

3. On another occasion, I asked a group of nine-year-olds to find out in how many ways they could fold or cut a square in half. They all found four ways of doing this, and marked in the four axes (a). John, however, triumphantly announced that he could cut a square into two halves in as many ways as he liked. After a good deal of discussion, John cut the

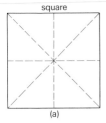
square

(a)

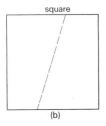
square

(b)

paper as shown (b), and gave it to the others to investigate. They agreed that John was right but asked: 'What kind of symmetry is it?' They pointed out that the square could not be folded along this 'axis' so that corresponding points matched as with mirror symmetry. I asked them how they would have to move one half so that corresponding points would match. At first, the children tried flapping one half over—but at last, on rotating it 'half a turn', they discovered how to do it. I quickly followed this by asking them to cut a postcard along its diagonal, and to find out what they had to do to make corresponding points match. This time, each child achieved it immediately. We then compared the four pieces made when a postcard is cut along its two diagonals. Are the pieces quarters or not? The children found various ways of folding and cutting to show that the four pieces were of equal area.

While experimenting, Mary made a new shape, with the two pieces of cord. (We gave it its mathematical name, parallelogram.) She discovered quickly how one triangle could be rotated through half a turn so that corresponding points matched.

We followed this with paper folding (and cutting) investigations. I asked the children to fold a sheet of paper into four. 'What shape will you get if you make a straight cut across the two double folds?' I asked. 'A square', was the immediate reply. Others said 'A rectangle'. 'Cut and see', I suggested. The children were surprised at the result. I gave them the mathematical name for a diamond rhombus. 'Tell me all about the rhombus', I urged. The children soon found all the important facts about edges, diagonals and angles. 'How would you have to make the cut to finish with a square?' was my next question. 'Make equal cuts', they said, and were soon able to differentiate between a rhombus and a square.

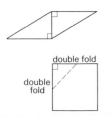
double fold

double fold

4. One of the difficulties teachers face, when encouraging children to investigate problems for themselves, is that frequently children make discoveries the teacher has not anticipated.

I was working with a group of eight- to nine-year-olds who had achieved very little in mechanical arithmetic. I gave each of them a large sheet of newsprint or brown paper, and asked them to fold to obtain the largest square. When this was done, I suggested they find the middle point of each edge, and mark in the new shape made by joining these midpoints either by drawing or by folding. Before I had time to ask them about the new shape, Margaret had discovered the area relationship between the outer and inner shapes. 'It's half,' she said excitedly, and continued to fold again and again, obtaining the midpoints of the edges of each new shape.

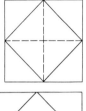

When I asked what the succession of shapes was, the first answer was, 'Squares and diamonds'. Later, using a 'square corner', the children found, to their delight, that 'All the diamonds are really squares'.

5. A group of eight-year-olds in Ontario, recently introduced to mathematical investigation, made some different discoveries from the same starting point. They were working with squares and were collecting examples of squares in the classroom.

I gave each of the children a sheet of paper, and asked if they could make the largest squares they could without using a ruler. One girl folded a piece over at one end until she thought the shape looked like a square. I asked her to check that the shape was a square, and, after some thought, she matched two adjacent sides and adjusted her square. By now, the six children in the group had made similar squares, cut off the odd piece at one end, and folded the square along the diagonal to check. I asked them what shape they now had. 'A right-angled triangle with two equal sides,' they said. 'How do you know they are equal?' I asked.

They matched the two sides of the triangle to show me. One said: 'Because we started with a square.' They found that they had made another isosceles triangle. Excitedly, they continued the sequence, making one isosceles triangle after another, each one smaller than the preceding one.

'What will happen?' I asked. 'We shall come to a very wee triangle, but we shall never get right to the middle point', was the reply. 'As the triangle gets smaller, the paper gets thicker', said another child.

I asked them to open the paper again, to see what else they could discover. They soon found that each successive triangle was half the preceding one, and began to give me the sequence of fractions

$$1, \tfrac{1}{2}, \tfrac{1}{4}, \tfrac{1}{8}, \tfrac{1}{16}, \tfrac{1}{32},$$

as we refolded our paper.

Then I asked them if they could make the original square into a triangle twice the size of the first triangle. Once one girl had thought of cutting the square along the diagonal, this was soon done. By now, we were all working on the floor; I asked them if they could make a triangle four times the original.

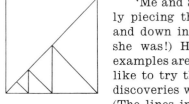

'Me and Scott will,' said Margaret, immediately piecing the triangle together, and jumping up and down in her excitement. (I was as excited as she was!) Here is the sequence—but the larger examples are not included, in case the reader should like to try this for himself. There are many other discoveries which can be made from this sequence. (The lines in the square mark successive folds.)

These eight-year-olds had met their first example of a limit; they had discovered some patterns (sequences) in arithmetic and geometry and, above all, they had become intensely interested in mathematics.

6. A group of girls, of ages nine to twelve years, were given some tongue depressors and thumb tacks and asked to make some shapes.

They first made these shapes:

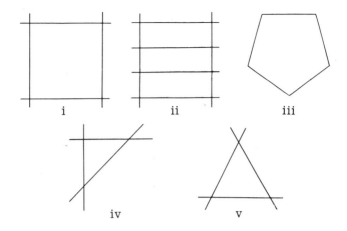

i   ii   iii

iv   v

They noticed immediately that all but one of these shapes was not fixed, and seemed quite determined to fix each shape. At first, they worked on the principle that, if they put in enough thumb tacks, the shape was sure to be fixed, and were very surprised to find that this was not so. For example, a thumb tack placed at each intersection in shape (ii), did *not* fix it. Then a ten-year-old made a triangle, putting the thumb tacks at the three corners, and was excited to find that at last she had made a fixed (rigid) shape (v). When she tried to make the square rigid, by fitting another tongue depressor as diagonal, she was disappointed that the square turned into a diamond. So she cut a longer straw to act as diagonal, in order to keep the outer frame square. (At this stage, we substituted strips of thick card, with holes punched at each end, for tongue depressors, and push-through paper fasteners for thumb tacks, to avoid more casualties.)

The group then decided to make a set of rigid

regular polygons. They found that there were various ways of making these frames rigid, but that it was easier to see a pattern when the diagonals did not overlap. Part of the sequence is shown.

When the group had finished, they made a table to show the patterns they had found.

No. of sides or angles	No. of diagonals	Total No. strips used	No. of triangles	Sum of angles in right angles
3	0	3	1	2
4	1	5	2	4
5	2	7	3	6
6	3	9	4	8
.	.	.	.	.
.	.	.	.	.
n	n−3	2n+1	n−2	2n−4

The twelve-year-old girl put in the 'n' pattern and, since she knew the sum of the angles of a triangle, she added the last column.

7. An unusual investigation was undertaken by a class of ten-year-olds. The starting point was four equilateral triangles, of different colours, fitted together to make a larger equilateral triangle.

'What do you notice?' asked the teacher. Here are some of the answers she received.

Four equal triangles; each is one quarter of the whole. The edge of each small triangle is one half of the edge of the large triangle, so the small ones are scale models of the large. The triangles can be folded to make a tetrahedron. They can also be folded flat, one on top of the other.

'Is this special to equilateral triangles?' was the next question from the teacher. By now, the whole class was involved, and all cut out four congruent triangles. They found that all the relationships discovered for the equilateral triangles were true for triangles of any shapes, except for the last relationship.

They also discovered other exciting properties from their triangles, for example: the sum of the angles of a triangle, whatever its shape, is always two right angles, and alternate angles between parallel lines are always equal. But the investigation with the tetrahedron thrilled them most.

Four isosceles triangles could be made into a tetrahedron; irregular triangles could not. 'But', said Martin, 'mine is irregular, and it will make a tetrahedron'. 'So will mine', said Marilyn. A few of the class were intrigued by this problem, and continued the investigation. They found that a right-angled triangle would not make a tetrahedron but it would make a flat shape. No four obtuse-angled triangles could be made into a tetrahedron, but this could be done with any four identical acute-angled triangles.

Shape fitting. Why do some identical shapes fit together and yet some regular shapes do not? Ten-year-olds

'Do we have to work with triangles?' asked Peter, 'because I prefer irregular hexagons', and so the investigation continued.

8. Tiling (or tessellations), with various identical shapes, provides opportunities: (a) for the discovery of angle relations of regular polygons, (b) for experiences which give children insight into why square units are normally used for the measurement of area, (c) for investigation of different kinds of symmetry, (d) for investigation of similarity (or scale). (See page 141).

A teacher in charge of ten-year-olds gave the children a variety of templates of regular polygons. She asked them to draw and cut out the shapes, and then to find the centre of each. They began with the easiest, the square, finding its centre by folding. Then they tried the triangle, pentagon, hexagon and octagon, marking in *all* axes of symmetry.

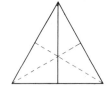

'Could you make your own sets of templates?' asked the teacher. This directed the children's attention to the angles at the centre of each shape. They recorded their results:

Number of edges	Angle at centre
3	120°
4	90°
5	72°
6	60°
8	45°

and so on

'What do you notice about these number pairs?' the teacher asked. 'One set goes up, the other goes down', was the first comment. 'What happens if you double the number of edges?' was the teacher's next question. 'The angle is halved', was the quick response. 'Do you notice anything about the *pair* of numbers?' persisted the teacher. At least two children found the relation: 'They multiply to give 360°, of course', they said. (The teacher returned to this relation on another occasion.)

The children then returned to the problem of constructing a set of cardboard templates. The

found that, once they had drawn in the angles at a point, they could draw large or small polygons (pentagon as shown) at will. They were by now well launched on a study of mathematical similarity.

9. A class of nine-year-olds became very interested in the blue whale. They searched in reference books for numerical information, and used this to make many comparisons which fascinated them. For example, they calculated that it would take forty strong men to carry the whale's tongue, which weighed two tons; and, 'You could fit twenty people with a height of five feet, lengthways on a whale.' 'You could fit a human baby sixteen times, lengthways on a baby whale, which is twenty-five feet long.' (See page 119.)

The teacher wrote subsequently:

You may be amused to hear of the continued interest in the blue whale in my class. One child had seen a model in a furniture shop, and, as she knew the owner, she asked whether she could borrow it. On the last morning of term, she arrived at the classroom door, carrying a ten-foot-long model! The children measured every part of it to see whether it was really a scale model. After lunch, we went to the Natural History Museum to see the full size model and a skeleton of a real one. The children took all kinds of measurements, using their own feet as measures. They were so interested, that an hour and a quarter had passed before anyone realized it.

The Blue Whale and another project, Big Ben, are continuing. One child has done pages of division because she wanted to see how many animals of various kinds would fit into the height of Big Ben. She discovered their length, and divided them into 3792 inches (the height of Big Ben is 316 feet), undeterred as to whether they were fractions, decimals, or involved long or short divisions!

The children wrote:

This all started when a girl saw a scale model of a

whale in a shop window, so she asked if she could
bring the scale model to school.

When she brought it to school we took the measurements and here they are:

scale model	whale
length: 4 feet	*length: 100 feet*
height: 10 inches	*width: 20 feet*
width: 9 in.
circumference: 2 ft. 6 in.
width of tail: 16 in.
width of fin: 6 in.

We worked out that four goes into one hundred, twenty-five times. Therefore, the model is 1/25 of the actual thing.

We did the same thing with the width, so the width of the model is about 1/26 of the actual thing. So we thought it was a good model.

10. Here is an interesting piece of work undertaken by two ten-year-olds.

Mirrors and images

Children are fascinated by mirrors at a very young age—and begin experimenting from the first moment they recognize their own image in a mirror —waving a hand, dancing, and observing the antics of the image. At a later stage, they are attracted by the beautiful patterns in the variety of kaleidoscopes now on the market. Children and adults view themselves in a mirror at least once a day. Why, then, are we so poor at understanding the principles of a simple mirror?

Mirrors usually form part of the equipment of an infant classroom—in the home corner as well as on the science table. A five-year-old made his first pattern showing mirror symmetry, when he dropped a blob of paint on his clean sheet of paper which he then folded in two to throw away. The pattern caught his eye as the paper fell on the bin. He was delighted with it and began to experiment, using paint in a variety of colours. Other older children were attracted by these patterns, and began to collect leaves and flowers which showed this kind of symmetry. The teacher used the name—mirror symmetry—and provided the children with mirrors. They experimented with many small coloured plastic toys, enjoying the reflections made by the mirrors and discussing what happened. The teacher also provided scissors and paper, and encouraged the children to make cut-out patterns with one, two, or more folds in the paper. There was much discussion—but little recording at this stage.

When an eight-year-old brought his kaleidoscope to school, his teacher took the opportunity of providing some free-standing mirrors and some scraps of coloured paper. At first the children used one mirror, but when their teacher asked them to find out how the kaleidoscope worked, they hinged two mirrors together and placed the pieces of coloured paper between. They changed the angle between the mirrors until they obtained ten half-sections, as in the kaleidoscope. When another kaleidoscope (with eight half-sections) was brought to school, they began experimenting again. 'The smaller the angle the more reflections there are', they announced.

When a spot of sunlight appeared on the wall, reflected from a mirror, the children's attention was diverted to experiments with one mirror, where they 'caught the sunbeam' and reflected it to various parts of the room. There was considerable discussion when the children tried to explain what was happening. Nine- and ten-year-olds joined in this experiment when the children took their mirrors into the playground. They found that they could move the spot of light (reflected image) steadily as they rotated the mirror. Some of the older children succeeded in drawing what had happened. Two ten-year-olds, working with hinged mirrors, found that by drawing a line between the mirrors and placing the mirrors symmetrically, they could obtain a series of regular polygons by gradually changing the angles between the mirrors. They measured the angle between the mirrors as they obtained each regular polygon. They recorded their results:

polygon	angle between mirrors
triangle	120°
square	90°
pentagon	70°
hexagon	60°
heptagon	51°
octagon	45°

(If the teacher had suggested that the children record the number of sides instead of the name of the polygon, the children might have found a pattern between the number of sides of the polygon and the angle between the mirrors, as the next piece of work suggests.)

The next investigation was the work of two boys of above average ability, with a background of three years' experience of 'Discovery Maths'. The teacher wrote:

Most of the work was done in my absence as, at the time, I was transferring from my classroom to the Mathematics Centre.

The starting point was the apparatus itself. No topic card was used and no stimulation from me was necessary.

The whole of the first experiment, and the graph, were done in my absence. When possible, we discussed the progress of the investigation. The children's own account of their work traces the development of the inquiry, and speaks for itself:

Children's work

Our mathematics this week was about mirrors and reflection. Our main apparatus was two mirrors hinged together and a pin.

First of all we played about with the mirrors, moving one mirror at a time. We thought of a way to make an experiment of this. We noticed, as the angle got smaller and smaller then we got more and more images. This we thought might have a relationship.

After this we did an experiment. We put the mirrors at 180°. We could not see any image. We moved one mirror at a time. We found that it was a long time before we could see five images (we started with five images and went on to thirteen). We recorded the angle of the mirrors and then recorded the angle when we could see seven. We found out that we could never see six or eight. When we saw the results we thought there was no pattern in it. Here they are:

images	angle between mirrors
3	127°
5	88°
7	59°
9	45°
11	32°
13	26°

With these results we were able to make a graph. This was a point graph meaning there are no points between the whole numbers.

We then discovered that the graph was the wrong way round. Also we found a relationship. The formula we wrote was

$$\frac{(180 \times 2)}{(\text{angle})} + 1 = \text{images}$$

[Here and elsewhere the children's thinking is ahead of their ability to express the relationships they perceive.]

Example: The angle is 90°. We divide this into 180°, answer two times by two and add one is five images.

Our teacher said that there was an easier way of writing the formula. This is it

$$\frac{360}{\text{Angle}} + 1 = \text{images}$$

From this we found out the right answers. Here they are

5 images	=90°		11 images	=36°
7 ,,	=60°		13 ,,	=30°
9 ,,	=45°		15 ,,	=24°

With these results we were able to make a better graph (see below). This was more accurate.

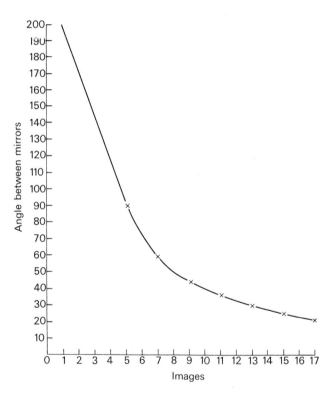

Mirrors and images

It is clear that the boys counted the object as well as the images—a natural thing to do (for values which give whole numbers of images: eg, when the angle is 90°). The formula is then $\dfrac{360}{\text{angle}}$ = total number of pins seen.

But, for values in between those giving a whole number answer, there is an extra image, so the boys' observations were substantially correct. The formula they obtained is true for 'in-between' values, ie, fractional values of $\dfrac{360}{\text{angle}}$. It is surprising that the boys discovered this, the more difficult form. The reader might like to experiment for himself.

What it is used for

When we had finished this work, we began to look for something that used this. A clue was shapes. We began to use the edge of a piece of paper so that the reflection made it look like a shape. First we made a pentagon and the angle was 90°. We discovered that the sides were images and we could find the angle by looking on our graph. Then we looked at a kaleidoscope.

A kaleidoscope has two mirrors at an angle so that it reflects images of one thing. In the kaleidoscope this made it symmetrical. We found the angle of the mirrors by the images we could see. We thought this an interesting piece of work.

Our graph

We plotted the results of our experiments on our piece of graph paper. Next we joined up the points on our graph. The sort of graph that we did is called a points graph. A points graph is a graph on which it is impossible to have a position between the points on the graph. For instance, you cannot have $2\frac{1}{2}$ images. We discovered a formula for finding the angle of the mirrors when a set of images are showing. This is the formula $\dfrac{360}{\text{angle}} + 1 =$ images. When the angle of the mirrors is 180°, there are no images showing in the mirrors. The imaginary line that we drew in will never reach the x axis for if it did, the mirrors would be closed.

It is interesting that these children actually joined the points they plotted, and then called the line an imaginary one because they realized that the points in between the plots could not be justified. Adults usually solve the problem by joining the points by a dotted line.

11. Similarity in three dimensions (eleven-year-olds).

This was accompanied by a well made, rigid three-dimensional model. Here is the teacher's description of the work:

The lesson was on how shapes grow by extending the sides, and by extending the diagonals. A discussion followed as to whether it was possible to extend the shape by projection from outside. I then drew a small square on the blackboard and we tried to see if this would work.

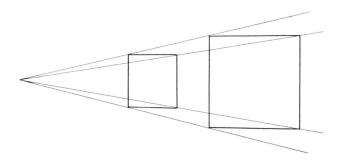

I then told the class they could extend any shape in any way they chose. One boy, Philip, asked if he could make a model of the diagram on the board.[1] I told him he could use anything he could find in the stockroom. He worked with a partner, and they made a similar model, using string for the projection rays. Later, I asked him if he could make it more rigid. In half an hour he had cut cane and fixed up the present model. Having made the model, he then took the graph

[1] It is interesting that Philip saw the blackboard diagram as three-dimensional (it needn't be), and that, having done so, he reproduced it back in two dimensions on his graph paper

paper and tried to reproduce a 'three-dimensional figure', and the result is shown. Work following from this has not been tried, as the model was made just before the course. When this work is returned to Philip, I shall put the question to him, do the two shapes always have to be similar?

This topic might well have been followed by a study of the shadows cast by a square on surfaces at various distances from the source of light. There is an interesting relationship between the area of the shadow and its distance from the light.

Both the examples of work which follow were undertaken by the same teacher.

12. Angles (unstreamed twelve-year-olds).
The teacher wrote:

After the 1966 course, I began to use discovery methods. But, because I was unsure of myself, and aware that some of these pupils would eventually take the CSE examination, [1] I decided on two guidelines.

(a) *The discovery must be syllabus-based, and directly related to work thereon.*

(b) *There would have to be a drawing together or formalizing of all topics, to ensure that all pupils had covered all the topics in one way or another.*

The present piece of work interests me from two points of view:

(a) *The obvious experiment and thought which has gone on.*

(b) *The 'strip cartoon' method of presentation, which shows that a logical analysis of the methods has been done by the group making the task card.*

[1] Certificate of Secondary Education—one of the two principal external examinations taken at fifteen or sixteen years of age

Task seven
An angle is the turning between two lines.

151

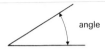
angle

Draw some, and then use a protractor to measure them. Draw an angle of any size, cut it out of sticky paper along the arms of the angle. Fold it in two to halve the angle. This halving is called bisecting the angle.

Can you find other ways of bisecting an angle, using set squares or compasses? Or a mirror?

Discuss the ways you have found, and give instructions for the method you think is most useful.

Can you find ways of making angles of 30, 45, 60 and 90 degrees without using a protractor or set squares?

Make instruction sheets to show your findings.

Find a way of copying a given angle without measuring it and include this in your findings.

13. Packaging (thirteen-year-olds) (see page 126). The teacher wrote:

The topic of volume came up on the syllabus and, in the light of earlier experience with discovery, I decided to pose a series of general questions on the packaging of commodities. (I find that involvement with a real problem is much more stimulating to a class.)

(a) _On entering a supermarket, what object is first to catch your eye? Try it, and see if you can explain why._

(b) _Are all packets bought by your mother full to the top? If not, how much space is there?_

(c) _Which do you consider the most efficient package? What do you mean by efficient in this respect?_

(d) _Have you considered bulk packaging, stability display, or economy in this respect? What other factors affect your choice?_

A period of general discussion followed, and various areas of interest arose. The class then split into their normal groups of four, to explore their theories, and to experiment in order to answer questions which had arisen.

The group which produced the particular piece of work following, was interested in (c) and (d) above, and began by examining packages already available from earlier work on equivalence of British and metric units.

Models of various shapes were made in thin cardboard, and initially a cuboid container was decided upon as holding the maximum for a given volume. However, in trying various materials in this, as 'goods', the children came to reject it as being not rigid enough and liable to split at the seams.

At this stage, they recalled some earlier work, done as 'interest' while waiting for others to complete an exercise, and sought out the relevant facts on plaited polyhedra. Their report, which eventually split into two sections (one unfortunately destroyed), included the work presented here.

In my opinion it shows considerable thought on usefulness (application to a product), packaging, costs, volume, etc.

'A packet of salt'

I found the best shape for a package was a triangular pyramid. This shape was very strong and the package I made had $219\frac{1}{2}$ cubic in. holding a maximum of 2 lb 4 oz. From a reference book I found I would have a very suitable package because salt is bought in $1\frac{1}{2}$ lb–2 lb loads. These packages could be put on display very simply, they could also be packed simply. I think that my basic package would have to be modified because the paper needed to make the package has to be 2 ft × 20 in. A package of this sort could probably be made from plastic, making the package stronger. From experience a package would have to be strong because sometimes our salt container is thrown in the cupboard.

[A cut-out folding model was attached to the work, and a net of this was drawn showing the fold lines.]

To find what happens to the volume if we cut cones from different sectors of 3 inch circles:

Method 1

The cones could be filled with sand and the sand then weighed. A paper cubic inch could also be filled with sand which is then weighed. By dividing

$$\frac{wt. \ of \ a \ coneful \ of \ sand}{wt. \ of \ a \ cubic \ inch \ of \ sand}$$

we obtain the volume of each cone if it were solid.

Method 2

Table

Angle	30°	60°	90°	120°	150°	180°	210°	240°	270°	300°	330°	360°
Volume	.19	.74	1.63	2.83	4.27	5.85	7.44	8.92	10.0	10.3	9.08	0

The volume of the cone is expressed as a multiple of $\frac{1}{3}\pi$ in cubic inches.

The maximum volume of a cone *cut from a circle 3 in. in radius is just over $10\frac{1}{4}$ cu in. and occurs when the angle of the sector forming the surface of the cone is about 295°. (This result was read from the graph.)*

Cone   *Radius of generating circle 3 in.*

$$r_1 = \frac{11}{12} \times 3 \qquad h_1 = \frac{\sqrt{23}}{12} \times 3 \approx 1 \cdot 2$$

$$r_2 = \frac{5}{6} \times 3 \qquad h_2 = \frac{\sqrt{11}}{6} \times 3 \approx 1 \cdot 65$$

$$\cdot \qquad\qquad\qquad \cdot$$
$$\cdot \qquad\qquad\qquad \cdot$$
$$\cdot \qquad\qquad\qquad \cdot$$
$$\cdot \qquad\qquad\qquad \cdot$$
$$\cdot \qquad\qquad\qquad \cdot$$

$$r_8 = \frac{1}{3} \times 3 \qquad h_8 = \frac{2\sqrt{2}}{3} \times 3 \approx 1 \ 83$$

$$r - 0 \qquad\qquad\qquad h - 3$$

Note to reader

The formula for the volume of a cone is $\frac{1}{3}\pi r^2 h$. In the table the actual values calculated are $r^2 h$. These values multiplied by $\frac{1}{3}\pi$ would give the volume in cubic inches.

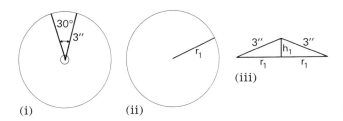

(i) (ii) (iii)

The first cone was made from a circle of radius 3 in. with a sector of 30° cut out (i). The circumference of the base of the cone is therefore

$$\frac{11}{12} \times 2\pi.3'' \quad \left(\frac{330}{360} = \frac{11}{12}\right)$$

(ii), showing the base of the cone, shows that this circumference is equivalent to $2\pi r_1$

$$\therefore \ 2\pi r_1 = \frac{11}{12} \times 2\pi.3''$$

$$\therefore \ r_1 = \frac{11}{12} \times 3''$$

It is appropriate that we should begin and end this chapter with three-dimensional shapes!

5 Patterns, Relations and Representation

Many examples have been given of children's awareness and appreciation of pattern, both in the natural and man-made environment, and in numbers, too. When children discover patterns which interest them and excite their curiosity, they look for ways in which to communicate their findings: in words, in tabular forms, and using attractive materials of various kinds.

It is very important, for sound learning as well as for a deepening understanding of mathematics, that the most important mathematical ideas are met over and over again in different contexts. The work described in this chapter gives frequent instances of the close links between arithmetic, geometry and algebra—links which can serve to reinforce important ideas in mathematics.

1. Some eight-year-olds used identical cubes in two colours to show their teacher that they understood the distinction between the 'two-times table (or multiplication table of two: ie, two ones two twos, two threes, two fours, etc) and the table of twos (ie, one two, two twos, three twos, four twos, etc). They also drew a block graph on squared paper to illustrate their discovery and wrote 'These tables both go up in equal steps of two.'

They illustrated the three- and five-times table in a similar way, and completed the work with tables:

multiplication by 2				adding twos	
	×2				
1	2			1	2
2	4			2	4
3	6			3	6
4	8			4	8
5	10			5	10
.	.			6	12
.	.			7	14
.	.			8	16
10	20			9	18
				10	20

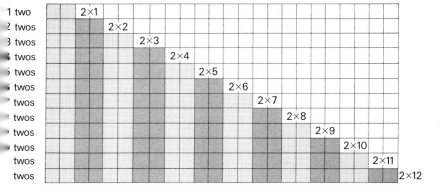

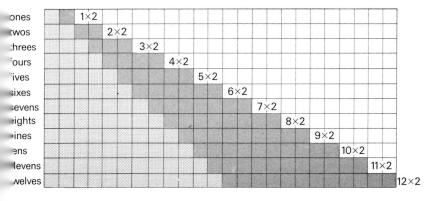

2. The same group of eight-year-olds built a sequence of squares, using unit squares of different colours.

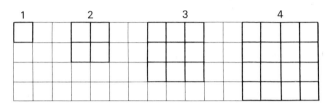

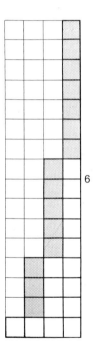

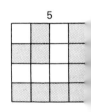

'What would you get if you made these squares into a block graph?' the teacher asked. The children re-arranged the squares and noticed at once that this time the steps between the columns were not equal. 'The steps go up in the odd number pattern,' one said. The children then arranged the squares to make different patterns showing their discovery

The one which delighted them most is shown in 5.

There comes a time, however, when children are ready to investigate other ways of representing number patterns as the following account shows.

3. Finding the place.
   The teacher wrote:

This followed some work on expressing changes of direction as compass bearings. Each child in a group of nine-year-olds drew a 'treasure island', on half-inch squared paper, with several interesting features clearly marked. The zero was placed in the bottom left-hand corner of the map; compass directions were inserted in the conventional manner, and intersections to the east and north of zero were numbered. The starting point for the search for buried treasure was given as an ordered pair. Here is one child's recording.

Land at dead man's cove.
Walk north to (16, 12)
Walk south west to (7, 7)
Go either due north or due south but it would be better to go through the trees to reach the coast.
Go due west to (9, 3) and to find the treasure go due north (3, 15) dig six feet down and remove the skeleton of the last man who tried to find it.

This gave a very interesting start to the representation of ordered pairs of numbers by co-ordinates. The children also enjoyed making picture puzzles for their friends, using ordered pairs, which gave them further practice.

4. The next sequence of work illustrates the close link between arithmetic and geometry, and shows how quickly children come to recognize certain important relations.

I was working in Ontario, with a class of ten-year-olds in which the children had only recent experience of learning mathematics by discovery. I gave each child a sheet of paper, which was plain on one side and had inch squares on the reverse side, and asked for the left footprint of each child. To my amusement every child turned the paper to the plain side in order to draw the outline of his foot. When I asked each group to find the child with the largest foot, each child cut out his footprint carefully and compared by matching, levelling heels on the table. But Mark noticed that, although Peter's foot was the longest in his group, it was by no means the widest. Next, the feet were placed in order of width. Finally, I asked the children to turn their paper feet to the other side to see if this would suggest to them another way of measuring their feet. 'Count the squares,' Elizabeth said. For some minutes, the children quietly numbered the squares, discussing with each other what they should do about the part squares. I turned to find Randy standing at my elbow. 'There's no need to count squares', he said. 'I've got a better idea'. He had found the perimeter of his foot, using a piece of string, made this into a square, and found the area of the square. I was as excited as Randy about his creativeness, and asked him to describe his method to the others. The children were delighted with Randy's suggestion. 'Will it give you the same answer?' I questioned. 'It will give a *better* answer because we shall not have to approximate to count the part-squares', was the verdict.

When it was discovered that all results obtained from the perimeter of the foot were considerably larger than those obtained by counting squares, some children expressed doubt. I then suggested that each child should make a paper crown, half-an-inch wide and twenty long, and should investigate the area enclosed as they made different shapes.

A boy announced that he could squash out all the area—so that nothing at all was left (not all children agreed with this!). Some children made a variety of odd, unmathematical shapes, counting the squares to obtain the area. One boy made a sequence of regular geometric shapes, and was delighted to find that the area grew steadily as the number of edges increased. Another group concentrated on rectangles (with edges measuring whole numbers to avoid tedious calculation).

Eventually, they made the following table. At first, results were not in any order, and it was only in response to a question from me that these were put in order.

W in	L in	A sq in
0	10	0
		>9
1	9	9
		>7
2	8	16
		>5
3	7	21
		>3
4	6	24
		>1
5	5	25
		>1
6	4	24
		>3
7	3	21
		>5
8	2	16
		>7
9	1	9
		>9
10	0	0

They were excited to find that the square was the largest of all the rectangles because this gave them the clue to their problem. Ann made the 'string perimeter' of her foot into a rectangle of the same length as her foot, and found that its area was close to that obtained by counting squares on her footprint.

Of their own accord, the children looked for a pattern in the area column: 'Because there are patterns in the other two columns,' they said. When they discovered the odd number pattern, they were delighted. Notice the 'mistakes' they made because they had not 'met' negative numbers.

I suggested that the group should cut out the complete sequence of rectangles in the table, and should arrange these in order. 'What do you notice about the rectangles?' I asked.

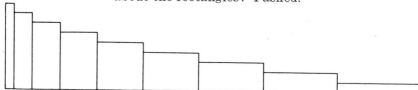

'Heights go down in ones, widths increase by ones,' was the immediate reply. 'What would happen if you overlapped the rectangles, pushing them all to the bottom left-hand corner?' I asked. Excitement ran high when the pattern below emerged.

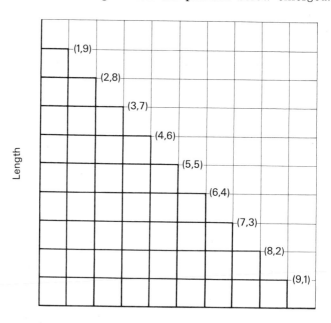

'What do you notice about the number pairs?' I asked. 'They add to ten', was the quick reply, and Paul wrote:

$$w + 1 = 10$$

Unfortunately, I was not able to follow the work through with these children, but some time later I told the story to another class of ten-year-olds (without telling them the answer of course). After they had made a table, I asked them what the area graph would look like. First they drew a rough sketch (as shown below), so I asked them to plot the ordered pairs (width, area) to check. Without hesitation they joined consecutive points as in the figure on page 164.

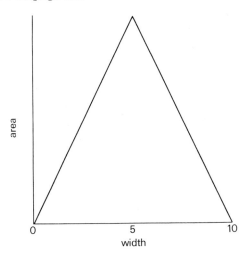

I asked them if they could give a meaning to the points in between. After some thought, Jennifer replied: 'We could have a rectangle $\frac{1}{2}$ in by $9\frac{1}{2}$ in, or even $\frac{1}{4}$ in by $9\frac{3}{4}$ in, couldn't we?' She checked that these rectangles would give points on the area graph, and used the graph to find dimensions of rectangles with area 10, 12 and 20 square units.

We then turned our attention to building a sequence of squares from unit squares. The children

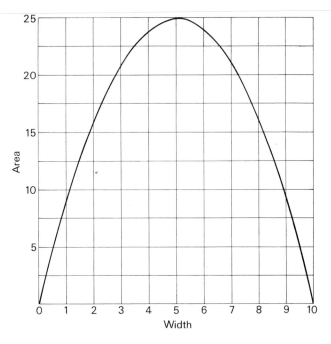

Width

soon discovered the perimeter and area patterns
(see the figure above) adding zero later.

length of edge	perimeter	area
1	4	1
2	8	4
3	12	9
4	16	16
.	.	.
.	.	.
.	.	.

They predicted that the perimeter, 'which goes
up in equal amounts and is the table of fours',
would be a straight line and that the area 'which
goes up in the odd number pattern' would be a
curve. (Once more we had to discuss the question
of the relevance of intermediate points.) They were
excited to discover that the differences between

areas of consecutive squares and between areas of
consecutive rectangles with perimeter twenty
units, were both odd-number sequences—'but one
goes up and the other goes down', they added. So
they expected the resemblance they found in the
graphs of the two relations. 'But where is the other
half of the squares graph?' they asked. 'Count
backwards and see', I suggested. So, for the first
time, these children met negative numbers. When
they had drawn in the other half of the squares
graph I asked them to find out what -3×-3 would
be. 'Plus 9' was the excited reply. The children also
extended both axes for the perimeter graph (and
inserted other multiplication tables as well) to see
what happened.

Since I was unable to follow this work further,
I asked the teacher to give these children another
example (below) of the 'constant sum' relationship

10										
9	10									
8	9	10								
7	8	9	10							
6	7	8	9	10						
5	6	7	8	9	10					
4	5	6	7	8	9	10				
3	4	5	6	7	8	9	10			
2	3	4	5	6	7	8	9	10		
1	2	3	4	5	6	7	8	9	10	
+	1	2	3	4	5	6	7	8	9	10

—to suggest that they made an operation table for addition for the numbers one to ten (see figure on page 87) and to ask them to investigate this table for number patterns. I hoped that among other patterns they would notice the resemblance between the pattern of tens in the new table and in the figure on page 162.

5. I was fortunate enough to be able to extend this work still further, with yet another group of ten-year-olds. I asked them if they could reverse the constant perimeter problem. 'Fix the area', they said. I suggested that each child should choose a number of squares, and make as many rectangles as possible, each one made up of the number of squares chosen. The children decided to use the square floor-tiles in the corridor. But Martin who chose five squares found my suggestion too restricting, and began experimenting on his own. He showed me the largest perimeter, 'with squares as spread out as possible', and the smallest, 'with squares as close together as possible'. We all became fascinated by this new problem, as Martin tried to fill the interval between ten and twenty units with as many different perimeters as possible.

Later we returned to our original problem, using first twelve, then thirty-six squares. While some children made the table and found the relation

| W | L | P |
in	in	in
1	12	26
2	6	16
3	4	14
4	3	14
6	2	16
12	1	26

between the number pairs, others cut out the rectangles and arranged these in order.

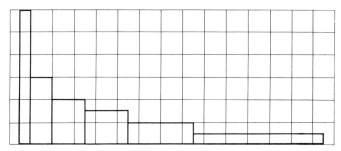

Finally, at my suggestion, they pushed the rectangles to the bottom left-hand corner, and obtained this symmetrical pattern.

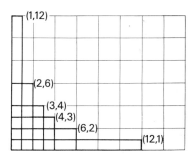

It was some time before the children who made the table discovered the relation between the number pairs (W and L). They pointed out that, when the width was doubled the length was halved, and that 'there is a kind of symmetry in the table.' I had to prompt them about the four operations they could perform on pairs of numbers to start them off. After first adding, then subtracting, without seeing any pattern, they were triumphant when they saw that the product of the pairs of numbers gave twelve every time. They recorded this: $W \times L = 12$, and later drew the continuous graph. They were intrigued to find that the graph for the constant product was so different from the graph for the constant sum.

I then asked the children to make an operation table for multiplication of the numbers one to twelve, and to mark the twelves in red. They were thrilled to find that this resembled the constant product of the figure on page 167, and justified this without difficulty. This multiplication table occupied the children for some time. They found many patterns which interested them.

If I had had time I should have followed this with work on regular polygons and on hinged mirrors (see chapter 4).

6. A class of eight-year-olds in Illinois had started on weather studies, and were making wind vanes. One boy was having trouble in getting his arrow, cut out from corrugated cardboard, to balance on a large nail. It was tail-heavy. I watched John remove the nail and move it nearer to the point of the arrow. The tail dipped more firmly than before. John removed the arrow and tried to find the point of balance on his finger. Once again he inserted the nail; this time the point of the arrow dropped down. He made another unsuccessful attempt to correct the position of the nail.

John was becoming frustrated, so I asked him to make me a see-saw (teeter-totter) using a trapezoid as fulcrum. By this time, other children had joined us, and a yardstick and a metre stick were produced. 'Where shall we balance the sticks?' I asked. 'In the middle', was the prompt reply. But the children had some trouble in finding the length of the metre stick. Both 90 and 99 units were suggested before John discovered that the metre stick was actually 100 units long (the last graduation was marked 99). Before we could continue, I gave the group some oral practice, first in halving, and then in doubling (to check). They had some difficulty in halving 90 and 99!

When the sticks were balanced on the wedges, we decided to use wooden cubes as 'children' for our see-saws. First the children experimented to see the blocks were of the same weight—they assumed

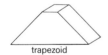

trapezoid

168

that children of equal weight would sit at equal distances from the centre. Then I placed a cube near one end, and asked John to find where a child twice as heavy (represented by two cubes, one on top of another) would have to sit to balance the light child. Without hesitation he pushed the two cubes towards the centre until balance was achieved. Peter then suggested that the distance from the centre had now been halved, and checked this, using string. 'What will happen if we have one child three times as heavy as the other?' I asked. 'The heavy child will sit one third of the distance from the centre', was the immediate reply. John tested and checked and repeated the experiment, using first four and then five cubes, one on top of the other. He then returned to his arrow and nail and, after some thought, moved the nail in the correct direction to achieve balance. This was an achievement, because moving the fulcrum is not the same as moving children.

When I had an opportunity of trying the see-saw experiment with some ten-year-old children, I asked them to make a table to illustrate the relationship they had discovered. Of their own accord they also plotted the ordered pairs on a graph.

number of unit cubes	distance from fulcrum
1	1
2	$\frac{1}{2}$
3	$\frac{1}{3}$
4	$\frac{1}{4}$
5	$\frac{1}{5}$

Here is another example of the constant product or inverse proportion relationship. This example illustrates how easily mathematics can arise in other aspects of the curriculum.

The topic of balance is one which requires reinforcement over and over again, each time in a different context. I quote two further examples, to illustrate some of the difficulties encountered by younger children.

I had discussed with a college lecturer the problem of introducing the topic of weight with young children. Should they be introduced to balance scales (a very sophisticated idea), or to 'weighing' objects on a homemade extension scale made from a plastic cup suspended from elastic bands, we wondered? The college lecturer decided to experiment with a class of seven-year-olds. He took in a plank which he placed over a brick, and then stood on the end which was farthest from the fulcrum. 'Can you lift me?' he asked. 'Yes' chorused the children, 'if we jump on the other end'. They tried, without success, and then had a second turn, jumping harder. A boy, sitting so that he saw the edge of the plank and brick, asked if he could move the brick. He did this, and lifted the lecturer with ease. This boy was so interested in balance that he subsequently made a balsa wood beam balance with equally spaced hooks, and continued to experiment.

A month later, I visited this class and asked the same question. To my surprise, the children gave the same replies—and jumped on the other end of the plank, as before—with the same results. This time, the boy who suggested moving the brick was absent—so we had no further stimulus. The other children had clearly learned nothing from their previous experience—possibly because their teacher had not given them further experience of this difficult idea.

The second example is of an eight-year-old American girl at her first experience of using balance scales. I asked her to halve a bowl of sugar. She poured some sugar in one pan and emptied the remainder (more than half) into the other. In order to achieve a balance (which she clearly recognized as a pre-requisite for obtaining halves), she transferred sugar from the lighter pan (which was nearer her). She continued to do this until the lighter pan was nearly empty. When I asked her to find half of a jug of water, she again poured the water into the pans and transferred water from the lighter pan to attempt to achieve a balance. This reinforces my previous impression that children require a great deal of informal experience of using balance scales before they are asked to find half of a given quantity.

Making a model— note lines marked for cutting

These stories suggest that children require prolonged and varied experience with see-saws and balance scales, and that they should be encouraged to put their findings into words to help the teacher to know whether they understand the underlying idea of balance.

7. A class of ten-year-olds who kept many class-room pets had noticed that the mouse seemed to feed for longer periods than any other animal. The teacher suggested that they should find out how much the mouse ate. So the children kept careful records daily for a month, and discovered that their one-ounce mouse ate, on an average, half an ounce each day. Mark, with a baby brother of weight eight lb, found out that the baby had six feeds a day of five ounces. 'That's nearly one quarter of his weight', Mark wrote. He then kept a record of the food he ate himself. He found this to be about 1/25 of his weight. 'Why do babies and mice, both small creatures, need more food?' the children asked. After much discussion with the teacher they decided that skin area and loss of heat might be part of the reason. The teacher (who had been doing some reading on the subject) suggested that the children should use a mathematical shape to find the relationship between skin area and weight (or volume). They chose inch cubes, and used these to build a set of cubes of edges one, two, three, etc, inches. They made a table showing the skin area/volume relationship.

edge (in)	skin area (A sq in)	volume (V cu in)	$\frac{A}{V}$
1	6	1	6
2	24	8	3
3	54	27	2
4	96	64	$1\frac{1}{2}$
5	150	125	$1\frac{1}{5}$
6	216	216	1

This showed that the skin area/volume rate was halved when the edge was doubled, and a graph helped to clarify this still further. Some of the children found this idea difficult, and repeated the experience using identical cuboids instead of unit cubes.

When the children compared the number pairs, they noticed that when the length was doubled the skin area/volume rate was halved. They did not find the constant product relation between the number pairs because the teacher herself was not aware of the relation, but they recognized that this was an example of inverse proportion.

edge (length) in	$\dfrac{A}{V}$ square units per cube
1	6
2	3
3	2
4	$1\frac{1}{2}$
5	$1\frac{1}{5}$
6	1

This chapter contains some fundamental mathematical relations; for example, direct and inverse proportion, square numbers and cube numbers and their properties. I cannot do better than end with a reference to the story in SCHOOLS COUNCIL CURRICULUM BULLETIN NO. 1 (pp 80–2, 3rd ed), once more. When Peter set out to find the pattern of areas under the graph of the squares at one unit intervals, his teacher asked him why he thought there should be a pattern. Peter replied: 'In mathematics there's always a pattern, you've only got to look for it!' If we, as teachers, can give our children this confidence, we have given them the best possible start in a subject which has sometimes been enjoyed by the few rather than by all the children. The delights of the patterns of mathematics are within the reach of all—we've only got to look for them!

6 Conclusion

The examples quoted in this book have come from classrooms on both sides of the Atlantic. It has been interesting to see that certain questions are of universal appeal, and also that children with different backgrounds and from different educational systems go through similar stages of learning when faced with the same problems.

Many of the questions included in this book arose in other aspects of the curriculum than mathematics. Frequently the children themselves asked questions about their environment, which captured their interest and provided the motive for the investigation which followed. Children's interests range far and wide, and the starting point for a mathematical investigation may arise in any aspect of their work. This integration of subjects is unforced and is, perhaps, of particular value in a subject like mathematics which, ultimately, is concerned with abstractions. It is important, therefore, that teachers should know enough mathematics to recognize a situation which has mathematical potential, and to be able to help the children they teach to exploit the mathematics of the situation to the full.

To assist teachers to obtain this knowledge, two appendices are included: (a) a list of mathematical ideas included in this book, and (b) a list of equipment which has proved useful in classrooms. A short booklist follows.

Appendix I

There are certain ideas in mathematics which arise over and over again throughout the elementary and secondary stages. These are powerful mathematical ideas which we should keep in mind at whatever stage we are planning our work. These comprise:

Sorting, classifying.

Putting in *order*, inequalities, equality, conservation.

Operations of additions, subtractions, multiplication and division.

Comparison—qualitative before quantitative—by subtraction and division. This leads to ideas of *ratio, rate* and *proportion* (direct and inverse).

Approximation in all fields of measurement, and in numbers.

Concept of a variable.

Patterns, relations, graphs.

Limits, greatest and least values.

Before listing the specific mathematical ideas included in this book, here is a note about 'sets', which have not been included as a separate topic. From their first day at school, children sort (and later classify) objects into sub-sets. Such activities involve recognition of likeness (correspondences) and of differences between objects or numbers (the elements of a well defined universal set). Children's reactions to these experiences are intuitive, and frequently remain so until the early secondary stage, when set language is often introduced. Examples of initial experiences are matching (one-one correspondence) of the elements in two sets, such as cups to saucers, or children to chairs. Such experience normally precedes counting.

It is important that, if set language is used, it should be associated with many practical applications. It can be used to describe clearly and precisely a variety of different mathematical situations.

Recognition of the laws of combination of the elements of two sets (their intersection and union) is not easy for young children, and they should not be hurried into representing these by set diagrams. Set diagrams are not an end in themselves. Children require extensive practical experience before they codify their learning in this way.

Summary of mathematical ideas covered

Number—see Chapter 1, for number knowledge which children need if they are to be efficient at reasonable written calculations.

Commutative laws of addition and multiplication:
$$a+b = b+a, \quad a \times b = b \times a$$

Associate laws of addition and multiplication:
$$(a+b)+c = a+(b+c) \text{ etc}$$
$$(a \times b) \times c = a \times (b \times c) \text{ etc}$$

Distributive laws:
$$\text{eg, } 37 \times 46 = 37 \times 40 \times 6$$
$$a(b+c) = ab+ac$$

Number bases.

Extension of number system to include fractions (ratio of two natural numbers or rational numbers).

Number patterns including squares and cubes and their difference patterns.

Ordered pairs and their position on a grid.

Measurement

Need for standard units.

Approximation appropriate to the task in hand.

Volume, weight, density.

Average pressure on feet.

See-saw relation.

Time and speed.

Pendulum and its variables.

Statistics and probability Ordering of information.

Interpretation of results.

Frequency (count) graphs.

Dice rolling—actual results compared with expected results.

Shapes Properties of cubes, cuboids, cylinders and cones, squares, rectangles, circles, regular polygons. Rigidity of skeleton framework.

Mathematical similarity (scale models).

Congruence and symmetry.

Patterns, relations and their representation Direct proportion: tables and graphs.

Inverse proportion: tables and graphs. Constant product relation.

Constant perimeter: relation of area sequence of rectangle to area sequence of squares. Constant sum relation.

Area of squares, relation and graph.

Volume of cubes, relation and graph.

Skin area/volume rate for cubes.

Appendix II

Material and equipment for learning mathematics

The normal environment possesses many possibilities for basic mathematical experiences which are provided as part of a child's total experience. There are four groups which teachers need to keep in mind.

1. Materials to excite curiosity, interest and enquiry.

2. Reference materials: books, pictures, models, globe, maps.

3. Tools and measures to use. These should be reliable and of good quality.

4. Materials for recording:
    plain paper, coloured paper,
    squared paper (squares of various sizes),
    coloured sticky paper,
    coloured beads and strings,
    identical coloured cubes,
    adhesive,
    powder paint and large brushes,
    felt tipped pens.

Other materials

(Some of these may be brought by the children themselves):

For operations on numbers
Collections of objects for counting, etc, as necessary.

Structural apparatus of all kinds
Abacus with nails and beads, square paper one-inch units, for children to make hundred squares and

number lines and strips). 100 one-inch squares, numbered 1 to 100. Interlocking cubes. Coloured rods, of length 1 to 10 units.

Length
Ribbon, lace, wool, string, drinking straws. Yardsticks and one-foot lengths from slatting 1 inch wide and $\frac{1}{4}$ inch thick, some unmarked, some marked in inches, some marked in $\frac{1}{4}$ inches and $\frac{1}{2}$ inches. Homemade tape measures from 1 inch paper, one yard long. Five-feet and six-feet tape measures. A six-foot measure, marked in feet and inches, can be fixed vertically on the wall as a height scale. An unmarked map measurer (opisometer). A globe.

Weight
Material for weighing: beans, rice, sand, marbles, nails, stone. Scales of all types: (1) balance type (suspended from above and not supported from below) and standard weights; (2) compression scales in wide variety from letter scales to personal scales; (3) extension scales. Assorted compression and extension springs, elastic bands.

Capacity and volume
Useful measures: empty milk and fruit juice cartons, plastic containers and boxes, cups, jugs, basins and pails. Measuring jugs: funnels and tubing. Sieves. Plasticine or clay. At least 100 coloured 1 inch cubes. Empty containers and bottles of various shapes.

Area
Scraps of textiles with repeating patterns. Square tiles. Coloured square inches, square feet, square yards. (In UK, square centimetres, square decimetres, square metres.) Leaves and leaf prints. Gesboards (wooden base—square—9 or 25 nails spaced at 1 inch intervals). Containers of various shapes to cut and press flat.

Time

Egg timer. Clock with sweep hand. Calendar.

Shapes

For constructional work: scissors. Waste material of all kinds: eg, boxes and cartons, cardboard, and corrugated paper, newspaper. Mosaic puzzles. Balls, hoops. Assorted wooden shapes. 1 inch cubes. Scraps of textiles. Hinged mirrors. Set of regular shapes: triangle, square, pentagon, etc. Constructional set, with rigid strips for making frameworks.

Booklist

Teaching of mathematics

MATHEMATICS IN PRIMARY SCHOOLS Schools Council Curriculum Bulletin No 1 HMSO 1965, 4th ed 1972; obtainable in the USA from Pendragon House, 899 Broadway Avenue, Redwood City, California 94063.

NOTES ON THE TEACHING OF MATHEMATICS IN PRIMARY SCHOOLS Association of Teachers of Mathematics, Cambridge University Press, London and New York 1967

PRIMARY MATHEMATICS. A FURTHER REPORT Mathematical Association, Bell 1970

Sealey, L. G. W. THE CREATIVE USE OF MATHEMATICS IN THE JUNIOR SCHOOL Blackwell, Oxford revised edition 1965; Humanities Press, New York 1965

Williams, E. N. & Shuard, H. PRIMARY MATHEMATICS TODAY Longman 1970

Structural materials

Dienes, Z. P. BUILDING UP MATHEMATICS Hutchinson Educational 1964; Humanities Press, New York 1964

History of mathematics

Ball, W. W. R. A SHORT ACCOUNT OF THE HISTORY OF MATHEMATICS Constable, London 1964; Dover Publications, USA 1964

THE GIANT COLOUR BOOK OF MATHEMATICS Dover Publications Golden Press, USA 1958. Published in England under title LEARNING WITH COLOUR: MATHEMATICS Hamlyn 1961

The geometry of shapes

Cundy, H. M. & Rollett, A. P. MATHEMATICAL MODELS OUP, 2nd edition 1961; also New York

Ravielli, A. ADVENTURES WITH SHAPES Phoenix 1960

Rowland, K. LOOKING AND SEEING Books 1 to 4 and Teachers' Books Ginn 1964; Van Nostrand-Reinhold Books, New York

Thompson, D'A. W. ON GROWTH AND FORM (Abridged edition) Cambridge University Press 1961; also New York

Weyl, P. K. MEN, ANTS AND ELEPHANTS Phoenix 1961; Viking Press, New York 1959

General mathematics (background)

Courant, R. & Robbins, H. WHAT IS MATHEMATICS? OUP, London and New York 1941

Land, F. W. THE LANGUAGE OF MATHEMATICS Murray, London 1960; Doubleday 1963

General

Davis, R. B., DISCOVERY IN MATHEMATICS; EXPLORATION IN MATHEMATICS Addison-Wesley

EXPLORING MATHEMATICS House of Grant 1964. Series of 12 books

Fletcher, T. J. (ed) SOME LESSONS IN MATHEMATICS Association of Teachers of Mathematics OUP 1964; Cambridge University Press, New York

Lockwood, E. H. STATISTICS. THE HOW AND WHY Murray 1969

MATHEMATICS IN COMMONWEALTH SCHOOLS Report of a Specialist Conference Trinidad, September 1968 Commonwealth Secretariat 1969

MATHEX: MATHEMATICS EXPERIENCE MATERIALS FROM CANADIAN SCHOOLS Encyclopedia Britannica Press Ltd, USA & Canada

Nuffield Junior Science Project MAMMALS IN CLASS ROOMS; SCIENCE AND HISTORY; AUTUMN AND WINTER Teachers Books 1 to 4, Collins Background Information Booklets 1967

Nuffield Mathematics Project series I DO AND UNDERSTAND (1967); BEGINNINGS (1967); PICTORIAL REPRESENTATION (1967); SHAPE AND SIZE (1968 COMPUTATION AND STRUCTURE (1969); ENVIRONMENTAL GEOMETRY (1969); GRAPHS LEADING TO ALGEBRA (1969) PROBABILITY (1969); PROBLEMS (Books and Cards (1969) Chambers/Murray, London; John Wiley New York

Paling, D. & Fox, J. ELEMENTARY MATHEMATICS. MODERN APPROACH Books 1 and 2 OUP 1966

Razzell, A. G. & Watts, K. G. O. MATHEMATICS TOPICS Books 1 to 6 Hart-Davis 1964

Whittaker, D. E. MATHEMATICS THROUGH DISCOVERY Books 1–3 and teacher's book. Harrap 1965

Whittaker, D. E. PATHWAY TO MATHEMATICS Harrap 1967

Williams, E. M. & James, E. J. NEW OXFORD JUNIOR MATHEMATICS Teachers books, OUP 1969

Wirtz, Botel, Beberman & Sawyer MATHS WORKSHOP Encyclopedia Britannica Press Ltd, USA & Canada

See also MATHEMATICS FOR YOUNGER CHILDREN, AN INTRODUCTION, SCIENCE, SPACE, TIME AND GROUPING, EDUCATING TEACHERS, ENVIRONMENTAL STUDIES in this series.

Suggested Audio-Visual Aids

1. *Dance Squared* and *Notes on a Triangle* are two 16 mm colour films, available from the Canadian National Film Board. The first runs for 3 minutes 30 seconds and the second for 4 minutes 56 seconds.

   These two films are available in the UK through the Canadian High Commissioner's Office, Canada House, Trafalgar Square, London S.W.1. and in the USA from the National Film Board o. Canada, Suite 819, 650 5th Avenue, New York N.Y. 10019

2. Two films from the series CHILDREN AND MATHE MATICS

   > *Checking Up*
   > *We Still Need Arithmetic*

   These are 16 mm black and white, each 30 min utes long. Com/opt/sound.

   All foreign enquiries should be made direct t BBC Television Enterprises, Television Centr London W.12, though some films are obtainab in the USA from Time Life Films (non-theatr cal division) 43 West 16th Street, New Yor N.Y. 10011.

3. *Maths Alive* is a 16 mm colour film, 30 minut long, which is available from the National Aud and Visual Aid Library, Paxton Place, Gip Road, London S.E.27.

4. *Donald Duck in Mathemagic Land* is a 16 mm colour film, 26 minutes long.

This is not available for purchase, but can be leased by local education authorities for a period of up to ten years, from Walt Disney Productions, 68 Pall Mall, London S.W.1., or in the United States from Walt Disney Productions, 500 South Buena Vista Street, Burbank, California.

5. A film from the series DISCOVER AND EXPERIENCE

No. 2. *Maths is a Monster*

This is a 16 mm black and white film, 30 minutes long.

All foreign enquiries should be made direct to BBC Television Enterprises, Television Centre, London W.12, though some films are obtainable in the USA from Time Life Films (non-theatrical division) 43 West 16th Street, New York, N.Y. 10011.

Environmental Studies

Melville Harris

The Author

After completing his Master's degree in geography, **Melville Harris** taught at primary and secondary level, and followed this by a long period in teacher training. During this time, he lectured in geography and environmental studies at several colleges, and also had some experience in East Africa and the West Indies. Since 1967, as Director of the Schools Council Curriculum Development Project on Environmental Studies, he has had considerable opportunity to witness the environmental studies approach in many different circumstances.

1 Three Studies

The lane   A study with a mixed ability class of six- to seven-year-old children.

The road outside our infant school was to be widened, so workmen, bulldozers and pneumatic drills arrived. Before long the inevitable trails of mud appeared in the school.

'Where is all this mud coming from?'

'Up the lane.'

'Well you must not walk on the banks, keep to the pavement.'

'They're digging up the road and pavement and the bank and . . .'

So it all began. Visits along the lane were made frequently, to watch what was going on, and to make a class book about the lane. Daily, the information was brought in and progress reported, as water pipes, drainage pipes and electricity cables were laid in the huge ditches. Sadness reigned when the news came that the trees on one side of the lane were to be cut down. Study books, on nature, mathematics and people in the lane, were made with drawings, captions and accounts—but mostly it was talk, talk, talk.

Then the hedge along one side of the lane was ripped out. A house-building scheme began, and a new interest arose. The surveyors with their poles and instruments, the laying-out of houses and roads, the machines, the bricks, cement, wood and glass that, in turn, moved onto the site, were all starting points of interest for the class, for small groups, and for individual children.

The class shop became a builders' suppliers where shopping cards and real money were used to purchase sand, nails, putty and the many other things needed by the house builders. Houses made of other material in other parts of the world—and houses in fiction—were studied. As a result of reading HANSEL AND GRETEL, *a cottage of cakes, biscuits and sweets, held together by icing was made and the whole school had a taste.*

The marsh A study with a mixed ability class of eight- to eleven-year-old children.

During the summer holidays I paid a visit to the marsh and took some slides of the river, the bridges, the dykes which kept the water flowing over the marsh, and the sluice gates which allowed the river to run out into the sea when the tide had ebbed. During the first week of term, these slides were shown to the children, and we discussed what we would need to take with us on our first visit. The children were also introduced to two folk songs which were concerned with the marsh.

On our first expedition, we visited the sea end of the marsh and had a good look at the dyke. Two of the boys measured the angle between the ground and the top of a large viaduct which crosses the marsh. Others measured the length of one of the arches, and from this worked out the length of the viaduct. We looked closely at three bridges crossing the river, made a note of the trains, and gathered rushes and wild fruits. While we were there, I took many slides of the marsh and of the children at work.

The following week, one of the boys brought a steam engine to school, and a group became very interested in how it worked and in the history of trains. They started experimenting with steam, and during the following weeks discovered how a steam engine works, and how to get clean water from dirty water, and they wrote a book about their experiments. Three of the boys were very interested in bridges and, after finding the height of the viaduct with a scale drawing in school they made models of four different types of bridge. They tested these to find which could support the greatest weight. Their experiments showed that an arch gives strength to a bridge. They experimented with other shapes, and found that a triangular construction gives strength to an even greater degree. From here they went on to curve-stitching, and wrote a book about this work.

A map of the area was made by using a one-inch Ordnance Survey map, and enlarging it to an eight-inch scale; this developed into an interest in Ordnance Survey signs and a study of maps and scale drawings. The children made detailed maps of the marsh itself, using conventional signs and a large papier mâché model of the island. The fruits collected were separated into their various colours, and a little suitably coloured ink was added after the berries had been boiled. Patterns were made on white cloth, using the tie-and-dye method. Models were also made using the rushes, for example, in whips, wigwams, chairs, and so on.

One of the folk songs said that water which had been used to wash a horse's hooves would wash clothes cleaner than ordinary water. Some of the girls tried to find if this was true. One of the fathers, who owned a garage, made a small hand-operated washing machine, and the girls brought a large white sheet to school. The sheet was put in a bucket full of tea and a mixture of red clay and water, after which it was dried, and it was then cut into thirty-two equal parts. One piece was washed for three minutes in one pint of clean, boiling water. Another piece was washed under the same conditions, with the single exception that the water had been brought along by one of the children and had been previously used to wash the hooves of his horse. Surprisingly, and as yet inexplicably, it was discovered, beyond any doubt, that the folk song was correct, for the second piece was much cleaner than the first. The girls then went on to compare all the washing powders they could find, making certain that the conditions remained the same for each sample. They recorded their results, and used them as a list of the 'best buys' for their parents.

Soon after our first visit, we again went down to the marsh, to the eastern end where we saw the site where the road crossed and, nearby, an old coal mine. We also watched animals and birds, and noticed that seeds were being blown about by the wind. We talked a great deal about the dispersal of seeds, and soon after our visit watched a programme on television which dealt with the distances seeds travel. One of the children observed that families spread from one part of the country to another. All the children made a family tree, showing where their mothers, fathers and grandparents were born. When we analysed the results, we discovered that families living in the village had come from all over North Wales, and some from South Wales and England. A large map was constructed showing the origins of families.

After the visit to the coal mine, the children read that many things could be obtained from coal. To see if this were true, two of the boys put three lumps of coal in a tin, and cut a small hole in the lid which they then replaced firmly. They then put the tin on a stove to see if they could obtain gas. After some time, they thought that gas was being given off, so they put a lighted match to the hole and watched a small flame which lasted for some minutes. When the tin had cooled, it was opened and coke and tar were found inside. These boys then went on to experiment with electricity, knowing it could be produced from coal, and eventually made a simple circuit. Other children wanted to know why a gap was left between the sections of railway track. This led to experiments from which they discovered that iron expands when heated, and that water and air expand in the same way.

While this work was going on, the other children were researching in groups, and as individuals, into other features of the marsh such as: animals of the marsh – wild animals of Wales – wild animals of the world; how the marsh developed; marsh and sea-shore birds; farming around the marsh.

On these and other topics, booklets were produced which were read and studied by other members of the class.

When these aspects of the study were completed, we made a taped commentary to accompany the slides taken of the expeditions and of the work produced in the classroom. We used this to finish off our study and to show the children's parents the work we had been doing.

An old industrial area A study with a mixed ability class of ten- to eleven-year-old children.

During the first week of the autumn term, the complete class, accompanied by the class teacher and head teacher, went for two walks out from the town to view the surrounding district. Both walks were taken in the afternoon and each was of approximately two-and-a-half hours' duration. The scenery consisted mainly of mountain grassland, derelict iron-stone quarries, small mines, and an excellent view, from above, of the town in the valley bottom. Six-inch and one-inch Ordnance Survey maps of the district were taken on both walks, and small river tributaries were noted and their names found on the maps. The children also noted the different types of trees, and examples of foliage were taken for later identification and classification. While passing some dumpings from derelict coal levels or drifts, the children found examples of coal fossils, and interest was immediately aroused in this field. The children went to the ruins of an old (1669) Nonconformist chapel. Approximate measurements of the chapel were taken, and the children suggested that they would like to excavate the site, in order to find out the width of the walls and entrances, and to obtain more accurate measurements of the foundations. The reforestation scheme on the mountainside was noted, and attention was drawn to the fact that the trees here were different from the natural trees of the lower slopes. At this stage, time did not allow us to enter the forest and investigate. The children's attention was drawn to the town in the valley bottom, and to the landscape of the adjoining mountain slopes. Some of the items they noted for further class-room discussions were: no tree growth on one mountain (limestone); a manmade mountain (waste dumping from furnaces of a derelict iron and steel works); crescent-shaped housing estates; new skyscraper flats; the town spreading out on to the mountain slopes; industrial sites; development of the new town centre.

As a result of these two walks, sufficient material and interest were now available for investigatory work to continue inside the classroom. The following weekend produced a mass of plant specimens and fossils, and the work of classifying and recording began. Reference books were now the centre of attraction, and help from the mobile library was sought over any problems.

Mapping on the six-inch Ordnance Survey map was now beginning, and a twenty-five-inch map was promised by the local town-planning office. Flashcards of one-inch Ordnance Survey symbols were prepared, and children tested each other on these. Soon, the

*children were constructing maps of their own, using
symbols they had taught themselves. The importance of
a key to each map was stressed from the beginning.*

*During the third week of the term, two 'digs' were
carried out on the site of the chapel ruins; walls were
now more accurately measured with tape measures, and
the removal of stones revealed spiders, ants, woodlice
and newts—arousing interest in a wide variety of
creatures. Back at school, a detailed plan of the chapel
was now drawn, and a model constructed of waste cardboard. From a sixty-inch map, a map was made of fields
and streams in the area around the chapel. Nearly a
month passed before a child asked why the chapel was
built in such an isolated and concealed spot; although,
because of previous studies, the children were aware
that it had been a place of secret worship. This led to
work on the growth of Nonconformity in the area. The
children drew graphs of places of worship that they
attended, and these led to much discussion.*

*The class was split into groups and taken to a
sheltered stretch of brook near the school. The valley
was divided up into lengths and the groups were asked
to count and classify the trees in their particular sectors.
Back in the classroom, these were plotted on a tracing of
the brook taken from a six-inch Ordnance Survey map.
Gummed paper spots were used to denote the various
species. Comparisons were made between densities of
trees in the various sectors. Why did one sector have so
few trees? We hoped to find this answer during the
summer term. Graphs of the number of trees were drawn
for each sector, and the complete length of brook was
measured. Towards the end of term, a set of aerial
photographs of the area was obtained and children were
able to check the work they had carried out on tree
distribution. During this work, two grass-snake skin
casts were found, and this led to one pupil undertaking
work on snakes of all varieties.*

*Owing to bad weather, outdoor work was now
limited, but two groups of six children were taken by car
to a farmhouse on the fringes of the reforestation belt
The cellar of the farmhouse had been used, before the
construction of the chapel, as a secret place of worship*

(1620). Out of doors, one group noted the markings on sheep and a new interest was aroused. Information on markings was sought from the local police station, but the children were informed that the record book, listing the owners of the different marks, had been lost! Some knowledge was obtained from the local inhabitants. It continued to be too wet to make a detailed study of the reforestation, but the children did note different leaf shapes. This led to class work on deciduous and coniferous trees.

The children working on a religious survey of the area brought up the question of lighting in the old chapel. Rush candles were made, and as no mutton fat was available in the school kitchen, margarine was used, and the children timed the burning of their candles against that of a modern candle. We discovered that the school premises site had originally been used as a chandlery, and so a group began studying 'light'. A letter was sent to a local factory where light bulbs were manufactured, and a representative called to give a talk and demonstration of the products made. Labels from export cartons were given to the children, and these were fixed on a world map, according to the addressed destination.

One group found that a dwelling house near the school had been a woollen mill. They were informed by the present occupant that distinctive waistcoats worn by the Chartists had been woven at the mill. Who were the Chartists? This led to stories on conditions of mines and factories in the nineteenth century.

On a visit to a present-day chapel, we were unable to gain admittance, so we spent a short time in the burial ground. From old grave-stones the children noted that families were once larger than at the present day, and that death occurred at an earlier age. They noted the children's deaths—at two days old, three months old, and so on. This led to a discussion on the social conditions of the late nineteenth century, and on improved conditions today. From reports made by the medical officers of health over the past fifty years, figures were obtained to show the decrease in deaths from cholera, diphtheria, tuberculosis, and so on, and the decrease in infant mortality. School milk, school meals, medical services and housing conditions were discussed before the end of the term brought the study to a close.

Throughout the work, a tape recording was made of various aspects of research carried out by the children. This tape, with a background of hymn tunes by local composers, and linked to photographs taken throughout the study, helped to bring the project to a conclusion for the class.

2 The Background

Throughout Britain today, young children are involved in similar studies to those described above, in **The Lane, The Marsh** and **An Old Industrial Area**. These are undertaken as a part of the normal routine of school life. In the streets and parks of cities, in the markets and churches of towns, and along the paths and streams of the countryside, children are to be found engaged in a great variety of activities. For many schools, this direct use of the environment is nothing strange or unusual but is just part of the general provision for the education of the children.

The use of the environment close to the school, as raw material for study and inspiration is, in itself, not new in British education. In fact it was suggested by HM Inspectorate of Schools in the 1840s. Considerable use of direct experience in the environment as a stimulus for creative work in language, art, craft and music has been evident in Britain for decades. Also, admirable accounts of localities have been made by children for many years in those schools where 'local studies' has long been an accepted part of the curriculum.

However, the recent scale of its development is adding a new facet to the activities of many schools. Examples of excellent use of the environment have, in the past, generally been rather isolated instances where individual teachers of talent have inspired children to high levels of creativity. There has been no widespread use of the environment outside the school itself until the last two decades, and even at present the schools using this approach are in a minority. What is clear is the growing interest of British teachers in an environmental studies approach. This development is due to a number of factors.

The 11-plus examinations

One cause of this growth is simply the general re-examination of teaching approaches which has accompanied the change in the form of selective examinations at eleven years of age.[1] These examinations have traditionally been made in language and arithmetic, though some areas of Britain used additional diagnostic tests. Children have been selected for more or less academic forms of secondary education and new methods of assessing children gain ground.

The '11+ examinations' greatly influenced the curriculum in many schools where, in order to attain the highest possible performance in the 'basic skills', other forms of study and communication became stunted or were ignored.

These examinations also influenced the form of teaching employed in many schools. The formal testing applied to language and arithmetic was often accompanied by a formal method of class teaching. In many schools, this formal approach was also applied to other subjects, such as geography, history and religious instruction, in which children were fed information which was to be repeated upon request. Many teachers did succeed in providing more varied, interesting and purposeful approaches with their pupils, but it was still possible to say of many schools in 1967: 'In consequence, curricula have tended to remain too narrow and teaching methods traditional and formal, rather than forward-looking and experimental.' (Central Advisory Council for Education (Wales) 1967.)

[1] See, in this series, THE GOVERNMENT OF EDUCATION by Maurice Kogan

New developments in the curriculum

The national movement towards a comprehensive system of secondary education is leading to the gradual disappearance of a selection examination from British primary schools. In some areas a form of ranking through various standardized tests is still undertaken, but overall, there is increasing freedom from formal examinations for these schools

One consequence has been the development of aspects of the curriculum not previously given much attention in primary schools, such as history geography and science. These subjects have long appeared on school timetables, and have consisted chiefly of information and stories concerning famous people and events, notable places and products; descriptions of plants and animals, and information about personal hygiene. There have been many instances of more perceptive, demanding and productive work; but generally this section of the curriculum has been limited. The methods of study and communication of the scientist, geographer, and historian have been regarded as secrets to be unfolded when a child is well into his secondary school life.

This view is now widely considered unrealistic and unacceptable. Information is directed at children through television, radio, books and comics, on a scale never before achieved. From an early age, children can see features of the far-distant areas of the earth, the surface of the moon, the remnants of past peoples and civilizations, and the wonders of biological and physical science. Children faced with this mass of material need to develop, before reaching secondary stage, a wide range of methods of dealing with it. As a result, many teachers are now giving more attention to the development, in their children, of the skills they can acquire and which they need in order to examine and interpret scientific, historical, and sociological and geographical data.

The environment as an educational resource

The fact that greater weight is being given to sections of the curriculum outside the traditional 'basic subjects' does not necessarily require an approach based upon the environment. A didactic teaching method within a classroom situation could be considered viable, but other trends in British schools have emphasized the value of an approach based upon direct activities in the whole environment.

First, there has existed since the nineteenth century, a considerable current of belief in the value of children's direct contact with the natural world 'through the soles of their feet'. In some cases this belief may have been due to an acceptance of Wordsworth's dictum 'Let Nature be your teacher.' Many educationists though, found more satisfying, reasoned statements, in the actions and words of Pestalozzi and Froebel, who emphasized the importance of experiences of the physical environment for the development of knowledge.

This tradition may well have contributed to the rise of such stock-in-trade clichés of British education as that good teaching moves from 'the concrete to the abstract', or from 'the particular to the general.' Though widely accepted, such precepts were practised by relatively few. In many schools, contact with the environment consisted of formal walks, in file, through parks or fields, as a reward for good behaviour and attendance.

In post-war Britain, new impetus was given to the 'concrete' view through increasing attention to the work of Jean Piaget and his colleagues. This experimental work appealed to many teachers who saw, in the conclusions relating to stages of intellectual development in children, an authoritative support for their long-held belief in the importance, for children's development, of direct experience of physical material.

Piagetian views of children's intellectual development are often taken as a framework of stages upon which teaching strategies can be based. The first areas of the curriculum to be influenced were those of mathematics and science, following the fields of study in which so much of the research work had been concentrated. In British primary schools over the last twenty years, revolutions have occurred in the teaching of mathematics and, to a lesser degree, science. In both these fields the provision of physical material within the classroom and the utilization of physical elements in the environment outside the school, have been bases of the method. It is now common in many British schools to see children working with wooden or plastic rods, squares and a great range of mathematical shapes and also growing plants, rearing living things and testing materials obtained from many sources.

A third element in the growth of the use of the environment in teaching is the growing desire in Britain to bring the child more closely into contact with the community within which he is developing. While a child is being made more aware, through mass media, of the features of the wider community of the country and the world, there are fears that his immediate social roots will become less important. The culture of the community in which a child grows is his heritage, and it is felt by many teachers that it is part of the function of schools to enable the child to experience this as something to be preserved, enriched and transmitted.

'That is where he belongs; his roots are there; and his affection for that intimate local community is the foundation of his affection for the wider community of the nation and later still, one may hope, for some understanding of, and possible sympathy with, other communities in different parts of the world.' (From a paper written for the Schools Council Committee for Wales, for internal circulation.)

This growth of awareness in a child, of the society in which he lives, his appreciation of his existence as part of a stream of humanity reaching back into the past and extending into the future is one of the major objectives of this approach.

Children need not only to identify with their society but also to recognize the importance of maintaining and improving the quality of the environment. As one of the long-term requirements for a conservation policy, at a time when the problems of conservation and pollution are concerning governments and planners, teachers want children to develop a respect and concern for the quality of their surroundings. Such respect and concern may best be served by direct active involvement with the environment itself, over a long period and as a normal part of school activities. While such involvement can provide ways of developing analytical modes of study and expression, it can also intensify children's visual perception of what lies about them in city, town and country.

A new approach Thus, several elements in the life of Britain today have helped to produce an environmental studies approach as a part of the ordinary curriculum.

To summarize, there is a growing realization that children and adults in the modern world require more skills than a command of language to interpret the mass of data presented to them in a variety of forms. Photographs, films, maps, tables, flow charts and graphs are frequently encountered, so that it is advantageous for a child to become fluent in their interpretation; such fluency was not likely to develop in the traditional pattern of schooling, with its limited curriculum. At the same time, the activities provide opportunities for further improvement in the quality of language as the basic tool for communication.

For child and teacher, direct and active investigation of the world around them is in itself an enjoyable experience. Excursions form only a small part of such studies but provide variety and interest in materials and methods of working. Children soon tire of purposeless jaunts, but maintain great interest when engaged in first-hand studies which they have helped to organize and conduct in co-operation with their teacher.

Through such experiences, children can develop the processes whereby to examine, interpret, communicate, and alter what they find in their world. Direct confrontation with environments can also develop in children an increased awareness of the nature of the areas they examine. Such awareness of the beauty and squalor of city and country, expressed through a variety of creative forms, can lay the foundations for adult attitudes expressing concern for the quality of the habitats we are evolving. Essentially, an environmental studies approach aims at helping to provide children with the tools and attitudes that are needed by an educated person in the modern world.

3 An Approach

The role of the teacher

Every teacher undertaking environmental studies is faced with a unique situation depending upon the age and nature of the children, the potentiality of the area in which the school is situated, the physical resources of the school, the regulations of the local controlling authority, and his own training and experience. These factors are among those interacting at any time, so no single answer to the problems they raise is to be expected, though some general suggestions are possible.

The first need is that of definition. A teacher must appreciate that environmental studies is only one of the approaches available to children at primary and secondary level. It is intended as a means of helping children develop a wide range of skills for observing, recording, and interpreting their world. Many of these skills will be those used by scientists, geographers, historians and sociologists, though these separate specializations are not relevant at this stage of children's development.

The activities in which the children are involved also provide experiences which will enable them to develop the varied concepts of space, structure and time through which they can relate to the physical and social worlds about them.

At the same time, involvement in direct investigation of the real dynamic world can itself be an enjoyable experience, giving children greater opportunities for appreciation of the quality of their environments.

The range of skills

The next problem facing the teacher is to identify the skills and techniques involved in this direct investigation. Especially is this true when his training and interest lie in a form of study different from those here utilized.

Before undertaking any work, he may draw up a list of the skills involved which includes the following:

1. Children need to develop techniques of collecting, grouping, and classifying material objects, such as plants, stones, snails, and cars, as well as non-material items such as pupils' ages, door colours, or the functions of different buildings.

2. The material objects will also have to be subjected to experiments, so that the children are given opportunities of experiencing stages of question-posing and record-keeping under control conditions during the activity and in the drawing of conclusions.

3. Ways of indicating the location of the material studied need to be developed, so plans and maps have to be drawn and interpreted, thereby aiding the growth of concepts of scale, direction, and so on. Often the interpretation here, as in other fields, will require the use of simple statistical methods developed in mathematics.

4. Use of books and documents by children to further their investigations may be seen as part of the essential development of language skills. This approach gives opportunities for the use of spoken and written language in many forms, though the primary concern may be the use of words for precise and accurate description and recording. Recording through pictorial representation (eg, forms such as diagrams, sketches, and photographs) needs to be developed, and careful interpretation of such evidence of the present and past as this supplies to be encouraged.

5. Underlying these study skills are the basic skills of language used for accurate factual recording and for personal creative expression. Language, together with mathematics and visual art forms, will be constantly used and developed by such studies.

The skills outlined here include most of those that can be developed with young children, so teacher may see environmental studies as setting out to cover almost the whole of the primary school curriculum. It may well be the ultimate aim of some teachers to base the school curriculum upon the study of the environment—widely defined. What generally occurs in the schools, however, is that the central core of study skills associated with collecting, experimenting, mapping, and examining documents is developed through environmental studies interacting with skills such as language and mathematics, the development of which is based partly on other approaches. The balance is a matter for each individual teacher, though it is valuable to recognize the need for variety of approach in teaching, thereby avoiding the dangers of replacing one dogmatic system with another.

The use of the environment with infants

The term 'environment' here is all-embracing, as it refers to all the experiences of the children at home and in school. The importance of making available to children a wide variety of objects for examination and use has long been a commonplace of infant teaching. This has resulted in many schools intentionally setting out to provide a varied environment within which learning can take place. Variety of colours, shapes and textures in the furniture and materials; living and growing plants and animals in the school building and grounds; real tools and equipment for hammering, sawing, and cooking; colourful attractive books and posters.

These, together with tape recorders and projectors, join to provide conditions in which children can form their own impressions of their environment and be led to improve the forms of communication basic to their existence as social beings. They talk, write, draw, model, and act out what they have seen and what they, their families, and their friends, have done.

Peter painted a picture of a gravel lorry arriving with its load. I asked about a little man handing something to the driver.

'What's that, Peter?'

'A nice cup of tea,' he replied.

It is the development of a fruitful environment, providing a multitude of possible experiences for examination and representation, that forms an important part of the core of our modern infant school practices.

Often, the extent of the environment to be utilized directly by the school is wider than the immediate building and grounds. Apart from walks on spring or autumn afternoons, visits are made to such places as building sites, bridges that are being repaired, the town hall, local ruins, city parks, and so on. These are visited partly for their intrinsic content but also because they are possible starting-points for the further development of the children's skills of expression.

Sometimes, starting points arise unexpectedly as in the case study of **The Lane**. That brief account shows a perceptive teacher using children's interests in the world outside the school as stimuli to develop speech, writing, reading, counting and drawing, in an atmosphere of interest and excitement. Attitudes of cooperation with classmates were encouraged through group-organized studies, while concern for the condition of the school, and the environment being developed outside, was frequently brought to the fore.

The main conclusion to be drawn is that these activities in and around the lane, activities that were fun to be involved in, had a purpose. The lane was a medium for the development of the children's powers of observation and the fundamental skills of language. A small part of the children's world had more meaning for them, and they had increased their abilities to express their thoughts and impressions.

The junior school A clear-cut differentiation between children in infant and those in junior schools is often difficult to make, especially when they are two departments of the same school. Generally, however, it is considered that the majority of children coming into a junior school (at 7+ years of age) will be reading with some degree of understanding and pleasure, will know some of the elements of number and will have a wide experience of materials and their use in visual representation.

As a result, teachers at a junior school may have a view of the use of the environment different from that of colleagues in the infant school. They will be looking to the environment for a more sophisticated use of language, art, and craft, and also as a medium for the development of the tools of observation, recording and interpretation. The general purpose of the use of the environment for learning remains the same, but the range of the use is widened, and the concentration of attention is upon these latter tools, together with frequent use of language, mathematical techniques, and art and craft, as the occasion demands. Language facility is, of course, indispensable for the conduct of any environmental studies, as it is through language that other skills are specified and developed. Through such involvement, the use of language is improved, as in mathematical skill when applied to practical observation and problems.

Case studies The detailed case studies, **The Marsh** and **An Old Industrial Area** illustrate the approach in two contrasting situations. Both studies, carried out during a period of ten weeks in the autumn, show teachers using particular features of the environment as raw materials, through the use of which children can develop and sharpen their tools of study. In order to achieve this, they have chosen situations containing a variety of potential interests which could serve as starting points for individual or group studies.

The resources available to the teacher involved in the marsh study included the marsh itself with its railway, roads, bridges, viaduct, ruined buildings and plants; several folk songs; a fairly extensive reference library; some scientific equipment; maps; a camera and a tape recorder. For the teacher starting the study of the industrial area, there existed the old coal mines, derelict iron-stone quarries, a variety of trees, historical ruins, a stream, reference books, copies of original documents, maps and recording equipment.

Neither teacher could anticipate or provide for every interest that could arise but, having examined the areas beforehand, they ensured that sufficient material was available for the studies to be launched. Attempts to cater for unexpected lines of enquiry could be made later, but first the class had to be involved.

In both studies, using the resources available the teachers set out to give the children opportunities to observe and appreciate the variety of things they encountered—flowers, birds, rocks, soils, trees, building materials—and where possible to try to use them in an artistic manner, producing sketches, paintings, and friezes. Also, measurements of different types were made and experiments undertaken under control conditions, as with the 'horse's hooves water', the coal, the rush candles and the bridges.

Another skill involved was that of mapping, to bring out the distribution element in the materials studied—so opportunities were taken, in some cases through unexpected incidents, to produce maps on a local, national and world basis. Plans of the old ruins, maps of the distribution along a valley of the birthplaces of older relatives, and of local and world rivers, were produced. In the drawing of all maps, attention was given to the essential requirements of scale, distance, key, title and direction, so that the map as a means of communication was emphasized.

The physical remains of earlier stages in the development of the localities studied were limited though where they existed, as with the early chapel coal mine, and Chartist mill, they were examined and used as new starting points for studies. Secondary reference material in book and document form was necessary to further this work, and though some such material was brought by children themselves it was forethought by the teacher that provided material to continue the momentum of interest. I was the manner in which the references were used—the methodical noting of facts and the careful arrangements of these in the written accounts—that was first emphasized, though poetry, painting and modelling were also used to evoke the past.

The overall effect of both studies is of children developing a wide range of skills of study and communication through a careful interplay of experiences in field and classroom. The approach is markedly different from a traditional formal lesson-giving situation, but is not made up of unorganized 'happenings'. It has structure and purpose, though much of the structure lies in the organization undertaken by the teacher prior to the involvement of the children.

The teacher and the study

In both these studies the teachers, perhaps unwittingly subscribing to Bruner's observation that 'discovery, like surprise, favours the well-prepared mind', played roles of major importance. They provided the conditions under which learning by the children could take place.

For those children's interests of which they were aware, they attempted to make reference material and simple experimental equipment available in the classroom. Study of the environment does not remove the need for books; rather it makes it even more important that reference material is available in which children can search for the information they require. Many children will require help in this, and it is partly as a guide to the process of searching, selecting and recording, that teachers need to function. The wider and deeper the range of references the greater the variety of interests that can be followed up by the children.

Other equipment that the teachers ensured was available for these studies included a supply of large-scale local maps, and wider-ranging maps and atlases on smaller scales. Also available was simple surveying material: tapes, clinometers, hypsometers, trundle wheels, compasses, string and plumb-lines, for accurate linear and angular measuring.

In both studies, provision for experiments that could arise was made through simple home-made apparatus, where more expensive material could not be purchased. So that children could develop their own test situations, the teachers ensured that a simple, safe source of heat was available, together with hand-lenses, water, a magnifying glass or simple microscope, filter papers, corks, batteries, bulbs, wire, and a great range of odds and ends. There would also be large supplies of the paper, cardboard, and paints that the approach demands for the making of displays and individual, group and class books.

For purposeful study using this approach, it is clear that the role played by the teacher is crucial. Whatever the process by which the general starting-point has been decided upon, it is the teacher who organizes safe excursions, sees that materials and references are available, encourages where imagination is lacking, discusses or questions when activities are becalmed, and generally provides conditions under which study and expression can take place. Without such organization and forethought, much of the work undertaken could earn the jibe that 'chalk and talk' have been replaced by 'walk and gawk'.

Environmental studies and the school

If such attention to organization is required from the individual class teacher, it is even more important for the headteacher of a school using an environmental studies approach as part of the normal school curriculum.

The headteacher has to satisfy the parents of his pupils and the local education authority that this segment of the school work, like all the other school activities, is developed to the advantage of the pupils themselves. This will often mean that there is an expectation of progression of some type over the school career of each child. This requirement especially when teaching staffs are frequently changing, is particularly difficult to meet in parts of the curriculum where careful grading, such as ha been established in mathematics and language schemes, is not in existence.

Thus, in order to provide some framework into which new or temporary teachers can fit, a head-teacher has a considerable task of organization to undertake when introducing an environmental studies approach into the school. This task is a difficult one, requiring as it does, the provision of a workable pattern which guides teachers without stultifying the freshness, spontaneity and original-ity which are essential characteristics of the prac-tice of the approach.

A number of stages in organization have to be completed before environmental studies can be established as a normal part of the school curricu-lum. Valuable individual studies may be carried out, without this overall planning, by gifted teachers in special circumstances, but if a broad age-range in a school is to be covered, something more systematic is needed.

Planning such a flexible framework requires three major elements. First, the examination of the potential of the environment; second, a clarification of the educational objectives of the approach; and finally, the suggesting of starting points in the environment that can be utilized in the attainment of the objectives. These elements are best illustrated by examining examples taken from urban schools containing a substantial teaching force. Similar problems are found in small schools, but it is in the larger urban school where many staff members are themselves strangers in the locality, that the great-est difficulties occur.

The potential of the school environment In a primary school of 365 children, located on a large municipal housing estate, the first requirement was to identify the general boundaries of the school environment. This environment was seen as the area around the school which could be used with relative ease on walking excursions, or short trips requiring some form of transport. Other experiences could be provided by day- or week-long visits to other sites, but problems of fatigue, bodily functions, and finance, severely limited such excursions so that the generally usable environment was considered to lie close to the school.

Within this environment, an attempt was made to identify potential starting points which could serve as stimuli for activities in mapping, collecting and experimenting, and in illustrating the material features of the society in which the children were located, as well as remnants of earlier stages in that society's history.

This examination resulted in a description of the school environment, summarized as follows:

The area has a variety of buildings with a limited range of designs of construction and an assortment of different functions—shops, houses, library, swimming pools, and factories making bricks, furniture, beer, leather goods and toys. Different types of roads are accessible and limited observations of people and traffic are possible from the school grounds. Opportunities to study variations in altitude are possible only by taking a thirty-minute bus journey.

Near at hand are a rural area and park, where an ample variety of flowers, plants, and trees is available for limited collecting and classifying. Animal life, however, is less abundant, though birds, insects, and stream life can be studied—the latter in a stream running through the school grounds. Rock supply is limited, as there are few exposures.

A castle, a fort and old churches are within easy reach by thirty-minute bus journeys. A railway is close by. A supply of documents, old maps and photographs of some local features has been assembled by local teachers. No museum exists, but there is a very good public library. Studies in a rural location are possible through the use of an Outdoor Pursuits Centre belonging to the local education authority.

This brief statement, together with an examination of the reference and equipment resources of the school, and the specialized knowledge and experience of the staff, served to identify the features of the environment of which use was to be made.

Similar exercises conducted in other schools reflect variations in the environment's potential for study. Schools in city centres may show little variety (together with many social problems), and may have to rely heavily on extensive transport provisions. Other schools, in small towns with long historical and industrial traditions, may have a high potential for studies. A small village school will be unable to provide studies in urban conditions. Each school environment is unique, and needs to be carefully surveyed as a potential teaching resource.

The objectives of the approach

As well as identifying the features of the environment to be used for study, headteachers and staff need to specify the purpose of the studies to be undertaken. The broad objectives are the development of confident, inquiring children, aware of the nature, variety, and beauty in the world around them, and having the skills to order and communicate their awareness in a variety of forms.

Such broad objectives also need a more practical statement of the means whereby their attainment could be aided. The means are best expressed through stating the skills children need in order to undertake active examination of the data and impressions arising from their studies.

The skills form three main groups which are constantly interacting in the conduct of environmental studies. The first group of skills, those most peculiar to the approach, are the 'study skills' including mapping, collecting and classifying of material, experimenting, preparing interviews, and questionnaires, and the reading of photographs and documents. These skills cannot develop without a strong support from the 'basic skills' of language and mathematics. Language and art, in all forms, are greatly reinforced by studies involving direct confrontation with the world outside the classroom. The third group of skills, those involving social conduct in groups, attitudes to people, and respect for the quality of the environment, are being developed whenever the approach is used. The view of the environment as the major resource for the development of study skills, as an important contributory factor for the development of language, mathematics, and art forms, and as an ever-present situation for the growth of social attitudes is a requisite for any school using environmental studies as an approach.

A framework An analysis of the school environment, when viewed against the stated objectives of the approach, provides headteachers and staffs with sufficient information to develop their own framework of studies. Each framework will be unique but should provide for significant development in part, if not the whole, of the curriculum.

The following example shows part of such a framework developed in a large city school; it demonstrates the way in which freedom and variety have been provided within an overall pattern. The staff has considered the potential of the city area and provided follow-up reference material and equipment. The particular starting points have arisen through children's interest or from suggestions by the teacher, depending upon the situation.

An analysis of two studies is given to illustrate the increase in complexity from Class 1 to Class 4, the intermediate stages having been omitted. These two analyses, while not showing the interest and enjoyment of the children, are examples of the objectives and means devised by the school in its attempt to provide a rounded curriculum.

Class 1: seven- to eight- year-olds

Starting points—'Our Homes' and 'Our School'

With these children, the emphasis is upon languag in many forms. They are encouraged to talk an write about their observations and impressions c how things feel, look, smell and taste; how heavy large, rough, attractive or unattractive they are and what happens to them in different condition. Impressions of the immediate and distant world ar expressed in writing, and in visual media of man types. In addition, simple study skills, required to clarify the location, structure and development of elements of the environment, are introduced.

Skills involved	Examples of activities
1. Oral discussion	Accounts of journeys, people we meet, things we see, ways of finding out, etc.
2. Factual writing	Accounts of journeys, written account of way to party, letter writing, 'How we tested the bricks', material derived from reference books and documents.
3. Creative writing	Through first-hand experiences at home, in the streets, on the building site, in school.
4. Drawing	'My House', 'A Street Scene', 'A Fire', machines on the building site.
5. Modelling	Local houses, foreign houses, furniture and furnishings for model houses. Fire engine, cars, etc.
Questionnaire & interviews	Simple lists of questions: 'Where do you live?' 'What type of house do you live in?' Simple yes/no questions. Children question each other on basis of questionnaire. Introduction of tape recorder for interviews.
Mathematics	Plans, measuring, shapes of articles, graphs, simple co-ordinate grids of rooms.
8. Mapping	Plans of rooms, houses and school. Compass points and local landmarks. 50″ plan of locality. Plans of furniture to scale. Designing room arrangements using simple co-ordinate grids.
Classification	Categories of houses—detached, terraced, bungalow, etc. Building materials—wood, metal, brick, etc. Furnishing materials—wood, textiles, etc. Family members. Garden produce. Work of people visiting us—milkman, policeman, home-help, etc.
10. Testing	Qualities of building materials—hardness, texture weight, etc. Qualities of furnishing materials—strength, design, texture, colour, etc. Conditions for growing plants.
11. Display	'Street Diorama', a frieze of house types, group books.

Class 4: ten- to eleven- year-olds

Starting point—A road survey

With these children the emphasis is no longer based as strongly upon language and pictorial representation as with Class 1. Language and mathematics are clearly involved, but the emphasis is upon observation, testing and recording, using plans and maps, keys, questionnaires, documents and sketches. These skills, resting upon a substratum of experiences gained through work undertaken in earlier years, provide a child with a wide repertoire of forms of study and communication. Particular use was made of a pack of resource documents, prepared in a local Teachers' Centre.

Skills involved

Examples of activities

1. Discussion

Why are particular building materials used? Are different materials used in different parts of the country? Why is there a camber on roads? Are some buildings more attractive than others? Do we need all the road signs? Could the area be made more attractive—and safer? How do different people travel?

2. Factual writing

Accounts of building materials. Factual information derived from Reference books and documents. Accounts of experiments. Conclusions from graphs. Accounts of visits.

3. Imaginative writing

'Roads in the Future', 'People Who Have Passed By' 'The Car Chase' (poetry).

4. Drawing and painting

Completing outline sketches of various buildings. Freehand impressions of quarries and bridges visited. Large-scale illustrations using photo-projector. Illustrations—of chariots, coaches, carts, cars, buses. Futuristic sketches of local streets.

5. Modelling

Cross-sectional models of road construction. Models of different bridge types and crossroads.

6. Interviews & questionnaires

Questions to be answered on excursions. Organizing question session with visiting surveyor. Preparation for interviewing pedestrians at road crossings. Taping of replies. Prepared interview with old inhabitants.

7. Mathematics	Measurement of width and gradients of roads and pavements. Graphical representation of information gathered.
8. Mapping	Street transect of gradients. Geological map of British Isles. Roman roads. The major roads network of Britain. Major world roadways. Local turnpike road maps.
9. Classification	Different functions of buildings—variations in building types throughout British Isles. Rock types on basis of colour, texture, hardness, etc. Types and origins of vehicles. Road classes.
10. Testing	Testing building materials—permeability, weight, thermal qualities. Drainage properties of road surfaces. Why have crossfall on a road?
11. Display	Page arrangements. Labelling and arranging general display panels.

Environmental studies and the child

Although the use of an environmental studies approach has the advantage of allowing teachers to continue growing professionally through their involvement in a dynamic exercise, it is the value of the approach for children that is its main feature.

The approach is no 'recipe' for education—many of the practical problems of ability-range and of supplies of material still have to be considered, while new problems, involving transport, safety and conduct outside school, inevitably arise as study outside the school area develops.

The approach does, however, have advantages that compensate for the effort required to combat the problems. Through active study, in cooperation with teachers, children can develop the range of skills needed for interpretation of the material world around them, and the representation of that world in the varied forms with which they will be bombarded in the modern mass-media society. Language may still be the main form of communication, but other forms are growing in importance, so that an educated person needs to know at least their basic alphabets.

A child who has these skills is better equipped, and is likely to be more confident, self-assured, and

A class of ten-year-olds in a city suburb made a model of the area around the shopping centre they were studying

A study of trees in the school grounds led these children to work on dating

A model of the local environment

Group activities arising from the study of a viaduct include
mapping, studying properties of rocks, and work in mathematics

involved than if competent only in the traditional limited range of skills. This confidence will be even greater if the studies have been of an active rather than a passive nature. The children who have been physically involved in direct examination, in field, laboratory and library situations, have been taught, over long periods, to seek out, sort and test material for themselves.

In the end, it is to the adults with this element in their education, that the world will look for improvement of the environment within which we all live. Awareness of the nature, the beauty and the shortcomings of our environment, as an accepted part of the educational purpose of our school system, may well be one of the means of improving the physical conditions under which we live. Environmental studies is based upon children learning through direct involvement in the study of their habitats; that knowledge gained should be used to make these habitats ever more attractive and stimulating.

Booklist

Bruner, J. S. TOWARDS A THEORY OF INSTRUCTION Belknap Harvard Press 1966

Doncaster, I. DISCOVERING MAN'S HABITAT National Froebel Foundation

PRIMARY EDUCATION IN SCOTLAND HMSO 1965

Sigel, I. E. & Hooper, F. H. LOGICAL THINKING IN CHILDREN Holt, Rine & Winston

STUDY OF ENVIRONMENT IN SCHOOL UNESCO 1968

Toba, H. CURRICULUM DEVELOPMENT THEORY AND PRACTICE Brace & World Inc.

Watts, D. G. ENVIRONMENTAL STUDIES Routledge & Kegan Paul 1969

Suggested Audio-Visual Aids

The following films from the series
THE EXPANDING CLASSROOM made in 1968 are available:

No. 1. *Elizabethan Village*
No. 2. *Eveline Lowe School*
No. 3. *Bucklesbury Farm*

These are 16 mm black and white films, each 30 minutes long.

All foreign enquiries should be made direct to BBC Television Enterprises, BBC Television Centre, London W 12, though some films are obtainable in the USA from Time Life Films (non-theatrical division), 43 West 16th Street, New York, N Y 10011.

Science

Peter Shaw

The Author

Peter Shaw is principal lecturer in Natural Sciences at the Froebel Institute. He is interested in fostering an active, practical, and involved approach to the learning of science. He enjoys teaching through field work, in any branch of science, but especially in biology, particularly marine biology.

Mr Shaw's interests have been developed through both his work at the Froebel Institute and his activities for the Natural Science Society, of which he was exhibition secretary for several years. He now edits the Society's journal, NATURAL SCIENCE IN SCHOOLS.

1 What is Science ?

To many people the word science conjures up a picture of white-coated technicians carrying out experiments in a well-equipped laboratory. Films and television frequently foster this impression with views of flasks and other glassware, in which chemicals bubble merrily, or of banks of electronic apparatus. All too often the popular view of science is of a complicated activity, reserved for specially qualified and trained personnel.

Nothing could be further from the truth. Science should rather be seen as a way of looking at the environment and building up a store of information about it. Every individual continually explores his surroundings in a scientific way, whether he is aware of it or not.

Scientific investigation begins with observations, using human senses and technical aids, as each is appropriate. As more and more observational records are built up, it becomes possible to see relationships between separate events, to classify the information obtained, to begin to make generalizations, and to distinguish between 'usual' and 'unusual' observations. Many observations or sets of observations need to be explained. Basically, a scientific hypothesis is an intelligent guess at an explanation, based on all relevant information currently available. A hypothesis is not true just because it sounds convincing; it must be tested by further observations and by experiment. The ultimate test available to science is the *controlled experiment* where the results of one experiment are compared with those of another, identical in every respect except that of the one factor being tested. Even a series of experiments do not prove that a hypothesis always holds good. However, it becomes increasingly credible where it remains valid in the light of information discovered after it was propounded, and especially if it has been able to predict such information. Nevertheless, every hypothesis remains vulnerable to even a single observation or experimental result which appears to contradict it.

Throughout history, man has explored his environment. When sufficient observations were recorded, it became possible to organize the information. Although the idea of a controlled experiment is a comparatively recent one, attempts were made to explain, and despite new developments in technique, observations remain the basis of all scientific investigations.

Science as we know it today is an uncompleted jigsaw puzzle, the pieces (large and small) which have been put together being the work of countless observers and investigators. These workers have been united by the compulsion of human curiosity, a driving force which has spurred men to major practical and intellectual efforts in tackling their problems. Both the endeavours themselves and the possibility of making discoveries, have been a source of satisfaction to a large number of scientists. Discoveries of facts, or relationships, new to the individual involved, have frequently resulted in feelings of intense joy, and in almost child-like behaviour. The story of Archimedes' unattired eruption into the outside world is probably merely an exaggerated account of his actual delight.

Over all, science is best considered as a vast body of connected knowledge and, at the same time as the relationship between this *expanding* knowledge and the method by which it has been obtained. Because so-called scientific 'facts' are always subject to further observations and to experimental test, the mass of knowledge is likely to continue to expand. Although the actual body of information is central to science and clearly important in its own right, it is the *method* which is so distinctive to science.

2 Science in the Primary School

Scientific development in children, like development in other fields, is progressive, and a very individual process. Thus any arbitrary distinction, such as that between various types of school (infant, junior, etc) is of limited value. It is important, too, not to limit consideration to the school situation, since the development of scientific knowledge and abilities begins long before a child reaches school age, and continues outside school hours.

In many ways, the development of scientific knowledge and abilities in children mirrors the historical evolution of scientific progress. At the earliest stage, observation, making use of all available senses, is almost the only aspect to be considered. As development proceeds, observations (and, later, second-hand information) will be analysed and classified, unusual features will be noted, and generalizations will be made. Some ideas will be tested both by questions to others and by further first-hand investigations. However, it is important to note that the idea of an experiment (and especially any concept of a controlled experiment) is rather subtle, and may not necessarily be discovered by any particular individual. Certainly one must not *expect* primary school children to engage in sophisticated experiments, although many children will see the need for 'fairness' in their investigations.

In the light of the above remarks it is illuminating to attempt to list some of the *working assumptions* (either stated or merely implied) which are made by 'progressive' educators in science;

ie, those who build up the learning framework from studies of the child and his behaviour.

These suggest that:

1. a child is very interested in his environment;

2. observation is the primary way of increasing understanding of the world;

3. related observations are progressively linked together to give greater understanding;

4. attempts to assimilate information give rise to problems—a child may want (indeed *need*) to know the answers to these, and an intense learning force may be provoked;

5. as it is impossible to predict which experiences will provoke interest and encourage observations in any particular child at any specific time, a wide variety of stimuli (provision) is necessary;

6. children have a need (and often a desire) to communicate the results of their observations, and the ideas which develop from them;

7. free discussion (both with other children and with adults) aids understanding, and provides a stimulus for further enquiry;

8. problems are best tackled by practical investigation;

9. the most effective learning is obtained when children's investigations are aided, rather than directed, by the teacher;

10. second-hand information is of greatest value when it can be integrated with recently acquired (or possibly, recently considered) first-hand experiences;

11. although the *integrated* body of knowledge built up by a child is important, it is not necessary (at the pre-secondary stage at least) to define which particular pieces of scientific information should be acquired, although some *concepts* may be considered necessary. There are many topics in which children are very likely to be interested.

However important science may be, it is only part of the learning process. Nevertheless, the enthusiasm generated in the course of an active first-hand investigation of the environment can be relied upon to provide stimulus for other aspects of learning, including the traditional 'three Rs'. (The relationship of these to science learning is shown in the diagram below.)

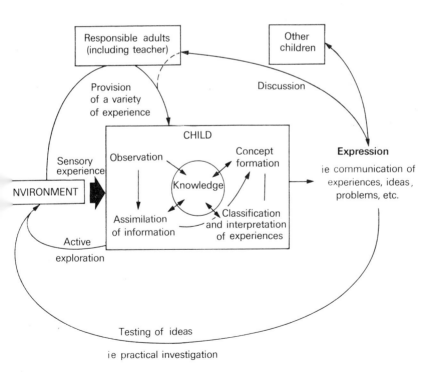

The techniques used to communicate experiences may be extremely varied. At the earliest stages of development, verbal expression will be of tremendous importance and may indeed remain dominant, at least for certain periods, later on. As other methods are seen to be of value they, too, are utilized. The *need* to communicate experiences gives meaning to writing, counting, etc, and provides some of the stimuli for expression in art, movement, music, and so on. Similarly, enthusiasm for finding out provides a strong motive to widen experience through the use of books and other written material. Thus the basic skills can be seen to be relevant to the process of living.

It is important to emphasize that the knowledge possessed by a child at a particular time (like human knowledge of science as a whole) will be incomplete and often inaccurate in parts. An active, practical approach to learning, however, will ensure that 'facts' are put to the test as necessary, and that ideas are progressively clarified.

Science is an important item in the 'curriculum' for young children, providing opportunities for learning which are co-ordinated within the child himself, yet arise from an almost endless list of possible interests. Paradoxically enough, this is perhaps best illustrated by indicating broad sequences of experience in comparatively limited fields of study. The topics will be considered under the following headings:

Invertebrate animals (small animals found under stones, logs, and in the soil)
Discarded materials (ie, 'rubbish')
Water

These areas have been selected because all or most of them provide material stimulus in the environment of every child. Thus they almost inevitably give rise to scientific interests (physical chemical, and geological, as well as biological) for each child who engages in practical study of his local environment. Each of these topics, alone, opens up vast fields, and the examples given are but a minute fraction of the possible developments of the studies. The 'knowledge' component of the educative process, like that of science itself, is almost limitless, and no one individual can hope to amass more than a fraction of the total.

For convenience the examples quoted here (which are taken from several schools) have been assigned to age ranges as follows: pre-school, 0–5 years old; infant, 5–7 years old; young junior, 7–9 years old; and older junior, 9–11 years old.

Invertebrate animals

Small invertebrate animals ('creepy crawlies') found in the soil and under stones are often of great fascination to young children. On the other hand, these creatures are often abhorrent to adults and, not infrequently, their distaste, even when not openly expressed, is noted and sometimes imitated by children. Thus, this is a field in which it may be difficult for a teacher or other adult to become enthusiastic or even to permit exploration.

Pre-school experience

Caroline's first known contact with a worm was at the age of nine months. Exploration was brief but intense and involved mainly the senses of sight and touch but was brought to an end when she placed the worm in her mouth! During the next year or so she came across many other animals. Often, earlier experiences seemed to have been forgotten and questions were frequently repeated but new facts were discovered and formulated.

What's dat? . . . It's a worm. Worm . . . wriggle. . . . Touch a worm . . . 'nother worm . . . wriggle.

One result of this experience was the, probably accidental, making of a plasticine worm, though the interest in this was short-lived. However, the experience was not completely forgotten, even though it was four months before the next worm was discovered and by then the word 'worms' could not be recalled. After hearing them named and before touching the worms now found, Caroline said:

What do we do with worms? . . . We could kiss worms. One worm, two worms, three worms . . . lots of worms. Big worm . . . baby worm. Worm live in the ground.

She was then willing to handle the worms, making no attempt to put them in her mouth, but jumped away quickly when she believed she was standing on one, and was relieved to find that it was only a piece of plastic tube. The tube was examined at length, but there was unfortunately no verbal expression of the way in which it differed from a worm.

At about this time, many objects, animate and inanimate, were being explored. Slugs, snails and woodlice were found, and a group of ladybirds was discovered among some leaves. Pebbles had been collected, the variety of shape and size noted, and preference expressed for rounded ones. During general exploration on waste ground, a tiny spherical object was discovered: 'A lovely stone'.

Then the object unfolded itself in the warm palm of her hand to reveal itself as a pill woodlouse. The horror on her face, not expressed in words, was due not to the fact that something was crawling on her hand, but to the fact that the *stone* was crawling. Attempts to discuss this with her produced the eventual reply, 'We want to play ball now.'

After a gap of a few days, the search for stones was resumed. Presumably this was now a period when ideas about living and non-living things were being reappraised and new concepts formed. No further pill bugs were found, but about a week later a snail was described as a 'stone with a little animal in it', and a few weeks later, when a broken snail shell was found Caroline said, 'It's an egg cup . . no, it's the skin off a snail. It's a bit like a petal' (a piece of apple blossom was picked up for comparison).

Of course, these experiences with snails and woodlice are but a fragment of the child's total experience at this stage, and much sorting out of information and progressive reclassifying is required as new information comes to hand. This record of Caroline's responses when attempting to name coloured pictures of birds illustrates this point:

... *pigeon* ... *pigeon* ... *dicky-bird* ... *quacker-duck* (correct!) ... *canary bird* (a yellow bird) ... *ladybird*.

Starting school

Interest in small animals does not cease when a child begins school. Adrian was a shy youngster, having attended afternoon school for nearly five weeks without saying a single word in class. The class was asked to find animals and bring them to school. At home, Adrian insisted on searching waste ground with his mother, and (somewhat to her—hidden—horror) decided to take a large spider. He selected this creature specifically because of its impressive size and shape, and took it along to school in a container. His excited words, shouted as he entered the classroom, expressed the uninhibited pleasure of discovery: 'I gotta spider ... I gotta *big* spider.'

He was then prepared to talk to the class in some detail about his find. There were many results from the number of animals brought into the classroom that afternoon, including naming, drawing, painting, counting, and model making. Probably none was more important than the development of Adrian's self-confidence.

An infant class

Young infants become progressively more ready to search carefully, examine in detail, and relate their findings to other experiences. A class searching in soil found a variety of creatures, and wanted to take them back and keep them in the classroom. Their interest and involvement is shown by some of the comments, writings and illustrations.

About a snail: 'It's got no feet.' 'It's like a slug with a shell.' 'There's a sticky mess behind it.' 'You can't pull it off.' 'A worm goes faster.' After watching the snail inside a glass jar: 'It's got its mouth in a funny place.' 'Sometimes snails climb over each other.'

More detailed examination followed, and Janet, having looked with the aid of a large magnifying-glass, told Angela that the things at the front were feelers: 'They've got blobs at the end.'

Angela was fascinated by the word 'feelers' and repeated it several times, trying to imitate their movement with her hands and body. Janet told her that there were eyes at the end of the feelers. She replied, 'They can't be eyes . . . they poke in when I touch them.'

John became fascinated by the empty snail shells he found. He brought several back to the classroom, commenting that they were to be homes for slugs. He ignored protests, from several children, that slugs didn't have shells, and put his collection with some slugs, examining them every day. He was delighted on the one occasion when he found a tiny slug right inside a large shell, and he drew it and wrote about it. He was quite undeterred by comments from his classmates that the shell was much too large.

The physical problems of housing the various animal finds had been discussed by the class as a whole. Suggestions for dealing with a snail were readily forthcoming. 'Put it in a big jar.' 'With leaves to keep it warm.'

Several children insisted that more than one snail should be put in a container, so that they wouldn't be lonely, and one suggested that they ought to have 'a mummy and a daddy snail', an idea which these children did not follow up. In helping the children to set up their vivaria the teacher without comment, added the necessary moist earth and some stones. Several of the children insisted that holes should be pierced in the lid so that the snails could breathe: 'Not too big or they will escape.'

A request for information about the food of snails produced a multitude of ideas ranging from 'dirt' (this child was probably thinking of worms) to a very specific suggestion: 'My daddy doesn't like snails. They eat lettuce.' Lettuce was brought to school that afternoon, and then daily!

Throughout their explorations and discussions the children were obviously concerned for the animals' welfare, which they related to their own well-being. No mention was made by the teacher of the necessity for moisture (or even for water to drink). However, they were quick to notice the behaviour of the snails in drier conditions. At first the suggestion was that the creatures were asleep but it was noted that: 'They come out when you hold them upside down.'

Suggestions were made regarding ways of making the animals more active.

'Make the holes bigger.' 'He doesn't need more food. He likes lettuce.' 'Put some *proper* soil in.'

This last suggestion came after the soil in the vivarium had been felt; the idea was followed up. When the snails were later seen to be more active, comments were made. One was particularly perceptive: 'He likes it better. It's more like outside.'

At the time this work was being carried out, a snail was being featured in a daily series of animated puppet films on television. Remarks from the children showed that watching these cartoons had probably enabled them to note more readily some structural features of the snails they found. However, the picture on the television screen may well have given rise to some confusion about the size of animals (at least two children were surprised by the 'small size' of quite large garden snails) and about the conditions in which they lived. It is interesting that no one suggested naming the snails found (possibly because there were so many other animals in the classroom at the time), so that the name of the television puppet was not mentioned.

A young junior group

A group of lower juniors were able to take their studies further. Many quite casual observations were recorded in detail: 'The noise of the aeroplanes does not frighten the snails.'

More detail of structure was seen: 'The snail has little feelers and big feelers.' 'A snail has a moth (mouth) with two lips. Its skin is slimy.' 'He has a breathing hole. It closes when it goes in his shell.'

While watching a snail eat flour, spread inside a jam-jar: 'It chews its food.'

Several lines of investigation into the behaviour of snails were followed. In the course of measuring how far snails moved, one child suggested putting one into the middle of the playground.

Andrew did not approve of the idea: 'He'd never get to the side. It would be like a million miles to him.'

Actual measurements were made, and records were kept for specific animals: 'The green snail walked one foot in 3 minutes 25 seconds.'

When commenting on the speeds recorded for snails of different sizes James wrote: 'We think that size does not have anything to do with the snail's speed and movement.'

Work developed to investigations of the progress of snails over various surfaces: 'It took longest on foam and ruff (rough) wood.' 'On the foam all the slime soaked in.'

Problems arose which needed to be solved or sometimes, simply accepted—animals did no always move in the required direction! Snail track were drawn—and these stimulated pictures an finger paintings. Sometimes snails became inactiv during the course of a test: 'In my picture I hav done two snails awake and two snails asleep.'

The noise of the
aeroplanes dose not
frighten the snails.

However, when snails were active, their movements could be examined in minute detail: 'Under the snail there is lots of little lines . . . they move up when the snail moves.'

When snails moved vertically instead of horizontally, their progress was timed; gravity did not seem to restrict their movements!

Alongside of this, studies of the many other invertebrates found were being developed. Life cycles were studied, including that of a pupa which later emerged as a moth. Much basic observational work was carried out and recorded, and details of structure and function were checked by reference to books. This in turn led to further investigations; the statement that woodlice lived in dark damp places led to tests to find out the conditions preferred by woodlice, and the results were set out in the form of block graphs and as 'sets'.

Investigations of the preference of invertebrate animals for moist places were further stimulated by the discovery of escapees from vivaria. Some of these had become stranded on the floor of the classroom and had become dry and brittle.

he took 5mns to wa-
-ot on this cardboard

A group of older juniors

A group of older juniors became involved in invertebrate studies when, at playtime, they found slugs, woodlice, and a worm, under a felt sheet left, following building work, in the corner of the playground. A thorough search indicated that the same animals did not seem to be present in other places, although spiders had been observed (but not collected) behind a drain pipe.

Encouraged by the teacher, the children recorded information about the animals and where they had been discovered, and drew a large plan of the playground to show exactly where they had made their find. Asked why they thought the animals were there, they put forward plenty of suggestions: 'They came with the sheet.' 'Because it's dark there.' 'It's wet too.' 'The animals are safe from birds.'

They eagerly responded to the suggestion that they should put out another piece of sheeting to see if animals came under that one, and they examined the sheet daily. After heavy rain one night, they noticed that the water remained longer under the sheet than elsewhere. 'It's wet now, there *should* be worms here.' 'Perhaps they haven't found it yet.'

The school caretaker threw away the felt sheet after four days! Although, later on, the children put down more pieces, and were eventually rewarded by finding life under some of them, they did not, at the time the experiment took place, continue to question *how* the animals had arrived there.

In the meantime, tests were devised to find out whether the animals were seeking darkness or wetness. The apparatus was basically simple, consisting of a transparent plastic container with a lid. To subject the animals to wet and dry conditions the floor of the container was covered, half with moist and half with dry blotting paper. Technical problems had to be tackled, as when, for example, water crept along the blotting paper from the moist half to the dry. This difficulty was eventually overcome by using two smaller pieces of paper, with a gap between them, and dampening one. A dark/light chamber was made, merely by covering one half of the plastic box with dark paper.

Woodlice showed a marked preference for damp conditions. The group concerned were so delighted by establishing this that they demonstrated their tests to all comers, almost as a party trick! The dark/light tests were not so convincing but, consequently, the children were ready to record results, repeat tests, and set out answers graphically. One girl concluded: 'We think the woodlice are happier when it is dark.'

When housing animals, the children were again ready to tackle practical problems as they arose, and seemed aware of the sort of conditions in which the animals would survive. Similarly, they were able to anticipate the results of searching for further specimens: 'There will be more in the wood' (a patch of scrub near the school).

Not only were more animals found, but so was a greater range of material, and this extended the interest to many other children in the class.

Animals were examined in detail, and intensive use was made of books. An elaborate scheme of grouping animals was built up, based on resemblances and differences, and approaching a real zoological classification. Some animals, such as the centipede, presented problems—it was not easy to count its legs: 'It's a centipede. That means it's got a hundred legs.'

Later (with difficulty) the legs were counted on a centipede, found dead. The number was checked and agreed.

Another older-junior group

Another group of older juniors became involved in similar investigations after being shown a film strip on 'Waste Ground'. Some interesting problems developed. Stephen commented that nobody had found woodlice anywhere except huddled under stones and solid debris: 'They *must* eat sometime.'

He decided that this must happen at night, and

he worked out that a jar sunk in the ground might 'catch woodlice when they are out hunting.' He probably got this idea from reading about pitfall traps used for capturing larger animals. He covered the top of the jar with a few strands of fine grass: 'If it's dark they won't be able to see much.'

After nothing was captured on the first night, he put out other traps just to make sure. He kept careful records and displayed them to the class. At the end of each day he remembered to check his traps to make sure that no animals had fallen into them during the day. Although few animals were caught in his traps he concluded to his satisfaction that 'woodlice hunt at night.'

However, there was one unexpected observation; the presence in one of the jars, of a centipede eating a small worm. Other children were fascinated by this, and several agreed to try to find out what their animals ate. At first, tests were crude, but refinements were evolved during 'discussion'. For example, children worked out that the animals might have gone towards some food items not because these were preferred, but because they were nearer or larger. In the case of some animals, for example, slugs, the children found it easy to see which foods had been 'nibbled' and could even examine 'teeth marks', but the results were very confused, as preferences seemed to change without apparent reason.

Stephen got nowhere with his tests on woodlice, and eventually concluded: 'Woodlice did not seem to have a preference for anything we gave them. I think they just like soil.'

Linda, in attempting to find out how fast woodlice move, discovered that they were more willing to run when put out on an open floor. At first, she had tried to channel them down a straight run made from strips of cardboard but found that they 'pile up on top of one another and creep into every corner'. She solved her problem by letting each animal loose on a large piece of paper and making a track behind it with a fibre-tip pen. She had intended to snake string over each mark and then measure the string. However, someone in the class had shown her how to use a Meccano wheel as what was described as a 'mini' trundle wheel (the class had made quite extensive use of a trundle wheel in work in mathematics). It is interesting, however, that Linda merely recorded her measurements in *turns* (of the wheel) and was only able to translate these into standard units following a group discussion. Needless to say, the 'mini' trundle found many other practical uses.

Colin, when searching waste ground, spent some time examining daisy heads. He later confessed disappointment that he had not found any earwigs on them. He had remembered one rather vivid close-up picture in the film strip, depicting an earwig on a daisy head, and believed that daisies were the usual habitat of earwigs!

Discarded materials   Man seems to be an animal whose production of rubbish is for ever ahead of his ability to dispose of it adequately. Some litter is, of course, unpleasant to handle, or even dangerous, but a substantial quantity of the discarded material which, unfortunately, forms part of our environment, is safe solid, relatively clean, and often almost indestructable. This material can be of tremendous fascination to children and may stimulate work leading to quite complex mathematics as well as to physical and chemical investigations.

An infant class

Some response seems inevitable when such material is found or displayed on an infant-class interest table. The initial reaction, 'It's all dirty', gives way to intense interest as sorting proceeds: 'This is heavy.' 'The tin is rusty . . . it crumbles in my hands.'

One group spent a lot of time sorting out and naming and classifying a whole variety of material including metal, plastic, rubber, leather, wood, etc. Various criteria were used in grouping, including size, shape, texture and colour, and the results were charted. Not infrequently there were discussions regarding the correct category for specific items, and sometimes this necessitated the creation of new groups.

Two children became quite absorbed in pieces of china, and brought along many fragments of that material. This resulted in strenuous efforts to piece it together and to assess exactly what each fragment represented. In addition, intricate details of pattern, glazing, etc, were commented upon and discussed. In fact, these children were getting the real feeling of being archaeologists, an impression which would have been reinforced, if they had been older, by the discovery of a large piece of a King George VI coronation mug!

A frequent response to scrap material, by infant children, is to use it for model making. Mark used a length of pipe, gauze, and various pieces of plastic and wood to construct his moon rocket. The string of verbal comments as he worked, and his later illustrations, indicated his plans for the journeys which his rocket would make. However, the actual construction, and the comment he wrote to accompany the displayed model, showed concern with more down-to-earth relationships. A metal bottle top attached to the side of the rocket was described as the steering wheel, and Mark wrote: 'My rocket is going to the moon. My rocket is ten inches high.'

Jane was fascinated by the fact that the world looked red through a piece of red plastic sheet which she discovered. She was able to relate this to the colours visible through pieces of cellophane provided by the teacher; she made more precise observations of apparent changes in colour which occurred when different objects were viewed, and of different effects obtained when looking through two differently coloured pieces of cellophane. Her interest declined in the face of difficulties she encountered when trying to make particular colours with powder paints.

Metals provoked a variety of activities. Alan

insisted, 'Metals go rusty. They go rusty when they get wet.' Further sorting threw doubts on this and, after discussion, various pieces of metal were left outside in a polythene-lined box. The children were, however, more fascinated by the method they developed for making records than by analysing results in any detail. The accidental discovery of the fact that damp rust would rub off on to paper focused attention on this as a technique of recording results pictorially as well as verbally. Other activities did, however, develop further. The provision of a small but powerful magnet gave impetus to a new kind of sorting and classifying: 'All the rusty things are picked up.' 'Even the crumbly bits of rust stuck to my magnet.'

When one of the boys brought a larger magnet, comparisons were provoked: 'Pins *leap* up to this magnet.' 'They jump much further than to the little one.'

Extensive pictorial lists, of what things were and what things were not attracted by their magnets, were drawn up, and attempts were made to weigh and measure some of the larger objects lifted.

An interest in sound (musical sounds) developed as a result of testing the noise made by some of the objects found. Objects were tapped, scraped, shaken and knocked together. A lot of interest was focused on a seemingly unopenable tin, and guesses were made as to the contents. The caretaker's wrench eventually revealed the contents as coarse gravel. One development of this discovery was the making of various musical 'shakers', using tins and rigid plastic pots as containers. In selecting contents for their instruments, the children were clearly mindful of the possibilities presented by the scrap materials they had found, and stone, sand, plastic beads, and pieces of metal were all utilized. In many cases the children attempted to forecast the sort of sound which would be made. Many of the children could make correct use of the terms 'high' and 'low' in describing the notes they produced.

Other children tried to make musical notes b

scraping and rubbing. Pamela brought to school a flat tin with elastic bands stretched across it. While she was demonstrating it, she found that it made much more noise when placed on a table than on a padded surface. An immediate explanation was forthcoming: 'The foam is a bit pinchety' (her word) 'and it stops the noise getting down.'

Further investigations were put in hand, and the volume of sound produced on various surfaces was assessed and compared. Pamela was then prepared to generalize as a result of her studies: 'The foam is soft to keep our feet warm but the floor is hard so it plays better on the floor.'

Artistic techniques were frequently used by the children to communicate information. Rubbing, done earlier by some of the class, was used as a way of listing some of the materials discovered. Shoe soles, window panes, a strawberry net, wallpaper, a sieve, and a loudspeaker grill were among the objects of which rubbings were made. The use of rust marks smeared on paper was extended, from mere recording, to a way of making pictures. Gear wheels were used both for printing and for rolling out patterns (the latter technique has since been developed commercially). Sometimes art and science were, almost literally, blended together. Materials found were sorted according to their suitability for grinding into powders, and the children readily responded to the suggestion that they might mix these with water and use them in their painting.

A backward infant group

A group of older (but below average ability) infants was able to extend some of the scientific investigations further (although their spelling left something to be desired!). Here are some of their practical responses to ideas put forward by the teacher:

'I think any metal sticks to magnets.' 'I thound out theat sum metals stick beta thean uvas.' 'I tooc a magnet and sor how meny nails I could get in a row 5.' 'I sor how meny nails I could get on a magnet.

111.' 'Magnets stil[stick] froo warta and glars and cardbord and me.' 'I ferst took sum bottels and filld eech one with a diffarant amount of water. Then I sor how meny diffarnt sounds I could mace. The les warta in it the hiya note I got.' 'I took a bottle and bloo across top. It made a thuny sound. Then I thild it with water it made no sound.'

magnets stil froo warta, and glars and card bord and me.

A backward older-junior child

With juniors, many further developments are possible, although many children, and probably especially those who have had little previous experience in this particular field, need to go through some of the earlier stages. For example, the book of rubbings produced by this older junior was to him as essential a part of the recording process as it was to an infant.

Often backward children get their important stimulus for effort from practical exploration. Charlie (aged ten) had been in trouble with authority (including the police) during his three years in the junior school and was barely literate. One of his pleasures was to be allowed to go with a relation to deliver coal, on some Saturday mornings. Perhaps his most sustained piece of work arose through finding pieces of coal and coke on a rubbish dump. Patiently he became involved, at times with a school friend (his only one, and intermittent at that), in crushing up coal for a model coal truck; in drawing, using coal and coke; in naming fuels from samples and illustrations obtained (by the teacher) from a coal merchant; and in building a model coal mine, using balsa wood, corrugated paper, and some of his crushed coal. This work may not sound impressive, but it involved him for lengthy periods, and he was willing to turn to simple reference books, especially to the pictures in them, for guidance. Some of his work was recorded in written form.

Later he began (as he put it) to 'find which coal is the heaviest' by weighing samples on the scales, but he was distracted from this by (rare) involvement with another group who provided him with a meccano lift to go with his coal mine. Other members of the group tried to test the hardness of some coal, using a hand drill, but this interest was, unfortunately, not developed.

An older-junior group

Able juniors are, of course, capable of much further progress in their physical studies, leading to quite advanced concepts. The response of one group to a rusty bicycle wheel, still in its frame, indicates the variety of stimuli which may arise.

'It's all rusty.' 'Not all; it's still shiny where there's chromium plating.' 'You can twang the spokes. It's like a harp.' 'There aren't many different notes, though.' (This interest was later followed up with wheels and individual spokes of different sizes.) 'It's like a spinning wheel.' 'It's stuck; it won't move.' 'It needs oiling.'

After the wheel had been oiled and eased: 'It takes nothing at all to turn it.' The ease with which the wheel moved when a very small piece of plasticine was stuck on, demonstrated this: 'It's a balance. We could use it for scales.' Several children followed this up and, with weights hooked on to the spokes, the sensitivity of the balance was assessed and compared with that of other scales in the classroom. So concerned were these children with solving technical problems and making their apparatus as efficient as possible, that many of the scientific possibilities of their investigation were overlooked.

Tests on rusting did lead to further work, beginning with detailed records showing which items rusted and exactly where rust was found on pieces of scrap. Tests were worked out to discover the influence of paint and chromium plating on rusting, and the effects of oil in preventing deterioration. Comparison of the effects of moisture on different substances revealed metallic changes other than rusting, and initiated practical studies of moulds. A textbook suggestion for demonstrating the need for air in the rusting process was attempted, but the absence of a clear-cut result reduced faith in this line of investigation.

An older-junior class

A completely different class, given very similar starting points, were able to exploit the mathematical possibilities of their physical observations more fully. Studies developed to include measurements of the actual force required to turn a bicycle wheel, using both weights and a spring balance; and the differing forces required at various distances from the centre of the wheel were not only noted but also recorded and graphed. This, in turn, led to an appreciation of the relationship between the circumference and diameter of various wheels, and of the use of linked wheels and of gear wheels in transmitting movement. Measurements were also made of the forces involved in putting on brakes and, in the event of brake failure, of the effects of crashes occurring on slopes of varying degrees of steepness.

Though these children did not neglect the possibilities for imaginative use of the material at their disposal, their 'inventions' showed appreciation of the real physical relationships between individual components.

Other members of the same class became involved in quite different topics. Many of the substances found were closely examined, and use was made of aids for magnification. For example, in assessment of the size of the threads in cloth-like materials, human hairs were used for comparison with the finer strands. After discussion, crude apparatus to compare and measure strengths was designed. Although their 'experiments' did not meet the rigorous standards of true science, the children were concerned to compare like with like, and realized the limitations of their results. Clearly, too, they were able to see their results in terms of the graphs constructed, and to use these mathematical displays to read and predict results.

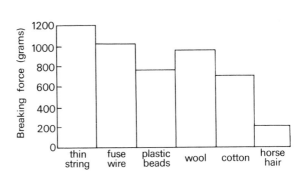

The fascination of these practical tests helped to encourage other practical work concerning, for example, the amount of stretching which could take place in different materials.

Another line of study developed into an investigation of the degree of slide (ie, absence of friction) produced by the soles of various items of footwear. A spring balance was used to measure the force needed to make a shoe move on each surface tested. Comparisons were made, both using the same soles on different surfaces and using different soles on the same surface. The work not only gave an appreciation of the nature and physical properties of a variety of different substances but also enabled numerical comparisons to be made, such as those shown in the following graph.

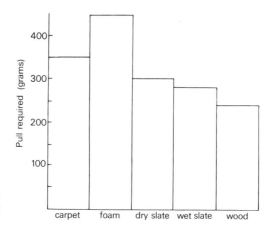

The force required to move a shoe on various surfaces

Another older-junior class

It is interesting to set these studies alongside of similar work followed through in another quite different class. Some of the children had commented on the increased strength of fibres when these were woven. (Initially, exploration had arisen from suggestions made by the teacher in connexion with observations of silk moths spinning cocoons.) Silk and nylon, in strand and woven form, were compared, using simple breaking tests.

At this time, David found some sodden paper sacks, and was surprised by how easily they could be torn; he had believed that they were waterproof and strong. He readily agreed to use the material test rig to compare samples, and he was most insistent on using pieces of exactly the same size in his experiments. The tests were repeated several times, but he was disappointed that the paper often tore at the point where it was attached. He improved the apparatus by adding rubbers between the pieces of ruler previously used for holding the paper, and demonstrated to his satisfaction that the wet paper was considerably less strong than the dry. (See the diagram opposite.)

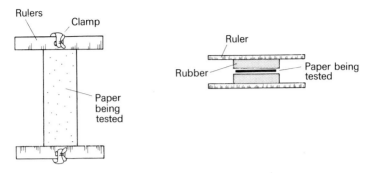

Apparatus to test the strength of paper: (a) top view of clamping
arrangements, (b) side view

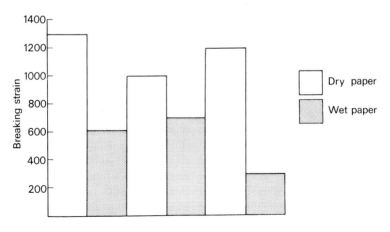

Graph to show the breaking strains of samples of wet and dry paper

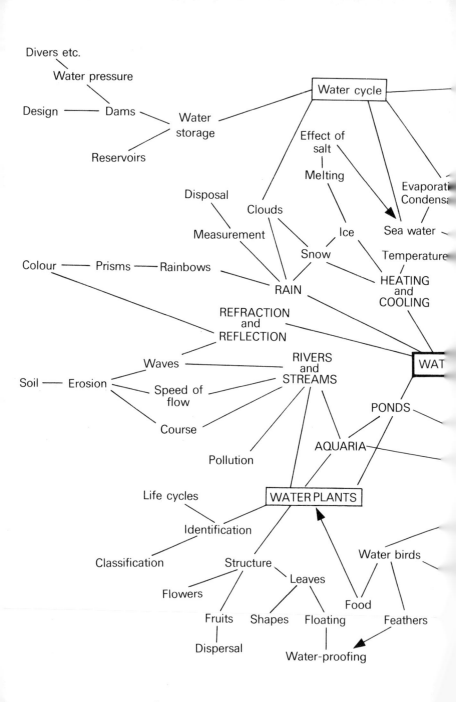

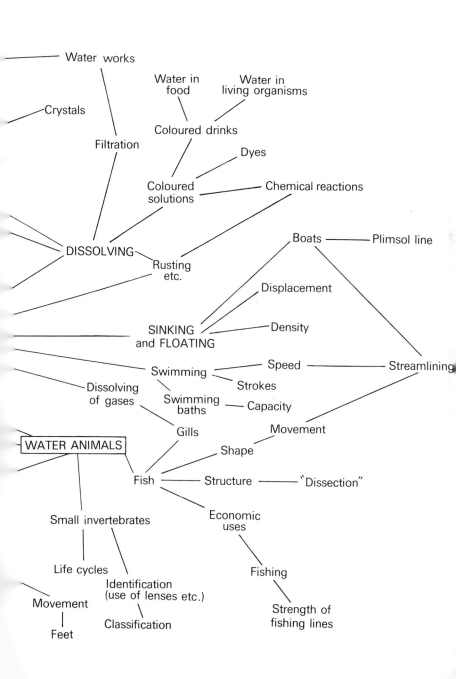

Water works

Crystals

Filtration

Water in food

Water in living organisms

Coloured drinks

Dyes

Coloured solutions

Chemical reactions

DISSOLVING

Rusting etc.

Boats ——— Plimsol line

Displacement

SINKING and FLOATING

Density

Swimming

Speed ——— Streamlining

Strokes

Dissolving of gases

Swimming baths

Capacity

Gills

Movement

WATER ANIMALS

Shape

Fish ——— Structure ——— "Dissection"

Small invertebrates

Economic uses

Life cycles

Movement

Identification (use of lenses etc.)

Fishing

Feet

Classification

Strength of fishing lines

Discussion with the teacher, and with a group, brought up the suggestion that sacks might be improved, and also produced ideas for carrying out and testing such modifications. Although many minds contributed suggestions, David was responsible for the practical work of trying out the effects of fat, oil, polish, and model aircraft 'dope' on the properties of the paper. He tried to assess whether water had been absorbed by a particular piece of paper by balancing it against another one of identical size.

Water　As water seems to have an irresistible attraction for children, it is perhaps fitting to use it in an example of the range of studies which may arise as a result of practical exploration of the surroundings. The flow diagram is often used by teachers to anticipate work which may arise as a result of environmental investigations—although a teacher must be prepared for the probability that some of his expectations will not be fulfilled, and that young minds may react with quite novel ideas and interests. The same technique for indicating radiating, and sometimes interlinked, sequences of work, may be utilized for summarizing events which have occurred in a single class.

The flow diagram shown on pages 252–3 incorporates the results of observations made in many junior school classes. It is still not complete, and only work in science is shown, because the range of activities is far greater than the space available in which to record them. It would be illuminating for the reader to try to extend the list of possibilities, or to develop the possibilities which arise when topics which have arisen are put at the centre of a new flow diagram. Many of the topics listed can engage (and *have* engaged) the study of infants and, indeed, even of pre-school children.

The extent to which work can develop may be illustrated by taking just two examples from this extensive range.

1. Pond life Fishing for animal life in ponds, ditches and streams seems to have an attraction for children from a very early age. The interest may be only short-lived, and often consist of no more than catching, and either releasing or attempting to keep, tadpoles, sticklebacks, etc. This comparatively superficial approach may persist but such interests, whether present or initiated, can be developed to encourage much more detailed studies.

2. Moving water Moving water seems to have a greater attraction than still water, for all age groups, and, when the opportunity presents itself, the youngest children will make use of moving water in their play. A fascinating example is 'Pooh sticks', the game described by A. A. Milne in WINNIE-THE-POOH. (The game consists of dropping sticks into a stream on the upstream side of a bridge, and seeing which stick first appears on the downstream side.)

Children may indeed make their first discovery of the fact that streams are in motion by observing objects floating on the surface (although other explanations are also put forward).

A class of older juniors, familiar with the above story, but of limited ability (and not renowned for their application to 'conventional' school work in general or mathematics in particular) were persuaded to measure, and later to graph, the speed of water flow in a local stream. Even before they made any measurements, they met and reported upon various problems—the presence of 'whirlpools' in the stream, places where the flow of water always carried objects to the side, and so on. Sticks did not always travel at the same speed, and particularly when they were irregularly shaped, got stuck, while pieces of polystyrene were blown to the edge. The children suggested the use of petals (although they were only partly able to express the advantage of these in being small, light, and reasonably waterproof), and it was their idea, too, to release the petals in a particular colour sequence, in order to

in my drop of water they were two aminals
one of them is long and thin and it is yellow
it keeps twisting and turning they ~~are~~ is
~~fofe~~ three strands on the tail end and it has
two ~~fet~~ feelers and it has no ~~lege~~ legs
when it was placed under a magnifying
projector we saw it had two eyes and two
suckers. and it was a Midge Larva

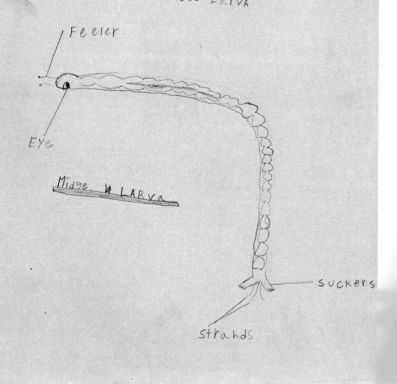

Feeler

Eye

Midge LARVa

suckers

strahds

'Midge Larva'

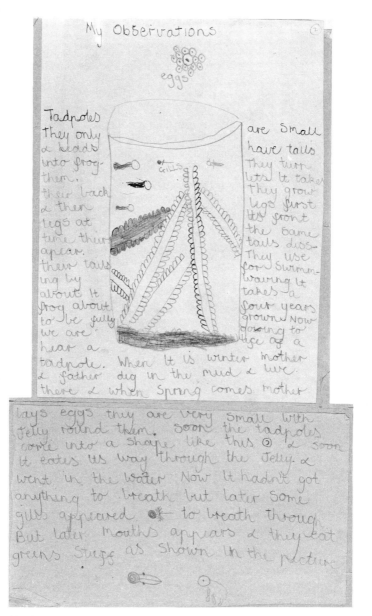

My Observations

eggs

Tadpoles are small
They only have tails
a heads They turn
into frog- legs it takes
them. They grow
their back legs first
a then its front
legs at the same
time their tails diss-
apear. They use
their tails for swimm-
ing by waving it
about it takes a
frog about four years
to be fully grown. Now
we are going to
hear a use of a
tadpole. When it is winter mother
a father dig in the mud a live
there a when spring comes mother

lays eggs they are very small with
jelly round them. Soon the tadpoles
come into a shape like this ⊙ a soon
it eates its way through the jelly. a
went in the water. Now it hadn't got
anything to breath but later some
gills appeared to breath through
But later mouths appears a they eat
greens stuge as shown in the picture

'My observations'

make it easier to follow their progress.

Perhaps more important than the work achieved was their attitude. As one remarked to a visitor: 'She don't know it's our 'obby.' Not only was 'she' (the teacher) fully aware of their interest but she was aware that they did not realize the extent of her knowledge! Thus, when at the end of the week she remarked to them; 'I wonder whether the rain will make the stream flow faster on Saturday', they did not guess that they were being 'set' weekend homework. Not only did they 'do' this homework but they came back asking how they could measure how much rain had fallen.

3 Conclusion

These examples, taken together, raise many interesting points. From the amount of enthusiasm generated, and energy harnessed, it seems evident that a study of the environment[1] in practical terms is so important that we cannot afford to neglect it. A scientific approach, being basically a method which helps an individual to retain his innate curiosity, and to use his developing intellectual powers in conjunction with this important characteristic, is surely one relevant to all human beings and not just to future scientists. The variety of topics available for study is so vast that it is hardly surprising that many people might wish to limit the amount taught. Certainly the individual has to limit his intake, but is it not perhaps *too* convenient to suggest that it should be limited *for him*, as is done by some restricted syllabuses? In some such cases it is all too easy for learning to take place without the necessity for individual thought. The willingness of human beings to learn is certainly not confined to accepted school subjects, and may often be greater in 'non-academic' pursuits.

The children mentioned in the examples above had to think for themselves and, usually, to communicate with others. Although help was always available to them, they were often prepared to accept the challenge offered by the problems in hand, and to seek solutions by trial and error, through discussion and from books, as well as by the seemingly simpler technique of 'asking the teacher'. They knew that the results of many of the investigations depended entirely on them, and in this situation the fact that some experiments didn't 'work properly' or produce the 'right' answer was

[1]See, in this series, ENVIRONMENTAL STUDIES by Melville Harris

259

of less importance than it might have been in a more formal situation. Unexpected results frequently provoked further interest, and failures of tests gave an excuse for repetition of observation—often very necessary if techniques are to be learned and information assimilated. Within the limited field each child studied, he became an 'expert', with the knowledge gained being relevant and connected.

In nearly all of the examples described, the activities were largely carried out by groups of children, rather than by the whole class, although discussions, and other methods of sharing experiences, by displays, etc, brought together larger numbers of children. Thus, at a particular instant of time there was a variety of work taking place within each classroom, not all of it necessarily either scientific or practical. Working in this way it is not possible, at the beginning of any particular term or year, to predict what scientific knowledge any child will gain (is it ever possible?). Consequently, conventional examinations are not practicable—in some fields a child would know more than the teacher setting the test! Much more reliance has therefore to be placed on the teacher's continuous records and over-all assessment.

This dependence on subjective criteria has advantages, as children cannot be graded merely on numerical evidence. The depth of involvement of the children in their activities is some measure of their achievement, as is the degree to which they themselves raise further problems for observation and investigation. Although written work may be assessed, it becomes essential to take into account other methods of communication, including the spoken word. Thus, evaluation of each child's progress is, of necessity, on a broad front.

Although the specific topics described above did arise in the classes mentioned, they need not have done. Even similar stimuli produced different responses in apparently similar classes, and variations in individual interests, in environment, and between teachers, ensure that each child will see different starting points. In general, it is probably true to say that the younger or less experienced the child, the more local his interests—which, as he develops, will expand geographically as well as intellectually. For this reason alone, the possibility that work already 'covered' at an earlier age may be repeated need not be of particular concern.

When what is to be presented is left so open, it is important to note that certain aspects are unsuitable at a particular stage. For example, it would not be possible for a child to have an appreciation of density and of, say, Archimedes' principle until he had grasped the concepts of both weight and volume, and a fair amount of practical experience is required before even this is achieved.

The examples considered show considerable variations in the ability of children to express themselves and, to be more specific, standards of grammar and of spelling may differ from what might be desired. Such variations are, of course, to be expected, and the development of scientific abilities does not, of itself, aid progress in the basic skills. However, the pursuit of an investigation does provide a meaning for the practice of such skills although, at times, the enthusiasm for what is being expressed may hamper the memory of some of the rules of English. Even so, the examples of work given have not always been the final reports, and the prestige of presenting a final report for a class book or for display has often improved the quality of presentation, including that of written English, beyond recognition.

The teacher has been mentioned rather infrequently, not because the role is unimportant but because it is relatively unobtrusive. The demands on the teacher are, however, great, as regards guiding children towards (sometimes away from) further investigations. The teacher needs to be aware of the stimuli likely to provoke a response, and to anticipate (supported by material readiness and some background knowledge) the lines of development which are likely to occur. Fortunately, the teacher's task is eased as children extend and bring to the classroom their interests and hobbies, and when children find that cooperation between individuals is a necessity, rather than something to be deplored.

It is all too easy to point to missed opportunities in the situations concerned. (Wouldn't it have been a good thing if Charlie had been taken to see the coal mining exhibit at the—not too distant—museum?) Undoubtedly, opportunities often were and are missed for many reasons, such as lack of experience on the part of a teacher, large numbers in the class, and so on. However, there is also much more to be learned about the best ways of harnessing the energy which children have available for their interests, and of avoiding excessive teacher involvement which may 'kill' interests.

It should now be possible to look back at the development of the children's work under the following headings.

1. The various starting points for studies including:

(a) children's own collections and interests;

(b) visits to the local environment; walks exploration, etc;

(c) the classroom interest table, which is bes seen as a selection (made by the teacher and th children) of items from the environment whic may be used for further investigation;

(d) books (including stories, etc);

(e) audio-visual aids (including television, soun broadcasts, films, etc);

(f) visits to special parts of the environmen such as museums, zoos, etc (the examples give have deliberately been restricted to the mor local environment).

2. The need for a variety of material to arous interests.

3. The importance of opportunities for caref

observations (including handling of material).

4. The various methods by which records may be kept and the relationship of science to work in the basic skills.

5. The importance of discussion both as a method of communication and as a way of clarifying problems.

6. The need actually to perform practical investigations.

Appendix

Classroom resources

Many primary schools have discovered that complex apparatus is not a necessary pre-requisite for scientific studies. Often, pieces of 'equipment' to hand are as satisfactory as their commercial counterparts, as well as being considerably cheaper; for example, transparent plastic containers and glass jars may replace beakers, although admittedly they cannot be heated over a flame. Frequently, materials discarded by an affluent society provide valuable equipment for school use. Collection of such materials may be a major exercise, but children and parents cooperate when given a lead by the teacher. Although storage may present a problem, this can be eased by the fact that many items may be of use in studies other than science and their lack of any monetary value means that they do not need to be locked away.

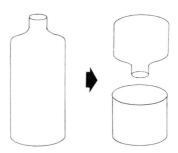

Beaker and funnel made from bottle

The list below represents an attempt to categorize some of the numerous items which may be useful. Many of these things will be found to have a multitude of uses, although some ingenuity may be required to realize their potential. The discovery that a plastic dispensing bottle may be cut in half to make a 'beaker' and 'funnel' has certainly been made independently on many occasions.

Undoubtedly many teachers and children have found uses for the 'nozzle' left over. One such use has been as a pan for a delicate balancing, also using a drinking straw, a pin, and a piece of bent metal strip:

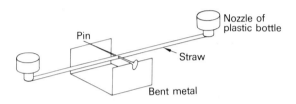

Another use for plastic bottles has been to make water wheels:

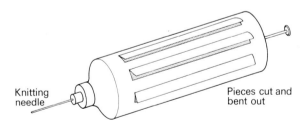

Another use is, combined with a large glass jar, to make a simple wormery. (See the illustration on page 266.)

Worms live in soil in the space between the inside of the glass and the outside of the plastic bottle.

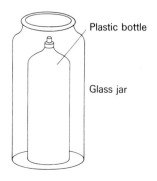

Plastic bottle

Glass jar

And so it may go on; the list of possibilities is almost endless.

Materials   Stationery etc: paper, cardboard, blotting paper (useful as filter paper), glue, paste, greaseproof paper tissue paper, adhesive tape, paper clips, drawing pins, pins, staples, string, elastic bands, scissors ink (red ink is a useful biological stain), old ball point pens and packages, powder paint, sealing wax, drinking straws, clay, oil-based clay, plaster of Paris.

Tools etc: hammer, saw, pliers, screwdriver, penknife screws, nails, washers, sandpaper. (A piece of timber can span desks or tables to make a work bench.)

Containers (usually discarded ones): saucepans trays, plastic bowls, plastic buckets, containers made of polythene, polystyrene, etc (eg, egg containers, ice trays, ice-cream tubs), polythene storage containers, plastic spray bottles, etc, jam jars and other glass containers (small bottles made to hold food flavouring make useful dropping bottles metal containers (including those which have held canned food), spoons, plastic bags, cardboard box (match boxes are particularly useful).

'Chemicals' (a) *from domestic sources;* common salt (sodium chloride), Epsom salts, baking powder, washing soda, starch, liquid detergent, detergent powder, bleach, water softener, methylated spirits, ammonia, vinegar, sugar, citric acid, talcum powder, food colouring;

(b) *from builders, timber merchants;* sand, cement, fine gravel, lime, asbestos sheet (for heat-resistant bench covers), offcuts of timber and surfacing materials, and *named* timber samples.

Domestic junk (excluding containers): needles, thread, stockings (for making nets, etc), cardboard rolls, metal and other bottle tops, expanded polystyrene packing and ceiling tiles, polyurethane 'sponges', old brushes (especially tooth brushes), sieves and strainers, pieces of candles, metal (wire) clothes hangers, corks, mirrors, clocks, electrical apparatus (beware of television tubes), eye droppers (pipettes).

Material from further afield: old bicycles; for gear wheels, steel tubes, chromium plated steel, rubber tubing, valves, metal spokes, ball bearings, dynamos, lamps, wire, brake levers, saddle springs, etc; old cars; for most of the above and for electric motors, coil, mirrors (plane and convex), pulley wheels, various metals and plastics, switches, speedometers and other instruments, etc.

Also materials from: (a) *plumbers:* piping of different materials such as copper, brass, lead, iron, steel, plastics;

(b) *electricians and telephone engineers:* wire, switches, fuse boxes, connecting boxes, etc;

(c) *opticians:* lenses.

(Many of the items listed above would, of course, not be in the possession of a teacher, but sources of such materials could be discovered.)

Some other equipment might need to be purchased, especially for work at the junior stage.

Simple equipment might include: thermometers, magnets, magnetic compass, corks, plastic tubing, pulleys, spirit lamp, lenses, and a simple microscope.

Booklist

Allen, G. E. et al SCIENTIFIC INTERESTS IN THE PRIMARY SCHOOL National Froebel Foundation 1960

CHILDREN LEARNING: THROUGH SCIENTIFIC INTEREST National Froebel Foundation 1966

Isaacs, N. EARLY SCIENTIFIC TRENDS IN CHILDREN National Froebel Foundation 1958

NATURE ACTIVITIES IN SCHOOLS School Natural Science Society 1970

Nuffield Junior Science Project: TEACHER'S GUIDE 1; TEACHER'S GUIDE 2; ANIMALS AND PLANTS; APPARATUS Collins 1967

SCIENCE AND MATHEMATICS FOR PRIMARY SCHOOLS Essex County Council Education Committee 1967

Science for Primary Schools: 1. CHILDREN LEARNING THROUGH SCIENCE; 2. LIST OF BOOKS; 3. LIST OF TEACHING AIDS; 4. MATERIALS AND EQUIPMENT John Murray (for the Association for Science Education) 1966

THE ESS READER by Elementary Science Study. Newton: Mass. Education Development Center 1970

Some useful addresses are:

National Froebel Foundation
2 Manchester Square, London W1. Publications are available from: East Sussex Office Equipment, 204–206 London Road, East Grinstead, Sussex.

School Natural Science Society
Publications are obtainable from M. J. Wootton, 44 Claremont Gardens, Upminster, Essex RM14 1RS.

Essex County Council Education Committee
Schools Department, County Hall, Chelmsford, Essex.

See also AN INTRODUCTION, ENVIRONMENTAL STUDIES, MATHEMATICS FOR YOUNGER CHILDREN, MATHEMATICS FOR MATICS FOR YOUNGER CHILDREN, MATHEMATICS FOR OLDER CHILDREN, A RURAL SCHOOL, AN INFANT SCHOOL, A JUNIOR SCHOOL, THE TEACHER'S ROLE, and EDUCATING TEACHERS in this series.

Drama

**Pamela Blackie, Bess Bullough
and Doris Nash**

The Authors

Doris Nash has done social work in a poor urban area with mothers and babies, and has cared for children with physical and emotional handicaps. Later she trained as a teacher. After eight years' work in a very old school, she was appointed headteacher of Sea Mills Infant School, Bristol, where the constant aim of the staff is to meet the children's need for all round development.

Pamela Blackie trained at the Royal Academy of Dramatic Art and has the University of London Diploma in Dramatic Art. At the outbreak of war she became Drama Adviser for the Yorkshire Rural Community Council, and was later Drama Adviser for the Council for the Encouragement of Music and the Arts (which became the Arts Council). She was later Adviser for the Community Council of Lancashire. In the 1950s, she wrote and produced many plays, mainly religious drama. She also taught drama in a boys' Borstal. She is author of A DRAMA TEACHER'S HANDBOOK (Blackwell, 1956). She now teaches drama, part-time, at Huntingdon County Primary School.

Bess Bullough taught in various schools from 1934 first as a general class teacher, and later specializing in English, drama and physical education. She became interested in the Movement approach to physical education and creative work, and experimented in the relationship between movement, sound and speech. During the past twenty years she has demonstrated and lectured on this work to training college students and at in-service courses. She has made teaching films for the West Riding authority and the BBC, and video tapes for training colleges. In 1968, she received the MBE, for work in the educational field. She is currently head of department for physical education and drama in a middle school in the West Riding of Yorkshire.

Introduction

Until fairly recently, school drama in England was
largely confined to secondary schools. In particular,
the big grammar schools in London, and some of the
independent boarding schools, have a tradition
going back to the beginning of this century or
earlier. In primary schools, however, drama has
been limited, with few exceptions, to a Christmas
Nativity play from a printed script and to a rather
half-hearted feature known as Dramatization
found chiefly in infant schools. In the last decade,
however, there has been a great quickening of life
and much innovation in primary school drama
affecting a substantial minority of schools all over
the country.

It is not easy to be sure of the influences which
have been at work behind this movement, but two
at least can be identified. The arrival in England
of a wartime refugee from Hitlerism, Rudolph
Laban, stimulated practical interest in his theories
and an increasing number of schools do a subject
which they call Movement. The object of Movement
in school is to provide a basic training in control of
the body so that all movements may be improved
and so that the specialized movements required for
particular sports and crafts may be more easily
learned. Movement is as much the basis of dance,
ballet, and drama as it is of football, swimming
and ski-ing, and Movement in the Laban sense has
developed in an artistic direction as well as in
more purely acrobatic one. It is a curious fact that
while Laban's influence in the USA has been mainly
in the professional theatre, displayed in particular
in the distinguished work of Martha Graham, in
England it has been almost entirely in schools.
Much of the most interesting dramatic work going

274

on at present in English primary schools follows the Laban principles very closely, and nearly all of it is affected by them.

A second influence has been that of the drama advisers. The first advisers had nothing to do with schools and indeed were forbidden to enter them. They were appointed early in the Second World War by the Council for the Encouragement of Music and the Arts and by the various Community Councils, to stimulate adult and youth drama as a contribution to civilian morale. Some ten years ago, however, they were transferred to the local education authorities with a responsibility which included schools. Some of the older advisers whose experience had been confined to older age-groups had little to offer the primary schools but, increasingly, they and their successors have become interested in drama for young children and, for the first time, professional skill and knowledge has been available to the teachers. The appointment, by the Department of Education and Science, of a Staff Inspector of Drama, in 1953, confirmed the growing importance attached to the subject by educational opinion.

These two influences have operated, so far as primary schools are concerned, mainly upon individual teachers who have initiated dramatic activity in their own classes, and who often seem to hold very strong views about how it should be done, and even stronger views about how it should not be done. Those who are strong adherents of the Laban Movement believe that children must begin by a purely physical approach, and learn the use and control of their bodies without any appeal to the imagination. Only when they have advanced a considerable distance along the road of physical mastery should they be allowed to use their imaginations. 'You must never *be* an old man,' they will say. 'You must move *like* an old man.' Others would argue that children will use their imaginations, whether the teacher likes it or not, and that the imagination provides one means of learning to move.

It is not necessary to follow out this argument here, but it explains the composition of this section which differs from all the others in that it consists of separate contributions by three different teachers. Each of them has evolved, not of course uninfluenced by others, but essentially for herself, a method and practice for dramatic work with young children. Each has written in her own manner, an account of what she does with her children, and two have given some indication of how they came to adopt their present practices. No attempt has been made to harmonize the three contributions, though it will be noticed that, despite some differences in approach, there is a great deal of common ground between them. Each eschews public performance. Each uses the whole floor space and will have nothing to do with a conventional stage. Each brings the whole class rather than a selected cast into the work. Each makes a maximum use of movement, with words coming slowly and at a later stage. None has any use for a play, in the sense of something written for children by an adult and published. All three, to a varying extent, link the dramatic work with other activities and experiences which go on in the school.

It must be stated, in conclusion, that there are schools in England where the dramatic work does not fit with what is described in this booklet. The initiative and independence of each individual teacher is no myth and those who wish to do formal production of scripted plays are at perfect liberty to do it. Here and there will be found very gifted teachers who make a success of this, though, i must be added, always at the cost of leaving out the majority of the children and using only 'the good actors'. However, it would seem that it is the type of work described in this booklet which represent the most interesting and the most important development in progress today.

John Blacki

1 Drama in the Junior School

by Pamela Blackie

I started teaching drama in a junior school eight years ago. Some children asked me to do it, and with their headmaster's consent I began by teaching a drama club in the school outside lesson time. After a term, it was decided that drama could be included in the curriculum, so I was able to do it in school hours. The experience I had to draw on when I started was a professional dramatic training, a university diploma in dramatic art, a brief time in professional repertory, a number of years taking drama classes for adults and teenagers, and the production of plays (some written by myself—dramatized folk tales, poems, and bible stories) among children, at home, in the village where I live, and on occasion in the neighbouring town.

The school contains nearly 600 children. It is one of two junior schools which serve a small but growing county town in a predominantly rural county. Most of the classes I take have about forty children in them, but usually I take half the class at a time for thirty minutes. I teach only one day a week, and classes I take have age ranges of seven to eight, eight to nine, and ten to eleven.

I made a great many mistakes when I started. I produced scenes with the children in a formal manner which I now think more suitable for boys and girls in secondary schools. I imposed my own idea of what was dramatic on them, rather than letting them try out their ideas of what was dramatic on me, which is what I try to do now. Very fortunately, I never made the mistake of boring them, so I was able to go on experimenting. Now, by a process of trial and error, the drama I teach has become an activity in which the children act for their own sake and for the sake of each other, not for the purpose of interesting an audience.

Imaginative play The other day I watched, unseen, some six-year-olds in their school playground. One discovered the cover of a drain; he beckoned to a companion and pointed, and the two looked at the cover; then the second boy picked up an imaginary key, fitted it into place and, using his whole bodily strength, turned the key. He then replaced the key on the ground and, in imagination, lifted the cover. It must have been heavy, for the muscles in his arms and shoulders came up. He put it on the ground, and then both boys knelt down and peered into the hole. By that time, other children in the playground had begun to watch them and to talk to each other about what they were doing. Then one boy rolled up his sleeve and put his arm into the imaginary hole (he had in fact to bend his arm flat over the ground as the real cover was still in place); he got up with an imaginary something in his hand and showed it to the other boy; they peered over it with their heads together. At this point, the rest of the children gathered round to look too, and the end of the story was lost to view as far as I was concerned.

I have described this incident in detail because it seemed to me to be a perfect example of the imaginative play, completely absorbing and real, on which one is building in teaching drama to children. The idea was suggested by a physical object, the cover of a drain. Some of the imaginary experiences involved in playing it out were physical: the effort of turning the key, the effect of lifting something heavy, the feeling around a hole in the ground. There were also emotional experiences involved: curiosity, determination to find out, and the excitement of discovery. The whole thing was essentially dramatic. The first boy saw the cover, called his friend, and pointed at it. There was no seeing, calling, and pointing, all at the same time, which is what children—and many adults—do when acting a character. The whole thing built itself up to the climax of discovery, the other children in the playground playing perfectly the part of all crowds in dramatic scenes, gradually becoming more and more involved, and then gathering round the principals at the climax. All this was completely spontaneous and unproduced.

Planning a drama class Drama then, must involve deeply the child's imagination, his body and his emotions, and it must be acceptable to his mind as well, which means that the experiences suggested to him must be suitable to his age and state of development. I did not, and do not, positively think of this when planning material for a drama class, but I think that the most successful work, when the children have been truly involved and absorbed, has been achieved when the material has measured up to such requirements.

When planning a first encounter with children who have not done drama before, I try to bring into it, first, the imaginative physical experiences, then the imaginative emotional experiences, and then to draw on both in working them into some kind of dramatic scene. The following was the scheme I used for a group of nine-year-olds who had not done this kind of drama before.

Lie down on the floor. Curl up into a ball. Make yourselves as small and tight as you can. Now stretch out and relax.

Now, with your feet on the ground, curl up into a ball, tightly. Leap into the air as high as you can! Curl up again. Now relax.

Next, I take falls and stabbing. I show all the children the technique of falling without hurting themselves; then, after they have all tried falling, they get into pairs, and A stabs B while B falls. In the course of this, they discover that, if you are going to try to hurt someone (ie, stab him), you must first hate him, and that hatred makes your body go stiff and tense all over, in the way it does when you are curled up tightly in a ball; also, that, at the touch of the stab, the victim goes stiff with shock but that he must relax quickly before he falls. They find these discoveries interesting. They find that the hatred has an element of 'menace' in it. This is a word that always seems to crop up sooner or later in improvised drama. Younger juniors usually don't know what it means, the first time they hear it, but they subsequently use it a good deal themselves.

Next I say something like this:

Now you can tighten all your muscles till you feel very strong. Make a slow, strong movement. How can you make a slow strong movement which is also 'menacing'?

At this point, one of the children will sometimes have something to say about why you might feel 'menacing' towards somebody else.

We then talk about the 'reaction' to menacing movements.

If someone bigger and stronger than you made a slow menacing movement, what would you do?—show me!

The response is usually fear, expressed by the quick nervous form of movement.

Now, show me slow, strong, menacing movements, with your partner reacting with quick nervous movements.

Gradually, the slow movements become more threatening and the quick movements more frightened.

Now let's make two groups; one group is strong fierce and menacing, the other is intimidated and fearful.

Then I tell them:

Four of you are rich people with food and money; the rest of you are poor and starving. How do you poor people feel about the rich ones? And what do you rich people feel about the poor ones?

They tell me.

Now, let's plan a scene with a climax.

(This is another word which sometimes needs explanation, but which they will use a lot in future.)

The poor people are sitting in the street, hungry and hopeless; they see the rich people coming; they approach them; they beg, beseech, cajole, and finally threaten, all to no avail; the proud, frightened, rich people hurry past them as quickly as possible, and the poor people sink down again, disappointed and apathetic.

We usually do this scene twice and, as this is the first day, we leave it there. But if this same scene were used with more experienced children, they would divide up into groups, discuss it, and perhaps use words, beginning with murmurs of resentment, developing into shouted abuse, and dying away into bitterness.

Using emotions It has been pointed out to me that this scheme for a first lesson makes great use of violence and feelings of hatred, and I have been asked whether I don't think that I am encouraging the children to behave in a violent way towards each other, and towards other people. My answer is that the feelings of hatred and violence are there already, somewhere inside the children, and they had much better bring them out and learn to handle their emotions legitimately, in the drama class, than discover them for the first time under the stress of real anger and bitterness.

The above are strong emotions, easy to discover in oneself, but they are not the only feelings it is possible to make use of at the beginning. This was another first lesson for a similar group of children:

Another first lesson

Lie down on the floor, completely relaxed, so that you feel the floor is holding you up. There is a nice warm fire beside you; you are relaxed like a cat; you are a cat. Stretch yourself! Now, move away somewhere else in the room . . . now relax again. Now—someone throws cold water at you!

At this point, a number of the children jumped up, arched their backs and spat, and then stalked away—those who didn't, soon got the idea from the others.

Now you are yourself again. Lie down and bask in the sun. A cold wind begins to blow; the wind is getting stronger; you begin to walk; as you walk, the wind gets stronger—and stronger—and stronger! It begins to snow; the snow comes down over your hair and into your collar, onto your eyebrows; you take shelter with your back against a wall; the snow goes whirling by; you begin to grow numb . . . to freeze. You freeze until you are an iceberg, and you can't move hand or foot. Then the wind drops, the sun comes out; you begin to feel again; your muscles straighten out; your fingers and toes hurt, but you can move your arms and legs. Feel them! They belong to you again! Now the sun gets hotter and hotter; you can hardly lift your arms and legs, they are so feeble. You can't stand any more; you collapse and relax.

This meteorological fantasy, and the 'getting under the skin of' a cat, are experiences of bodily relaxation and tension, and the way in which circumstances affect these. In the 'weather' lesson, we went on to discuss other weather situations.

You have just experienced walking in a buffeting wind; how about other things which you may have to do in a wind?

The girls try out unpegging and bringing in washing from a line; the boys try bringing a boat ashore and making her fast. Then, the boys become fishermen in a storm, and the girls become fishermen's wives waiting on the cliff top. The class ends with the children sitting down in pairs; the boys telling each other how worried they were that they wouldn't be able to get to the shore, and the girls talking about their anxiety that the fishing boats might be lost and the men drowned. This prepares the way for the next class, which might involve making up a scene about a shipwreck, or a cliff rescue, or some other happening with a wind and sea setting.

Starting from the physical In planning a drama class, I try to make the beginning a physical rather than an emotional experience; emotions creep in inevitably, since all physical experiences must have some degree of pleasantness or unpleasantness about them, but the aim is to give the children something to limber up on, something which, if possible, can be used in a dramatic scene taken later on in the lesson. Here are some examples of beginnings:

You are seaweed, draped over a rock, which rises and falls with the tide.

You are in a room where the walls and floor have magnetic currents which can be switched on and off.

You are marionettes with strings attached to your head, back, wrists, and feet. You are completely floppy until I pull your strings.

You are candles (or matches) which someone lights (or strikes), and you burn down.

You are a mechanical toy which can be wound up, and which stops when the clockwork runs down.

You are a Jack-in-the-Box which is set off, and then put back in a box.

With your partner: one of you is a kite, the other is the person who puts the kite together and then flies it.

With your partner: one of you is 'Action Man' and the other the person who tries out the various attitudes 'Action Man' can assume.

You are running after someone, when he suddenly produces Medusa's head and turns you to stone in the attitude of running.

You are a spaceman arriving on a planet with little or no gravity.

An imagined situation The main part of each drama class is usually concerned with some imagined situation, which may be something in itself or may be developed into a more elaborate scene.

It is difficult to select examples of imaginative situations because the possibilities are so numerous and varied. Literally almost anything is possible, but the best scenes happen when the children build up the situation themselves.

You are in a wood at night, what can you hear?
The children say: *Owls, wind in the trees branches creaking, twigs cracking, leaves scuffling.*

Oh—what time of year is it then?
Autumn—we can hear wolves howling.

Where is this wood then?
In some mountains where there are wolves. It i beginning to snow. We are walking by lantern ligh and the wolves see the lantern and follow us. The stand among the trees watching us, with their ey

glittering in the moonlight. We run and run, and then we see the light of a cottage in the distance. We run through the wood, falling over the roots of trees, and reach the cottage door, and bang on it. We're exhausted! The woman inside is frightened and doesn't open the door at first, but after a bit she lets us in just before the wolves catch us. It's warm in the cottage, and then we faint with exhaustion on the hearth rug.

By now the scene is well under way, and full of possibilities. With an inexperienced class, I should encourage them to act it in pairs, one partner being the traveller escaping from the wolves and the other the woman in the cottage. With an experienced class, some children would probably be trees in the forest, animated trees that claw at the traveller, and others would be the pursuing wolves. In a class new to drama, the 'wolves' will always catch the 'travellers' and bite them—often, to begin with, working off private feuds in the process! But usually, a general feeling in the class that 'it spoils the story' prevents this happening again.

Disasters   The dramatic possibilities of disasters such as earthquakes, erupting volcanoes, shipwrecks, fires, floods and avalanches are obvious. To begin with, the children usually act them out as themselves, or else as a group of people such as fishermen, peasants, or explorers, but after a time the portrayal of character can be introduced.

The gentle old man who returns to find his cottage flattened by an earthquake and his family dead in the ruins—how about him, does he accept it with resignation or does he curse God for letting it happen?

The twisted avaricious old man who returns to find that the earthquake has buried his bag of gold deep in the ground, and that from now on he must be dependent on the charity of the neighbours he has neglected and despised; how about him?

An emotion
With older juniors a situation can sometimes be evolved by thinking about an emotion such as loneliness, homesickness, anxiety, temptation or fear. The boy or girl returning after an air raid to a house that has been destroyed by bombing may experience utter loneliness as he/she sits among the ruins, thinking of the days when this was a home. But loneliness implies that the family are dead; if they may be alive somehow, somewhere, then anxiety must be the main emotion, because anxiety is connected with hope. This is sometimes discovered in a drama class. Usually, quite early on, children will make up a scene which involves a clash between 'good' people and 'bad' people, and will discover that the 'bad' people are always the more convincing and interesting. Why? 'Because', said one inspired boy aged ten, 'You can't just be good by yourself; you can only be good *to* someone.' After that, the scene had to be replanned, and the 'good' people given objects for their charity.

Other sources of drama
The seasons and festivals of the year give plenty of scope for dramatic situations, particularly Hallowe'en with its legends and witches. Beginning the class by 'being a cat', as described earlier, (or any other suitable 'familiar') makes a good preparation for a story involving witches.

Another way that I find fruitful in getting children to build up a situation is to take a number of objects and give them to groups of children. I gave an old fox fur to a group of boys; they put it in the middle of the room: then, from all four corners they stalked it, and finally killed it by stabbing. The same fur, given to a group of girls, was tried on, passed from hand to hand and, finally, quarrelled over. A brooch I brought in was 'valuable' because it contained (a) real diamonds, (b) smuggled drugs, (c) a secret agent's message, and (d) because of the person who gave it. It was lost or stolen, and found (a) buried in the garden, (b) in the churchyard, (c) in the crop of a chicken, and (d) in Piccadilly Circus on Eros' left ear.

Music   I often use music to suggest ideas, to start the children limbering up at the beginning, and either to create or to enhance a situation during the main part of the class. Since I am not a musician, I am obliged to use music which has not been written specifically for this purpose, and which, therefore, is being to some degree misused in being employed to stir and canalize emotion in a drama class. I try to use music which is appropriate to what we are doing, and which I consider to be good of its kind—and, if it is any consolation to a musician reading this, many of the children have learned to enjoy listening to composers such as Debussy and Stravinsky because they originally heard them in the drama class. Music greatly helps a child to feel his own emotion in a situation, without being embarrassed by it. For example, Ravel's PAVANE FOR A DEAD INFANTA has helped many children mourning a dead kitten, or even being Hans Andersen's dying Little Match Girl, to weep real tears without any sense of incongruity or any desire to giggle.

Using speech   In the drama class, using speech as a vital part of a scene sometimes presents difficulties. In my class, one of the more successfully evolved situations using speech occurred as follows. The children were concerned with the state of the fishing trawlers, and were sitting in pairs, discussing the conditions of work and the state of the boats, the boys as trawlermen, the girls as their wives. At my suggestion, and unknown to the other members of the class, one of the boys, who was a natural leader, got up and said loudly, 'It's no good just talking. Come on, men, we've got to do something about it!' The boys and girls all looked at him for a few seconds of stunned surprise, then another boy got to his feet and said, 'Yeah, we've got to do something.' Then a girl shouted, 'And about time too!' After this, a thoroughly lively scene was under way, the children generally all talking together, though occasionally a leader topped the others with his or her voice. When I broke up the scene, ten minutes later, to discuss it with them, several of them said in tones of surprise, 'I say, that was *fun*!'

I find that, until children are fairly experienced in improvised drama, to suggest improvised conversation between individuals tends to make for self-consciousness, which in its turn produces charades instead of drama. Occasionally, charades have their place in the drama class. Very often the children want to act stories of their own making, and it seems to me to be wrong to prevent their doing this simply because it produces a charade situation. The children often become conscious of this situation themselves, and one has to guide them through it, or take them back to spontaneous crowd scenes or improvised acting in pairs, until they are more self-confident.

The study of an emotion, referred to earlier, led to a scene involving spontaneous speech. In this case the emotion was homesickness; the class was a group of ten- and eleven-year-olds. I did not make any suggestions for the use of speech. The situation began with the children talking together, in pairs, about occasions in their own lives when they had been homesick. Then they became a group of refugee children in a strange country. I waited to see what would happen. A girl, self-appointed as a leader, stood up and said, 'Let's go home!'

'Yes, let's!' said the others.

'How can we do it?' she asked. From a spontaneous series of suggestions, a plan for creeping out of an orphanage at night and crossing a frontier unseen was evolved, and this they proceeded to act.

Extent of children's contribution

I think that a drama class should aim at handing over as much as possible to the children, and that by the time they are about to leave the junior school, they should have a good deal of say in what they do in their classes. I find that, at this stage, they have a great many ideas for situations and scenes, and are prepared to write these down so that they can be acted in class. They usually want to have some kind of an 'occasion' before they leave school, which, if the drama that we did were suitable for an audience, would take the form of a performance to their parents. Since they are all agreed that our drama is not meant primarily for an audience, they usually invite their parents to an open drama class at which they act scenes and situations that they have planned out beforehand. In order that they should not start off in too self-conscious a 'state', we sometimes begin by using the audience in the scene. For example, the children planned out a scene about a witch hunt, in which their parents, from their seats round the room, joined in the hue and cry, 'She's a witch!', 'Burn her!', etc. The witch was then burned at the stake, some of the children being the fire that killed her, and the whole audience, children and parents alike, being the crowd watching the execution.

Evaluating work

I have been asked how I would evaluate a year's work with a class; what signs I would look for that would assure me that it had been, on the whole, a success. One of my first assurances is my own feeling in the class. For instance, to begin with, I had disciplinary difficulties, I was obliged to supply most of the ideas myself, and to keep a very tight hand on the class, or they would have been not only very noisy, but 'all over the place' as well. Towards the end of the year, the older juniors, at least, took more and more responsibility for the class themselves; they saw to it that the odd disruptive child was kept in his place, and I was consequently able to relax, and to be much more observant.

I would next try to judge just how involved the children had been in what they were doing. I have found that not every class is equally successful, and that things like the weather, the children's state of health, and tension over exams at the end of term,[1] or the lack of such tension, affect them. I have found that material which is tremendously absorbing to one group of children will leave another group comparatively cold, so that is is necessary to abandon it and try something else.

[1]The Selective Examination (eleven-plus) still exists in certain areas and also some schools set internal examinations

The most successful classes have been thos where the children have developed and worked ou an idea for themselves, and have become complete involved in it. This has usually been in some i tensely human situation, such as the loss of a hon through disaster, or the death of a dearly love animal (the death of a person being too dreadful contemplate dramatically), or in some entire fantastic situation such as the discovery of strang animals, or unexplored country, or the putting of curse on someone. The more involved the childre become, the greater is their creative experience ar this manifests itself in their growing more ready show initiative in coming forward with useful idea in taking over the running of the class, and disciplining themselves in it. They also show greater sympathy towards all kinds of people a circumstances and, in their criticisms, the gradu evolution of a scale of values.

2 Basic and Expressive Movement

A World of Action, Thought and Feeling

by Bess Bullough

I started my teaching as an English and drama specialist in a senior school (age range, eleven to fifteen years). To me, then, drama meant a stage, acting techniques and an audience. I taught the techniques, set standards, and demanded results. I produced and directed well-ordered plays. The results were pleasing to me at that time, but I realize now that the majority of the children were never wholly involved, and that very little contribution was made to their growth and development.

From the senior school, I went to a mixed junior school (age range, three to eleven-plus), as a general class teacher. This school is situated in one of the most depressing areas of a mining town. The district served by the school is some two miles from open country, and there are no open spaces where the children can play. The district is in the shadow of two chemical works, a gas works and a colliery. The houses are small, were erected eighty to a hundred years ago, and are now slums. Some of them are being cleared, and their occupants moved to new housing estates, but most of the children attending the school live in slum conditions.

We had to find some means of bringing colour and vitality into this grey world; ways of making the school an exciting place where there was pride in achievement, and of helping the children to become more aware of their surroundings, and so increasing their sensitivity. We were eager to do anything that invited the children's involvement as feeling, thinking beings. So we concentrated on physical education, drama, music and art.

I began to experiment and explore the possibilities of a 'movement' approach to physical and creative education. The following are some of the observations and experiences which are the result of working in this way with the children at this junior school.

Basic movement

Every movement we make, moving part of the body or all the body, involves three basic fundamentals —the use of space, weight and time.

Space
Use of much space, little space
Moving at different levels
Moving directly, moving indirectly

Time
Moving at various speeds—moving quickly, slowly, coming to stillness, being still, leaving stillness

Weight
Control of weight
Transfer of weight
Relaxation

Expressive movement

Expressive movement develops from exploring and experimenting with these basic fundamentals.

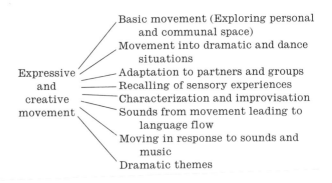

Expressive and creative movement
- Basic movement (Exploring personal and communal space)
- Movement into dramatic and dance situations
- Adaptation to partners and groups
- Recalling of sensory experiences
- Characterization and improvisation
- Sounds from movement leading to language flow
- Moving in response to sounds and music
- Dramatic themes

Introducing movement

The first introduction to basic movement must b approached with patience and understanding Instructions must be simple and clear, given i words the children can easily understand. The children must not be rushed into situations that are beyond their understanding or control. The awareness, self-discipline and control at which we are aiming cannot be expected from the start. If the movement experience is to be of real value, helping a child to become a *feeling* as well as a *thinking* being, then this must be a gradual process. The teacher must be prepared to accept what the children offer and then, through her observations, present them with situations that invite their interest, capture their imagination, and encourage their exploration, so helping them to become fully involved in what they are doing.

Throughout all the children's movement and dramatic experiences, they should be given frequent opportunities for observing each other's work. If this 'watching each other' is introduced sympathetically by the teacher, the children will accept it readily, and soon will comment on and discuss what they see. This class observation is of great value, for it helps to increase a child's awareness, clarify his movements, and deepen and widen his experience.

Exploration of personal and communal space

When I begin to work with a class of children who have had no previous movement experience, I first ask them to move about the hall in any way they choose. Invariably there is chaos and confusion. So we come to a halt. Then I ask the children each to find a space of his own where he is not touching anyone. Now I draw the children's attention to their own *personal space*. It could be in the following way:

We are each standing in our own space. Let's look at it. How much space have we to move in without touching anyone? Look right up to the ceiling and down to the floor. That space is yours. Stretch out as far as you can in all directions without touching anyone or 'stealing' anyone's space.

Now, move in any way you like in your own space
but take great care that you don't touch anyone else.

At this stage of exploration, a child's movements will have little control or inner effort—it is
just a game, which at this stage is right. But, from
this stage, a child should be helped to become more
aware of his own movements, to work with increasing control and absorption. Here I find it helpful to narrow the field of movement by directing the
child's attention to one part of his body: eg, feet.

Look at your feet. Move them anywhere in your
own space. Try standing on your toes, heels, sides of
your feet. Watch your feet all the time. See how they
move. Feel *how they move. Can you move your feet at*
different speeds? Sometimes quickly, sometimes slowly?
Now try touching the floor lightly with your feet—
anywhere in your space. Watch them carefully. Are
you using all the space around you?
Can you let your feet sink into the floor . . . hit the
floor? Can you feel the difference right from inside
when they touch, sink into, or hit the floor?
Now explore your space with your feet, sometimes
touching, sometimes sinking into, and sometimes
hitting the floor. See how many different ways you
can move your feet—but all the time watch how they
are moving, feel *how they are moving.*

Here, and throughout all their movement
experiences, the children should be given plenty of
time to explore, select and consolidate. They will
become more and more interested in watching and
feeling what their feet can do. Their minds begin to
direct their movements with increasing absorption,
inner effort and control.

Now, return to further exploration of communal
space. Ask the children to move around the hall
again, finding for themselves how many different
ways they can move on their feet. Remind them
that wherever they go they must think of their own
individual space, taking care not to touch or 'steal'

anyone else's space. Now narrow the field again by giving definite instructions: eg, walking at varying speeds, looking for spaces; running in a straight line, and making a sudden stop (*feeling* the suddenness of the stop); running on a curving path, gradually getting slower until stillness is reached (*feeling* the stillness), and so on. After repeated moving around in this way, awareness of others in the group is increased, and moving with ease and control without invading another's territory becomes a habit.

Now, return to further exploration of personal space, perhaps this time concentrating on *transfer of weight*, aiming at increasing body management and flow. Remind the children that, so far, we have been moving mainly with our weight on our feet. Now we are going to experiment, taking our weight on other parts of our bodies—big parts and little parts: eg, hands, feet, back.

Stand perfectly still, so that you know your weight is on your feet. Think about lying down in your space. Now find out how slowly and smoothly you can get there. Feel the slowness and smoothness from inside as you are moving. Where is your weight now? Can you put your weight onto another part of your body? Think where it is going and then try moving it there quickly. Can you hold it there? Now relax so that every part of you sinks into the floor.

As you are lying there, think of two or three different parts where you could take your weight. Now, find a good starting place and work out each transfer, separately if you like, but somewhere trying to bring in quickness, slowness, and stillness. Now, repeat the same movements, trying to join the three transfers easily and smoothly into one sequence.

Here the children have been concerned mainly with controlling their movements in varying degrees of time. At the same time they will have been working at different spatial levels and in different directions, since it is impossible to isolate the fundamentals. During these movement sequences, without being actively aware of it, the children will have experienced different qualities of movement: eg, curling, stretching, and so on.

Awareness of movement qualities

To help the children to become consciously aware of these movement qualities, I introduce them to what I call 'shape-making'. They start by simply moving in their space to make shape patterns. They draw on previous movement experiences, using varying speeds, tensions, levels, and directions. They are invited to think about the movement qualities in the shapes they are making.

They readily make and feel the different movements in changing from a small, curled shape to a big stretching shape, finding different levels and directions within their own space. Other movement shapes can be suggested and explored: eg, a big, flowing movement, followed by a quick, straight movement, or a slow, strong movement, followed by quick, jerky movements. The children will soon begin to experiment on their own, letting their shapes flow from one into another. Through continued exploration and repetition, they begin to appreciate difference in movement qualities. Their work becomes increasingly expressive and, depending on how they feel, their shapes move towards dramatic and dance forms.

And so these practical movement experiences gradually establish a language of movement that is the basis of creative work in drama and dance.

Reasons for movement qualities

Simple ideas or reasons for moving in certain ways can now be introduced: for example, ask the children to move, as quietly as they can, anywhere in the hall. When they become really involved in this moving quietly, I should probably continue as follows:

You have been moving quietly because I asked you to. Now can you think of any reason for moving quietly without making a sound? Work out your own ideas and I will watch for the pictures you make.

This could be followed by a sequence of given movements: eg, moving quickly, stopping suddenly, and then moving slowly. Ask the children to repeat this pattern, trying to make clearer to themselves the variations of time; *feeling* from *inside* the sudden stop, the stillness, and the slow moving growing out of the stillness.

As they work with increasing inner effort, the movement sequence will become dramatic, and ideas will emerge. Now, encourage them to let their ideas take over, reminding them that every movement they make should help to build up their picture. They are now becoming more aware and appreciative of the qualities of movement, and simple situations can be given for the children to work out in their own ways: eg, moving through a wood without being seen; using stepping stones to cross a stream; crawling under a fence; looking for a gap in a hedge and forcing a way through; pushing open a heavy door and closing it quietly.

Adaptation to partners and groups

During these movement exercises, the children, while being aware of others moving around them, have been working individually. Through her own observations, the teacher will know when the time arrives for the children to work with others.

First let each child work with a partner. Start by asking them to walk together, looking for spaces, sensing changes of direction and speed without touching. Follow this by asking them to share a space with fingers lightly touching, making flowing shapes at different levels. Now they can share a space without touching, each child making his own shapes but being aware of his partner's movements. Now invite them to find different ways of meeting and leaving each other, such as coming together slowly, and leaving each other quickly. Out of these moving patterns, dramatic or dance forms may emerge. If this happens, encourage dramatic and dance development.

Now give them plenty of opportunity to explore definite situations that they can share and work out together: one helping the other across stepping stones; exploring a dark cave together; Bedivere helping the wounded King Arthur down to the lake.

Working in groups
After working with a partner, sharing a space, responding to another's movements, and sharing ideas, the child can begin to work in similar ways with increasing numbers.

1. Ask five or six children to share a space, weaving in and out at different levels, using varying speeds and movement qualities.
2. Ask them to walk around the hall, following a leader, feeling they are moving as a group, and avoiding contacts with other groups.
3. As their group feeling increases, encourage them to think of movement patterns: eg, making big, flowing movements, followed by a quick, downward movement; quickly forward, sudden stop, slowly backward. Encourage any resulting dramatic or dance form, giving time for development.
4. Let them move around with common feeling in their groups: eg, groups of frightened people, strong people, angry people, happy people. Develop these further by asking why they are moving in these ways. Give them time for discussion within their own groups so that they can work out their own situations.
5. Find out what happens when one group becomes aware of another group: eg, two groups meeting each other slowly; the meeting of two strong groups; the coming together of a weak and a strong group. Give time for discussion between the groups on resulting situations and working for further development.
6. Now give definite situations in which such groups are involved: eg, a meeting of groups of conspirators in the Gunpowder Plot; King Arthur and his followers facing Mordred and his men.

Recalling of sensory experiences

Sensitive observation and awareness give colour, shape and meaning to the world around us. To develop greater depth and feeling in expressive work, frequent opportunity must be given for sensory experiences and recalling of these experiences.

Handling of objects and materials from observation and discovery tables helps to pin-point the child's observation. Ask the children to pick up shells, fossils, pieces of wood, glass, cinders, pebbles; to look at their shape and colour in different lights, to feel and contrast their textures. After giving children time for delight in the handling of an object, ask them to recall their feelings in words or paint. Later, ask them to imagine that they are holding the shell, the piece of glass, etc. Can their eyes and their fingers recall the shape, texture, colour?

Ask them to perform various actions involving vivid sensory recall:

Put your hands into a bowl of sticky dough. Feel them sink in. Feel and watch the pull of the dough as you lift your hands out. Pull and scrape the dough from your fingers.

Think of a holly leaf. Let your fingers feel its smooth, glossy surface. Now touch its sharp, pointed prickles.

Think of snow. Watch the snowflakes falling, see how lightly they move. Feel them falling on your face, your hands. Watch them disappear as they melt on your hand. Let your feet sink into the snow. Can you feel and hear the crunch under your feet? Gather up some snow, feel its coldness. Press it firmly into snowballs. Feel the hardness and the shape.

Lie down. Imagine it is a warm, sunny day and you are lying on grass. Feel the warmth of the sun on your face, arms. Let your fingers touch the grass. Perhaps if you look carefully, you can see a ladybird on a blade of grass. Look at its colour as it moves. Hold out your hands. See if it will move onto your finger. Watch and feel it move on your hand and arm. Watch it disappear between the blades of grass. There is a sound overhead. What is it? A plane streaks across the sky leaving a white trail. Watch it disappear.

Think of King Arthur's sword. See it lying at your feet. Look at the length and strength of it, at the jewel-encrusted handle. Lift it carefully. Feel its weight. Move it around in different ways, watching the tip of it. Can you see the sparkle of the jewels as they catch the light? Feel the dryness of the rushes as you hide the sword on the edge of the lake. Hear the lapping of the water.

Characteriza-tion

During the exploring of personal space, the children will have had countless opportunities of finding out how their own bodies move. When the time is ripe, draw their attention to how other people move, and how the way they move depends on how they feel and on what sort of people they are.

1. Start by directing their attention to parts of their own bodies: eg, feet, hands:

   Feet *As you look at your feet, try to make them feel like the feet of an old man. How does this make the rest of your body feel? Move about inside this old man's body. Try to think like the old man. How does he speak? What does he talk about?*

   Hands *Look at your hands. Watch them grow into the greedy, grasping hands of Scrooge. What does this do to the rest of your body? How do you feel inside? What are your thoughts? Count your money, feeling like Scrooge.*

They can be asked to make their shoulders those of a boastful or arrogant person, a timid or weak person; the head that of a proud person, and so on. Explore and experiment as with other parts

2. Now try developing characterization from shape making.

   In your own space, grow into the sort of person who takes up a lot of space. Change to a person who takes up a little space. Try walking in these shapes.

   Think of a witch shape. Feel this shape from inside. Grow into it. Prepare your spells, keeping this shape. Talk to your cat.

   Make up your own character. Can you move in this shape, think in this shape? Can you meet another character and have a movement conversation, still keeping your shape?

3. Develop group characterization. Invite small groups, after discussion, to grow into the same sort of people, to walk about together, trying to keep the group character.

4. Start improvization. For example, take the theme of a family on the beach. The group discusses this situation. Then talk about the different people in the 'family'. They decide what sort of person each of them will be. They work out the situation.

Sound and movement leading to language flow

During all movement experiences, feeling is all important. As a child becomes more absorbed in his movements, there is continual searching for the right movements to express his feelings. The time comes when a child feels the need to communicate his experiences still further. Intense movement feeling develops into sounds expressing the same feeling. There is joy and life in this sound since it comes from within and is not imposed. Through further exploration, out of these sounds, come words and phrases leading to language expression, and natural communication that has vitality and flow.

1. At some point in 'shape-making', ask the children to concentrate on one movement shape: eg, a strong, straight movement. They should repeat this movement with increasing inner effort until they *feel* the sound that grows from it. Next they should let the sound accompany the movement, and then develop this sound into feeling a word, or phrase.

2. After this, get them to think of a word, feel it, say it, and let the movement come out with it: eg, 'explode', 'stealth', 'wonder', 'fireworks', and so on.

3. Start with a word or phrase and let it come out with *different* feeling and accompanying movements. For example, take the phrases 'Go away' and 'Come here', and suggest the children say them in a strong way, an imploring way, and a frightened way.

4. They can develop movement conversations with partners in the same way.

5. They can toss, flick, throw, and so on, movements from one partner to another, letting appropriate sounds develop.

6. They can experiment, sharing space and ideas with a partner, letting sounds, gibberish, and words develop.

7. Work with small groups in a similar way, for example, a group moving quietly. After they have moved together and felt movement quality, allow time for the group to discuss reasons for moving in this way, to bring ideas into their movement plan. As they work on their plan and feel the need to communicate still further with each other, sounds growing into words will follow.

8. Experiment further with characterization and improvisation, encouraging the children to let their sounds and words come from the movements, feelings, and thoughts of the character they are interpreting, eg,

   (a) Ask them to think of one of the strange creatures in *Jabberwocky*; to grow into the shape of the creature, move like it, think like it, feel like it, to feel the sounds that would come from it and let them come out with its movements.

(b) Two such creatures meet. Each child maintains his own characterization, with resulting movements, feelings and sounds. Two can then work on ideas arising from the meeting, and develop gibberish conversation.

(c) Three people meet: eg, three witches. The children assume witches' shapes, movements, sounds, etc, and develop ideas and language flow in this situation.

(d) Larger group improvisations are possible: eg, at the hairdresser's or barber's shop; groups round market stalls; a family picnic.

Here give time for defining individual characterizations before working out group improvisations.

The selection of the right words with the accompanying movement effort, the development of language flow between members of a group, will become a natural part of working out improvised situations and later will help to build up situations within dramatic themes.

Responding to external sounds and music

From an early stage in their movement experiences, children will respond readily to clear and direct sounds such as clapping, the beating of a drum, or the clash of cymbals. As they become more involved in movement qualities, as their sensitivity increases, they will respond to more subtle and varied percussion sounds, weaving patterns of movement that are either dance-like or dramatic.

Again, these movement sequences should develop from working individually to working with a partner and then with a group.

Careful choice of music is essential. From the beginning, children must have plenty of opportunity for listening and should be directly encouraged to listen.

I find that the most suitable music for an introduction to this listening and moving, is a simple tune with an easily recognized rhythm: eg, an English or Scottish country dance tune.

I ask the children to sit down and listen to the music. To direct their observation and concentration, I first ask them to let their hands 'listen' to it.

Make your hands listen to the music. Can they touch the floor, the space around and above you, while you are listening to it? Now let your head, fingers, shoulders, feet, listen to it. Can you feel it inside?

Now, on your feet, move in your own space, making every bit of yourself listen to the music. Can you still listen to the music and move around the hall?

Next come short musical passages with clear phrases, for shape-making. Here the children listen directly for phrases, feel them and interpret them in movement shapes: phrases that demand, for example, big, flowing movements, quick jerky movements, curling and uncurling shapes.

After working individually, the children work with partners and groups, finding ways of meeting and leaving, sharing a space, developing a pattern

During these experiences, the children concentrate on rhythm, pattern, and shape of the music, and find their own way of interpretation No dance techniques or steps are taught. These the children discover for themselves.

Frequently, we listen to music, concentrating on its mood and feeling. Here the selections are carefully chosen so that, over a period of time, the children have the opportunity of hearing music of many contrasting moods and feelings.

1. The children may interpret the mood suggested by the music, first by feeling it as they walk and later by working out dramatic movement pictures suggested by the mood. Often these dramatic pictures are developed into group themes.

Working out a drama theme

2. Sometimes characterization grows out of this listening.
3. Often music is selected in this way as a background for situations within dramatic themes that are being built up.

After the children have explored the varied avenues of movement experience, the working out of dramatic themes with the entire class can be attempted. They now have a movement vocabulary, their movements are expressive and controlled, their imagination has been stimulated, and they have a sensitive awareness of individuals and the group.

Sources and materials for themes can be sparked off by some situation already worked out in movement; they may arise from the children's imaginative and creative writing; they may come from stories from literature, history, scripture, etc.

Whatever the source, all the children should be thoroughly immersed in the fabric of the theme and excited by the idea of working something out together.

There should be no definite or set plan to begin with. Gradually this will develop, as individual characterizations are drawn, situations and group reactions are worked out, and creative ideas are introduced through movement experiences.

Here we will consider how a theme could develop from THE PIED PIPER OF HAMELIN.

1. Read the poem for the enjoyment of the story.
2. Let children select and read aloud words, phrases, sentences that excite them, so that all the class can share in 'tasting' the colour and life of the words.
3. Now let them choose situations in the poem which they feel are dramatic and exciting.
4. Talk about the different feelings of individuals and groups within these situations—the changing attitudes and feelings as circumstances change.

5. Draw from the children their opinions of the different characters in the story. At this stage, the children will be eager to start working together.

6. Ask the children to move and feel as the harassed mayor who senses the townsfolk's anger, then as the jubilant mayor after the rats have disappeared; as the piper as he walks up the street; as a man or woman surveying the destruction caused by the rats; as the lame boy when he is left alone, and so on.

7. Work out situations in groups: the troubled councillors moving up the street; an angry crowd advancing towards the council chamber; rats creeping out at night; children following the piper. Contrast the group feeling of rejoicing when the rats have gone, with the sorrowing crowd when they realize their children have vanished for ever, and so on.

As the children become more absorbed, there will be increasing development in characterization group feeling, and reaction. Ideas will grow within situations, sounds will come from movement, and the sounds will develop into speech.

At different stages in the working out, time should be given for observation of individuals and groups—followed by discussion and selection of the most dramatic interpretations.

A loose framework will then be drawn up and certain locations fixed: eg, the street, the council chamber, the river, the mountain.

In this framework the situations already worked out will be placed, and the theme will begin to take shape. As it develops, it may be felt that music could be introduced at some points to deepen the feeling: recorder music for the piper; FANTASY ON A THEME OF THOMAS TALLIS (Vaughan Williams) as the rats creep out at night; NIGHT ON THE BARE MOUNTAIN (Mussorgsky), as the lame boy stands alone.

Since all the children will have explored all the characters, and will have shared in all the situations, they can at any time take any part, and at all times will act with real understanding in the situations and react sensitively to others around them.

The purpose of movement experience

Movement experience gives a child a remarkable control over his physical movements. It compels him to concentrate; it stimulates his imagination; it makes him react sensitively to other individuals and the group. As he explores and experiments with different qualities of movement, he develops powers of control and concentration. The more deeply he feels, the more his movements become an outward expression of his thoughts, feeling, and imagination. As his movements become more controlled, the more easily he moves. He lacks strain, and develops poise and awareness, becoming more sensitive and observant. As his concentration and absorption become deeper, he feels the need to communicate his experiences. He searches continually for the right movements, the right sounds and words. So, out of this sensitive awareness and observation, comes natural communication that is colourful, full of vitality and flow.

3 Drama in the Infant School

by Doris Nash

The importance of drama in contributing to the full development of children up to seven years of age is now widely accepted by teachers and parents. How this is achieved must depend on the sensitivity of the teacher and the skill she brings to daily working with young children. A few of the ways children have been helped are noted here—all from direct observation—in the hope that more children may be enabled to discover the exciting world of language—gesture—sound—communication.

Arrival at school Children, when they enter school as five-year-olds, take periods varying from two days to two months to adjust to the new situation of living and learning[1]—vastly different from preceding experience in home and street.

The skilled teacher's preparation of a room must include provision of a corner or large wood chest (at least 2 ft × 2 ft × 4 ft high) where a child can withdraw, alone or with a self-chosen friend.

It is in the private areas in the learning situation that the most exciting dramatic situations arise—always observed by the teacher, and guided by her, through provision of lengths of material for 'dressing-up', through her decision to equip this area as either a dramatic corner, or home corner and so on. Observation of children in these private areas suggests that all children need such experiences. Language between child and child becomes much more precise. Here it is that persistent communications through gesture and head-nodding are noted.

[1] See, in this series, FROM HOME TO SCHOOL by Alice Murton

308

Encouraging speech

Once such communications have been noted, the teacher can contrive ways to encourage direct speech. Sometimes the dramatic corner itself is enough. However, if the child with a speech problem is sensitive and withdrawn, then many, many different ways may have to be tried before a response is found. Simple puppets have helped—one emotionally disturbed child was eventually prepared to use the puppet as a medium for speech, while still unable to speak directly to anyone.

Similarly, a child who had an uncontrolled voice and shouted everywhere learned self-control of his voice through making a puppet out of plastic containers.

In the group, a teacher can help a child gain control of his voice by sharing sound-making of vigorous quality—eg, wind roaring—with whole body movement, and gradually contrasting sounds with voice, or by blowing balloons or thistle-down. Children enjoy listening to adults using 'surprising voices', and once the child can listen, a whole new world of sound-making by the child—using stones and sticks, metals and air—opens up.

Exploring sound

The sensitive use of natural objects indoors and outdoors is an essential stage—though it should always be remembered that such experiences are just leading towards greater discoveries in quality of expressing speech and sounds.

Where does singing fit in most appropriately? Children, we know, have a great feeling for rhythm and sound. Watching a child in the dramatic corner, we note how sustained his breath-control is when he is mimicking a mother singing to a baby (the 'baby' may be anything from a doll to a roll of paper). The child's dramatic use of the material around indicates to an observant teacher: the imaginative child; the child who has no control of voice or gesture; the child with no ability to concentrate.

As the five-year-old develops and explores the

opportunities provided, the teacher is daily adding stories, well-read poems, and songs. She is deliberately adding words and sounds to help the child listen more carefully to, and communicate more easily with, peers and adults.

Many children come to school from a background of continuous sound of industry, radio, television, and traffic, and it is becoming increasingly difficult to achieve thoughtful listening. Only the teacher can determine whether a child needs the opportunity to listen to stories in isolation, in a small group, or in a large group.

Group situations

Manipulation of group situations by the child, through building, painting, dramatic play, excursions, and endless other experiences within the school, enables him to operate more fully. With more experiences and observation, children interpret and communicate in painting and language and movement. As in language at this stage, so much of what is creative is based on an experience or observation. The picture on the right shows life around the school, recorded in paint. Over seventy children painted something personally experienced, and their knowledge of space in movement and drama was here used in a creative presentation.

Children and teachers deliberately plan the outside area around the school to encourage observation. *All areas* are capable of exploitation.

In one, children have planted bulbs and saplings, and so have ceaseless opportunity for discussion, observation, and talking—even a handicapped child benefits (one of the children is a five-year-old mongol, living and sharing in a normal school day), contributing fully.

Structuring situations

Increasingly, the daily experiences within the school are structured by the teacher to obtain more precise and careful observation of growth and *shape* within and outside the building.

Plant growth fascinates children of six-plus years, who are sensitive to, and aware of, three-dimensional shape and pattern, both of which are so essential to drama.

Six-year-old children taken into the country for a day on a farm, use their earlier experiences of lifting, and are able to adapt to a real situation and move a heavy bale of hay. The farmer has a far greater skill, but the group of children solve the problem at their level of skill with such obvious enjoyment (see the picture on page 312).

In spontaneous discussion in the classroom, following a story, children show animation, and desire to communicate and share their personal experiences. Notice the sensitive hand gestures. (See the picture on page 313).

In the hall, children cluster around the teacher until they have experience of use of space. Many children are unwilling to undress, for several weeks after starting school. Some watch from the side until they have enough confidence in themselves and the teacher to explore movement more fully. (See the picture on page 314).

(American readers may query some references in this booklet to children's undressing for movement. This means that boys and girls strip to the waist, the latter, at the onset of puberty, also wearing a vest or singlet. This goes back to 1933 when the Board (now the Department) of Education published a book of suggested exercises and activities involving headstands, cartwheels, climbing, etc. Hitherto, primary school children had done their physical exercises in their ordinary clothing which was exceedingly hampering to the kind of movement now required. Furthermore the problem of decency, so far as the girls were concerned, which had hardly existed in the old days of drill, became

self-evident. The girls' PE class in the early 1930s was often, to say the least of it, lacking in decorum.

Attempts by teachers to induce the girls to shed their skirts and to wear suitable pants were, in the early days, resisted by many parents and, when the boys stripped to the waist, their mothers frequently feared for their chests. Gradually common sense prevailed, parents saw the reasonableness of what was being done and the practice is now general, if not universal.)

Gaining confidence, the child will gradually become aware of his entire body. He will start moving at low levels, using space and speed and direction with concentrated thinking and effort, making self-disciplined movements.

Five-year-old girls use junk material to make

puppets. The teacher will use the puppets for direct communication with the girls as *one* way into drama. (See the picture on page 315).

Some children's records

This section contains the ideas of seven-year-old children as expressed by them.

How children record experience
It seems important to note how much the environment conditioned by the teachers, becomes part of the child's dramatic and recorded language. Some

children record in speech, in singing, in movement, in paint, in clay. Children need freedom to select *their* most creative way of recording.

For example, Marie, unable to achieve academic success, inspired and influenced the entire group through her sensitive movement and her choice of a gay golden gown. Simon, with a sung tune, and creative use of voice and body, inspired music and language.

We have learned that children are able to extend an original idea (they seldom if ever enlarge or change the idea), and each development complements the preceding episode—any number of children can be accommodated and the children show respect for any creative effort.

Discipline appears to be maintained by them through: music, recorded or sung; language, spoken or sung; movement, gesture and mime.

They have ability to group themselves as the drama demands—a very sensitive awareness of periods of repose following vigorous movement or sound. These qualities seem part of a seven-year-old's skill in drama.

The criterion for teacher and child, must be absorbed happiness, reflected in dramatic movement and individual creative interpretation. (See the picture below.)

After many such experiences, we see how children's own written records reflect the impact drama has on the young child.

Children's records

Words, tune and movement sequence by Simon:

GG A♯ A♯ A D GG A♯ A♯ AA A CCC A♯ G CCCC A♯ C

In the moonlit sky
A lightning dragon came
with a flutter of a wing.
It was morning again
and with a mysterious swirl
He rose into the sunlit sky.

In the dreary mist
A blue-winged, green-backed dragon
came swirling in curves
His way out of his cave,
and with a mighty flap
He rose into the moonlit sky.

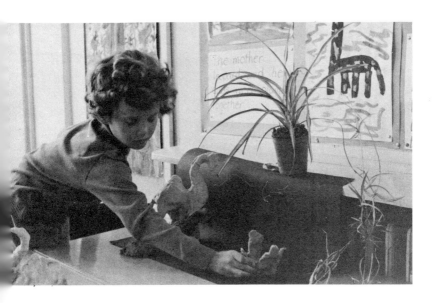

Crying Spell by Sarah Jane (words, music and dance):

Crying . . . crying . . . crying . . . crying . . .

(This dance sequence reminded adults of Greek drama.)

By Graham:

At school after dinner all the girls go in the hall and they dress up in gowns. When I do my spell it is broken by a laughing spell. We do lovely movements when we are in the hall . . . some boys join in and they are horsemen.

By Dean:

During the dinner-hour I go in the hall to do the Play—we had to wear a cloak and we have to get in position and then the horseman start to gallop and then the horseman go back to the stable and the horseman lie down because the music stops—the music is the tambourine—the musicians used little shoes to make the sound of the hooves hitting the ground.

Laughing Spell by Victoria (words and tune):

Abracadabra Ha! Ha! Ha!
    Abracadabra He! He! He!
Wherever I go I dance with glee!
    Abracadabra He! He! He!
This is my sung spell.

We do all kinds of spells in our school hall. We play instruments for our spells. There are about forty people in our hall with spells—not all of the people have good spells.

We do our play nearly every day now—the instruments we use are called chime bars and a xylophone.

Spell by Paul:

In this school we do a play and we have a wizard in the play and the wizard has a spell, it is
    '*My magic, my magic,*
        Her magic, her magic,

Oh Wizard, OH WIZARD!'
*These words are the words of the wizard's spell
that she sings while she is dancing about, and when
she casts her spell everybody near her goes to sleep.*
And we have a spell called 'Fiddle de ree':
'Fiddle de ree, the magic of the night
Fiddle de ree, the moon we see,
Fiddle de ree, a silver sphere,
Fiddle de ree, an upturned boat,
Fiddle de ree, as black as a cat.'

*These words are the words of the spell and it makes
two cats dance around the room.*

By John:
*In our play I am a creature and there are seven
more and we try to break the spell and some of us are
kangaroos and I am a tiger and we go about on the floor
and we do some long movements and we do some nice
movements and we go around the moonbeams and we
go in between the boxes and we go around fast and the
moonbeams move us away.*

Words and Dance Sequence by Ruth:

*Blue I am
Blue as mist
    Swirling softly
Over clouds.
Blue I am
    Blue as mist.*

*In the play I sing this song and while I sing the
song I do movement and I swirl and turn and lift my
skirt and look as though I am floating in the air and
Frank is the blue-winged green-backed dragon and
Simon is a blue-winged green-backed dragon too and
Debbie is the wind dragon and she does movement like
me and she wears a yellow skirt and I wear a green
skirt.*

For this particular drama by Ruth, movement

came first—then came the words. The tune was composed by another child, and eventually the words were sung as Ruth controlled a group of children during lunch-hour drama—either in the hall or out in the field. Dramatic communication, at this age, is never finished.

It should be noted how the growing awareness of other children in the group comes through clearly in the child's own writing.

By Christopher:

Lorry driver you're big and strong
Going faster and faster as you go along
*   past trees and houses early in the morning*
And you see the grass heavy with dew
And making magnificent patterns.

By Murray:

On the desolate sands the seagulls scampered
And left footprints small and footprints thin
I walked along and I heard them screeching
And when I got near they flew away.

By Neil:

The roaring waves hurtled upon the shore
But when it got dark the waves went down
*   When we went to see the boats*
They bobbed up and down gently.

By Susan:

I heard the wind roaring through the trees
*   The angry voice of the wind on the sea*
I saw the waves tossing and turning
*   And running quickly back to me.*
I climbed some rocks to find some pools
*   The rocks were very pointed*
I saw a crab—it was moving quickly
*   Trying to get out of the pool.*

By Fiona:

We went to a wild-life park
Where I saw some lovely swans
They stretched their necks and made themselves

tall

And it was quite windy.
All the trees were waving happily
Bending over a river was a big willow tree.

By David:

Noise
I like noise
The thud of a hoof
The clang of a door
And the crash of a train.

By Debra:

The Howling of the Wind
The howling wind blows through the open tree-tops
The rain pours through the tree like thunder
It rattles through the rain-pipes hurriedly.

By Mark:

Sounds I like
The crunching of leaves in Autumn
The chime-bars ringing
The growling of a motor-bike racing
The glide of birds flying swiftly through the air.
The pattering of rain on a roof.
These are the sounds
I like to hear.

Instruments, and sticks and stones used in rhythms, as well as the teacher's sensitivity in use of voice, contribute to children's awareness of sound.

By Elaine:

When we do movement we do all different kinds of things. Sometimes we do circular movements and sometimes we do sharp short movements—sometimes we do twisty movements. Mrs Patterson sometimes asks us to relax and then she says a strong shape—now! We curl and then we let go and sometimes we move along like that.

You can speak with somebody by moving your arm in the direction you want them to go. You can make up a story in movement. I shared my story with Pippy and Jane—in our story we were witches and we were trying to make other people into witches.

Elaine's writing, I feel, reflects how important the relationship between teacher and child is. I do not expect many seven-year-old children to be capable of self-analysis. (See the picture below.)

By Vivian:

Happy birds fly everywhere . . .

That is the beginning of my poem and Elizabeth plays for me and the instrument she uses is the tubular instrument and it has a bell noise and it has the right sound for my bird poem and I like the sound because it has a jingle in the sound and it sounds like birds chattering and I like the music which Elizabeth plays for me and I read my poem while Elizabeth plays.

Happy birds fly everywhere
We never know where
But when the blackbird sings his song
*   We know he's very near.*

And when we look at the long, long grass
We know the pheasants come here
Above the grass I see his head
*   He looks so beautiful and big.*

Then we go to the dark dark wood.
We find the tree creepers here
Then when the dark falls on us
*   We hear the owls loud hoot!*

Composed by five children and used to control forty children in the drama:

Search the curving branches of the leafless tree
*   Search the cracking bending bough*
Hear the rumbles of the storm
Hear the roaring of the wind
*   See the angry clouds so grey*
*   See them sweep across the sky*
Watch the twisty willow bend
Watch the gliding of the birds.

Search the secrets of the snow
*   See the crook shaped icicles*
*   See the foot print of a fox*
Feel the bitter bitter wind
Feel the softness of the snow

323

By Sarah Jane:

At school in the lunch-hour the girls go into the hall and do a play. The play has got spells in it. I am in the play and have got a spell. My spell makes the girls cry. Boys come into the hall and they are horsemen.

When I have done my spell someone else does their spell. I like doing the play.

When we have done the play we put our gowns away. My gown is mauve. My spell is sad. (See the picture below.)

David's story of a ballet:

I am a moonbeam in our play. We come from a crowd of little planets: the planets are really six boxes in a circle.

The other people are—king, queen, prince, lots o

princesses, four prison workers, a cloudy witch, two thunder witches.

The new climbing apparatus is the castle where the Prince lives. The big grey mattress is the thundercloud—the small blue mattress is a lake.

The witches want to keep the Princesses from the castle, so they can live in the castle instead of their thunder clouds—when people are forced to trip on the mattress by the witch you are dead. The witch does not touch you—she does the movement of pushing.

We dance to the music of Bach—there are two pieces of music the moonbeams do not dance to—the other children dance to them.

After their pieces they go to sleep and we come down from our planets to search for the castle in the clouds. When we find it we wake them all up after their deep sleep. It takes quite a time to do this. I go up on a planet and make the movement of two circles with my arms. Then they get into groups and do a dance.

Drama, a unifying influence

How does drama help a child to represent his learning more completely?

From our many observations of children, we are aware that once a child in infant school understands how to place himself in 'space' in relationship to other members of a group,[1] then other things follow. For such understanding expresses a certain level of conceptualization, of thinking, which becomes part of a child, and which permits a teacher thereafter to expect this quality to be expressed in all areas of this child's learning.

Preparation

In her movement periods, the teacher will quite deliberately help this quality to develop on the basis of her specific knowledge of a child's needs. This will involve the teacher in concentrated preparation before the lesson. She will not only need to plan the language and quality of movement she knows she can expect from her group, but she must understand young children's need for self-disciplined movement in restricted areas as well as

See Bess Bullough's essay in this section

for expansive movement.

Language will be used only to inspire the children to think for themselves, translating it into terms of whole body movement, and enabling them to make instant decisions. This is essential; for each child has his own rhythm, and the teacher must allow for each child to experiment with this rhythm. Instructions, too, must be phrased to permit each child his unique interpretation. It is not enough, for example, to ask children to 'move'. Until a child knows quality of speed, and understands direction, and levels of movement, as well as space, he cannot fully interpret such an instruction, and the period becomes occupational rather than educational.

Confidence

When a child has awareness of and skill and confidence in body movements, in relation to the group environment, then this is reflected:

1. in his general attitude to all school situations and the ability to share his learning with adults and children;
2. in his painting—particularly in spacing of colour and design on paper;
3. in arrangements of 3-dimensional objects in space—working either in isolation or with his selected group (the objects being selected and arranged to show the growing ability to discriminate, and see relationships):
   (a) shapes in clay—made by children
   (b) shapes in wood—found by children
   (c) solid glass shapes linking directly with precise mathematical language.
   (d) shapes in colour
   (e) skeleton shapes
   (f) fossil shapes
   (g) growing shapes, and so on
   (the choice is endless, and is only valuable when related to the all-round development of the child),

4. in presentation of his work in an interesting and exciting way.

Contact with the teacher

Teachers of five-year-old children will be aware from their own observations that most children at this stage of growth will need a close contact with the teacher—and may be quite unable to explore even the environment of the classroom without adult support. These children must be given confidence and time to develop their own rhythms—even though the teacher may wish them to 'join in fully'. I have seen five-year-olds just 'watching' from the fringe of the group for even a term.

If the *rapport* between teacher and child is related to a child's individual need, the child will be absorbing and learning. To date I have not encountered a child who did not eventually join in.

Even a six-year-old, in a new situation, must have time to adjust to a new teacher and new peers, before he is able to use his thinking fully in movement and drama situations. The skilled teacher gives extra opportunities but no pressures until the child is adjusted.

Watching can be an essential part of absorbed learning for both child and teacher. In fact, watching and listening by the teacher is an essential part of her preparation of the environment. The more we observe children, the more we realize how learning must relate to the total child.

Ways to creativity

While it is quite impossible to determine which of them should come first in a child's experience, enough observations have been made to show that any of the following can help a child to a creative experience:

1. listening to music, stories and poetry;
2. gaining skill in gesture;
3. making rhythmic patterns with natural things;
4. making tunes on musical instruments;

5. making puppets;
6. awareness of textures, and observation;
7. thought for other people—adults and children;
8. props, costumes sometimes help, sometimes impede movements.

These are some of the ways into drama, for young children. But how does drama, this specific experience, become generalized, and lead to learning in other areas?

A unifying experience

The effect of drama on the daily life of a school can be noted. Most important, the creative uses of dramatic experiences are reflected in the language of the children. (One can discover in the children's vocabulary in the examples quoted earlier, the influences of T. S. Eliot, John Clare and James Reeves, among others.) In addition, the staff's thinking is clearly influenced by the experience. Being open-ended, communication between children and adults is continuous—sharpening thinking, and enabling concepts to be formed.

Moreover, the actual use of the language—in other words talking and listening—is essential to all children's full development. Children who don't talk, or whose experience in talking either to adults or their peers is limited, will have extra difficulty in learning to read.

Finally, recording and writing are expected when appropriate. For only when a child is fully aware of himself within the class community, and is thinking for himself, can we reasonably expect that communication through the written word will be well presented. And all children can present their own work in an interesting way, whatever their academic limitations.

Thus drama enables a child to represent his learning and understanding to others in many different ways. In particular, it gives a child extra confidence in dealing with day-to-day problems of growing up. In effect, drama unifies the total child

Booklist

Garrard, Alan and Wiles, John LEAP TO LIFE—AN EXPERIMENT IN YOUTH DRAMA Chatto & Windus, London 1969

Haggerty, J. PLEASE MISS CAN I PLAY GOD? Methuen, London 1966

Way, Brian DEVELOPMENT THROUGH DRAMA Longman, London 1971; Humanities Press, New York 1971

See also AN INTRODUCTION, ENVIRONMENTAL STUDIES, TOWARDS INFORMALITY, MUSIC, THE PUPIL'S DAY in this series.

Audio-Visual Aids

FREE TO MOVE

This is a 16 mm colour film which runs for 35 minutes. It was made for the Schools Council by Southern Film Productions and is available in England from: Southern Film Productions, Brockenhurst Film Studios, Brockenhurst, Hants SO4 7RD, and in the USA from: The Film/Play Data Bureau Inc., 267 W. 25th Street, New York, NY.

MOVEMENT IN TIME AND SPACE

A black and white film which runs for 30 minutes. It is available in England from National Audio Visual Aids Library, Paxton Place, Gipsy Road, London S.E.27, and in the USA from: Time-Life Films, 43 West 16th Street, New York, NY 10011.

Art

Henry Pluckrose

The Author

Henry Pluckrose, who is head of a London primary school, has particularly concerned himself with the part which the arts play in the education of young children. He has written a number of books on art in education and is currently the editor of the monthly magazine ART AND CRAFT IN EDUCATION.

1 New Approaches

A change of role Over the past forty years there has been in England a gradual but profound change in the role which the arts play in the education of young children. It does not fall within my scope here to trace the development from 'drawing' (often unrelated to most of the other things which occupied the child while at school) to the conditions which prevail today—for now picture making and modelling permeate almost every aspect of the curriculum. Nor is it relevant to comment at length upon the work of educationalists who have been responsible for creating a climate of opinion in which these changes could take place—writers, lecturers and teachers of the standing of Richardson, Gardner, Catty, Isaacs, Tomlinson, Nairn, Holbrook, Marshall and Tanner. Suffice it to say that the changes (though dramatic if viewed over a decade) were gradual, never constant or uniform in pace, and varied tremendously from district to district and from school to school (and even within individual schools).

That change took place at all was somewhat surprising. 'Workshops' in which teachers could experiment with materials before introducing them to their classes were almost unknown; moreover, as there were few art specialists at work in the primary sector, the majority of the teachers were probably extremely hazy as to the implications of the changes they were implementing (for instance in the organization of the timetable and in making the spread of activity possible). For example, a teacher might hesitantly begin to introduce potato printing, and be surprised to discover that 'printing' had taken over the school day, that from the mean potato, children had developed an interest in printing with wood, lino and plaster. Yet it was from such beginnings that just such teachers, sometimes working with large classes in cramped conditions which lacked even running water and adequate storage space, discovered that children were capable of using a wide range of materials with unexpected flair and tremendous sensitivity.

Finger painting, 6″ × 9″, by a three-year-old girl: 'Two People'. The picture was worked in acrylic paint on thin card.

New materials and tools   Pencil and water-colour were not rejected. They were simply seen for what they really are, merely two ways of communicating an idea through line, colour, texture, and form. One still finds children drawing with pencils, or applying pale washes of colour with squirrel brushes on sheets of cartridge paper. Far more significant, however, is the fact that these traditional media have been supplemented with wax crayons, oil pastels, chalks, dyes, stains, and paints of all types (oil, powder, poster, water, acrylic).

The advent of new materials resulted in a greater range of tools being made available for children's use and this had quite unexpected results (quite unexpected, that is, for those adults who had not watched children at work). Lino blocks, for example, are inked with rollers. Could the same rollers be used to apply some other sort of paint to some quite different sort of surface? Papers patterned in broad swirls of colour offer quite a different challenge to the young mind, from that posed by paper virgin white or slatey grey. Palette knives, essential for oils, offer yet another way of applying paint. Can anything be added to powder colour to make it less fluid . . . would gum do . . . or flour . . . or cold water paste? And if it is possible to apply colour with roller and knife, as well as with brush, what other things could we use? Fingers, perhaps, or sponges, or twists of paper, or straws, or sharpened sticks? These particular questions are typical of young children's thinking, and indicate something of their response to an environment rich in tools and materials. The teacher's role in this connexion is to observe children at work, and to intercede when necessary, by giving further stimulus through introducing new materials or extending the technique which is being undertaken, or to withdraw and merely observe the group's intuitive response to materials.

Children have a way of communicating that is uniquely their own—for they have not been sophisticated by adult standards, and are uncluttered by the cultural conventions of the society in which they are growing up. String and newspaper, feathers and pulses, fir cones and leaves, fabric scraps and packing boxes, tin cans and chipped plates—all are materials which a young child handles with tremendous enthusiasm. They provide an additional outlet for his innate desire to handle and to fashion, to make and to do. 'I'm going to make these pieces of leather say Owl,' one six-year-old announced, 'and he can have these foil bottle tops for eyes because he must see in the dark to fly.' Imagery and fantasy wrapped up in reality!

Brush painting, 15″ × 20″, by a four-year-old boy: 'Man'. This was painted during his first week at school. Notice the well formed face lacks ears (though it has hair). The body is very small and there are no hands or feet. This picture took less than five minutes to complete, only one colour being used.

A comparison of the photographs on pp. 336–8 is of interest. All three children were members of the same school group. Although each wishes to express a similar idea (a person), each chose different materials to convey it. Note also that, even at four years of age, distinct ability variations are already noticeable (compare the simplicity of the illustration p. 336 with the sophistication of that on p. 338).

Paint and fabric collage, 30″ × 20″, by a four-year-old girl: 'My Mum'. A highly developed picture for so young a child. Here we have hands (coming from the neck) and a body. It is interesting to compare the face with that on page 336.

Discovery and direction

In the seven years that a child spends at the primary school he is encouraged to undertake a wide range of activities which, for successful completion, depend upon his intuitive response to materials. Moreover, the nature of these materials imposes a discipline upon a child. For example, it is possible to model a boat in clay and in wood. John is making a boat in clay. His response to his material will be utterly different from that of Peter who is working in wood. John's boat will grow from a soft easily shapeable mass, its form slowly changing under his finger tips. Meanwhile Peter is bound by the hardness of the wood, the sharpness of the tools that are available and the degree of control he has over them. Although Peter and John may each end up with something which says 'boat' to the onlooker ... the problems which they had to overcome (and the skills which they had to employ to do so) were quite different.

Paint, paper and wool collage, 30″ × 20″, by a four-year-old girl: 'A Lady'. Here all manner of material has been incorporated into the picture. This was worked at the same time as the previous illustration. The body shape here is very developed, although so textured as to become almost abstract in conception.

It is in such situations that the teacher has an especially significant role to play. One does not want to destroy a child's innate curiosity with technique lessons unrelated to his particular needs and accomplishments. At the same time, some materials have to be understood before they can be used fully and to leave expensive materials out 'to be played with until their properties are discovered' is both unrealistic and foolhardy.

How the balance is achieved between the two contrasting aims of child discovery and adult direction is virtually impossible to describe. It happens if the climate in the classroom is such that the teacher is one who inspires rather than dictates, it happens where discoveries about the nature of materials are discussed so that children learn through each other's experiences as well as from the teacher. A group of ten-year-olds, for example, might discover that wax crayons resist water-based ink. From this starting point (simple wax resists), the gifted teacher will try to create situations in which the process of using wax to repel water is examined in as many contrasting ways as possible. What would happen if we tried to dye a piece of waxed fabric? How could we wax a length of cloth? What would we need? How could we apply the dye? How could we remove the wax? Can we apply more than one colour? The teacher might initiate the discussion but his aim should always be to provoke questions from the children which *they* (not he) will attempt to answer. (The sad thing is that many teachers feel ill-equipped to fulfil this role—to suggest a starting point one has to be aware of the various options available. If teachers have in fact 'played' with materials themselves, they will be far more likely to be able to ask these 'developmental' questions in a sensitive and perceptive way. This might involve regular attendance on courses, and reading professional magazines. The development of new materials surely makes this an absolute necessity!)

Thus, throughout the whole time the child is at primary school, he is learning about materials, the way they behave, and the things for which particular materials are suitable. At the same time, this rich variety of experience is helping the child to discover his own individual gifts. Every child has his own personality and, because of this, particular materials will have a particular appeal to individual children. Mary might find that she can express herself most satisfactorily with size 12 hog brushes on large sheets of paper; for John, scraper board provides the ideal surface for fine line drawings, which for him are an important aspect of visual communication. Peter, on the other hand, prefers modelling and enjoys the discipline imposed by paper sculpture. Iris finds chalk carving far more satisfactory, and Jaki, imaginative and unconventional, is never happier than when building weird constructions from junk material.

Moreover, the variety of materials available not only makes it possible for each child to discover his own gifts but also to deepen his understanding of the ways particular materials behave. That is, he comes to terms with a process (or craft) at a much deeper level than he would ever do if the teacher imposed an identical art situation on every member of the group.

Jennifer, for example, had a penchant for weaving and this interest took her, in two final years at primary school (9+ to 11+), from using cardboard looms, to working on large two-heddle wooden table looms, to carding, spinning, and the use of the warping board, to woven patterns and to a study of the woollen industry in Britain (including a brief historical survey, types of sheep, raw wool imports, textile exports, knitting patterns and folk lore).

Aspects of the teacher's role

This development of specific interests does not mean that experiment in other media is discouraged —rather, it means that teachers are prepared to shape their art programme to meet the needs of individuals rather than the supposed needs of a group. There is nothing worse, for example, than to make Stephen paint for seven years in the hope that his pictures will eventually be something more than muddy grey splodges. Usually, after a much shorter period, Stephen discovers that he can't make paint say what he wants it to—and his interest in art atrophies accordingly.

Underlying all that has been written so far, is the assumption that the teacher himself is prepared to continue to learn about materials and the way they behave, for the horizons in art education are not static but continually expanding. The teacher (however expert his professional training) will need to keep abreast of new developments by reading, by attending refresher courses, and, most important of all, by experimenting for himself. To take a typical classroom situation: a teacher is introducing lino block cutting to a group of nine-year-olds. She has prepared the lesson thoughtfully, has all the tools and equipment readily available. Yet is she really in a position to answer all the 'why?' and 'how?' questions if she has not, quite recently, experienced for herself the same sort of 'doing it' situation, laboured under similar difficulties, suffered similar frustrations, and, finally, been elated at the success of her design? The *raison d'être* for art practice lies in personal involvement. John Newick, whose interest in art education took him from a teaching post in an English boarding school to central Africa, and then to London University, makes this point very succinctly: '. . . unless we are mysteriously fortified by the problems of a craft at a level which draws sleepily upon our personal resourcefulness, we have no defence against the intrusion of the commonplace.'[1]

And yet—as in all learning situations—the teacher cannot sit back and just expect 'something' (ie, art) 'to turn up'. Some form of organization is essential. Although, in many British primary schools, the 'art period' (in which all children in any one class 'do' art at the same time) is a thing of the past, let us assume that it is in such a situation that we find ourselves. How can we cope? Firstly it is essential to break down our class of thirty children into much smaller groups—say five groups of six children each. Let us assume that four of these groups are already engaged upon an activity which

[1] POTTERY by John Newick. Dryad Press, Leicester

they can manage without too much adult help (eg, making papier mâché puppet heads, doing wax resist, carving in soapstone or chalk, colour cutting into oil pastel). The fifth group consists of children who have been concerned with fabric decoration (block printing, tie-and-dye). The teacher now wishes to introduce them to batik, and this will require direct teaching. The teacher might begin by explaining the process and the tools, following this by working alongside of the children as they in turn experiment. Such teacher-led discussion as takes place should have the aim of consolidating the children's understanding of the activity.

Brush painting, 20″ × 30″, by a five-year-old boy: 'Witch'. This painting followed upon a story about a witch. It is somewhat unusual for a young child to try to paint in a background—still more unusual for him to succeed as he has here. This picture took twenty minutes to complete (cf photograph on p. 336).

From time to time the teacher must, of necessity, move to other groups, offering help and advice as and when appropriate, but he will continually return to those children who, for that period are his especial responsibility (the batik workers).

Marbled pattern over wax drawing (resist) 15″ × 20″, by an eight-year-old girl: 'A Boy in my Class'. This was the result of experiment with wax resist drawings. After simple wax and stain techniques had been understood, an attempt was made to pattern a resist drawing by laying it in a trough of marbling colour (oil on water).

This pattern will be repeated during subsequent lessons. The batik workers will become reasonably conversant with the process, and will then need time to deepen their appreciation by further experimentation. But the puppet heads will be dry, and will need painting and clothing. Is the teacher's main responsibility here, or with the children who seem to have exhausted their interest in wax resist and soapstone? Could these two groups merge for some supportive work on the theatre project from which the puppets grew? Herein lies the teacher's role: a professional know-how, supported by an understanding of the children for whom he works.

Pastel drawing, 20″ × 30″, by a nine-year-old girl: 'Pat Fenn'. A carefully observed pastel picture drawn from life. Many children can draw who cannot paint, and for these children soft pastels are ideal.

Photographs on pp. 342–4 illustrate the development of children's art. Paints remain popular (p. 342) but experiment is now commonplace. Wax drawings might be resisted with a simple wash (see below) or in marbling colours (page 343) so that overall texture is obtained. While one child prefers fabric, another will find tremendous satisfaction in pastel and chalk (page 344).

Wax resist, 15″ × 10″, by a six-year-old girl: 'My Pet Cat'. Here the motivation was provided by a record of T. S. Eliot's *Practical Cats*. This was one of the pictures which was produced during experiments which eventually led to the figure on p. 343.

Of course, the example developed above does not only apply to art-orientated subjects. One could in the same way have the groups following quite different programmes (eg, maths, science, creative writing, weaving, individual research work). The teacher then becomes rather like a master juggler at a circus, whose aim is to keep thirty plates spinning on thirty poles. This he does by moving to where he is most needed when he is most needed, increasing the momentum of individual poles to prevent the plates falling to the ground.

As the young child learns about materials he is

better able to relate them to the particular things he wants to do. He becomes comparatively expert in some, whilst in others his knowledge is sketchy and peripheral. Children with knowledge are able to share ideas and technical know-how with less gifted members of the group. Leaders emerge, and often these include children who in other spheres (for example, games, drama) have much less to offer.

Environmental studies

Knowledge of materials, however, is of little worth unless it is used purposefully. Environmental studies[1] play an important part in the curricula of British primary schools, and out-of-school visits to places of interest are common. A visit may be linked to a study of the area around the school—its factories, the shopping area, the town hall, the police,

[1]See, in this series ENVIRONMENTAL STUDIES by Melville Harris

Brush painting, 20″ × 30″, by a seven-year-old girl: 'Man in the Red Moon'. Here we have a picture by a child who could paint but could not draw. All her paintings were strangely abstract—and the titles she gave them merely served to emphasize the fact.

Oil pastel drawing, 20″ × 30″ by a nine-year-old boy: 'My Holiday from School'.
While, for instance, the figures on pp. 336 and 342 were completed fairly
quickly, as the child grows older his concentration span increases. John took
four hours (unbroken save for lunch) to complete this picture.

The impact of these free imaginative pictures (pp. 345–7) is dependent largely
upon the media selected by the children concerned. Whereas Iris (page 346)
could only use paint, Jane (page 345) and John (see above) found the viscosity
of paint quite impossible to master.

fire, and ambulance services. It may take in a local
farm, a church, an old building or a museum—or it
may be (with small children) nothing more than a
visit to a nearby park, to walk through autumn
leaves, or to feed the ducks on a pond. Any of these
experiences will trigger off discussion, and this will
invariably lead to a desire to paint, to write in prose
and verse, to model. In other words, to a desire to
communicate. 'We went to the museum and this is
what we saw . . .'

Each visit will give each child a unique individual experience, and, because it is individual and
unique, each member of the group should be given

the opportunity to express himself in his own way. It is worth remembering that the impact of any visit depends largely upon the child's previous experiences. A quite commonplace happening for one child can be utterly shattering for another. Barry, a lad of ten, who lived in a downtown slum, was taken to the seaside. Stunned silence was followed by a torrent of questions. 'Look at all that water. Does it go all over the world? Is it cold? Can I touch it? Why does it make that noise? Why does it move?' On returning to school, Barry looked in the library for as many 'sea' books, from atlases to reference books, as he could find, and he made an anthology of 'sea' drawings and 'sea' poetry.

The group experience—written work, pictures and models—is taken by the teacher and displayed so that a variety of viewpoints is presented—each child contributing something of himself to the overall effect. Photographs, maps and diagrams are also added and the final display should be a synopsis of the children's experiences. 'We went to . . . and this display is our way of showing you what we saw, what we learned, how we felt.'

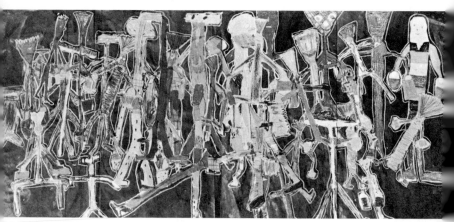

Paper collage and wax resist, 20″ × 60″, by a group of eight-year-olds: 'The Dance of the Brooms' from *The Sorcerer's Apprentice*. This picture really began in the free dance lesson when the group moved to Dukas' music. The fact that the children had moved like brooms made it far easier for them to capture a feeling of wooden stiffness in their picture.

Girl, by Harriet. age 5

Painting on fabric, 36″ × 12″, by a five-year-old girl: 'Girl'.

Display for five-year-olds, following upon a visit to some tower blocks near the school. The pictures (varying in size from 30″ × 20″ to 30″ × 15″) were painted in acrylic. Compare this with the photograph on p. 352.

Norman knight and lady. Life-size paper and fabric collage made by a group of eight- and nine-year-olds. The mounting paper was also prepared by the children, using acrylic paint applied by roller.

This picture was painted following a visit to Rochester Castle by eight-
and nine-year-olds and forms part of a display which included writing and
rubbings

Tissue paper and acrylic paint, 20″ × 25″, by a seven-year-old boy: 'Autumn Trees'.

Work for display   When selecting materials for display, be they reproductions of the work of great masters or pictures painted by the children themselves, thought has to be given to those which are 'hung' and those which are 'rejected'. It is important, for example, that the children are not so influenced by the teacher's tastes that they lack discrimination, and do not discover that the work of every artist will affect each onlooker in a very personal way. 'However did he think of using all those twirls to say "tree"?' asked an eight-year-old as he gazed at a Van Gogh painting. 'There aren't twirls in trees . . .'

(long pause) '. . . or trees in twirls . . . but he makes it sort of right for twirls and trees to go together.' Thus, a teacher whose first love is Paul Klee must ensure that the group for whom he is responsible is as much aware, for example, of Tintoretto, Gauguin, and Sutherland.

Children's paintings and models need to be selected with equal care. Each child, when he paints or draws, conveys something of his inner self, his personalized vision of the world. As teachers, we must not simply select pictures that we can live with—but pictures which represent something of the child who painted them. Sometimes the selection can be left to the children themselves—and often the discrimination they show is quite remarkable!

Teachers need to take trouble in mounting children's work, for if the display looks slapdash and tatty, the fact that the 'teacher does not really care' will quickly be communicated to the children concerned. While engaged in any creative activity the child is at his most sensitive to praise and to criticism. The adults in the child's world need to take this into account when handling his work.

The integrated curriculm If art is approached in this way, as a vital part of an integrated curriculum, it becomes almost impossible to regard picture making and modelling as a self-contained subject. Obviously, if a display is being mounted to consolidate and clarify work based upon the local railway station, pictures must play a prominent part. However, children do not compartmentalize in this way. If a locomotive merits a picture to support a piece of writing, why should not a piece of writing serve as the starting point for the picture, for a piece of embroidery, or for a model? Let us examine for a moment how children are led into writing. The teacher might begin with a piece of music, Smetana's MA VLASTE for example, being taken as the starting point for a discussion on water or of a river in all its moods. The evocative sounds of the music might then be extended by an extract from a poem or a book (for example TOM SAWYER or HUCKLEBERRY FINN). A group of children might then attempt to improvise a dance based upon an excerpt from the music, or to mime a scene from the reading. Another group might go to look at the river which runs through the town, perhaps wandering along a grassy bank and through the drab streets near the docks. The aim of the initial exercise—to help the children towards sensitivity in their oral and written expression—has not been forgotten. It has simply been supported by a whole range of other closely related experiences—emotional, visual, verbal; experiences actual and vicarious.

Wax drawing, 20″ × 30″, by a ten-year-old boy: 'The Fox Screen'—Chichester Cathedral. This picture—which captures something of the spirit of the medieval builder—took two-and-a-half hours to complete and was worked entirely in the Cathedral.

Model making in clay—by a three-year-old. Synthetic clays are now widely available, and these make it far easier for the teacher to preserve children's models. 'Newclay', which was used by the child photographed here, is hardened with a liquid (applied by brush)—thus no kiln was required.

An awareness of the traditional crafts plays an important part in the aesthetic development of young people (photographs on pp. 359–360). These traditional crafts are supplemented by a wide range of free modelling using 'junk' (or waste) materials (see photographs on pp. 362 and 364).

As suggested above, the teacher would not dictate the particular methods which individual children employ in their efforts to express themselves. By providing experiences and the means through which these experiences can be expressed, the teacher will have come a long way towards realizing an environment in which creative work will flourish.

There are, however, two other important aspects of the teacher's role which are often ignored. First, the teacher must be prepared to plan his work programme so that the child is given time to assimilate new experiences and then to extend and develop them. An 'art period' which is fixed and immovable rarely allows sufficient time for really creative work to develop. A creative act cannot be bound by time. It is in schools where syllabus and timetable serve to indicate direction, rather than to instruct and command, that creative work flourishes. Thus, in such a school, one might find a group of girls spending a whole morning labouring over a piece of embroidery, while, in the same period of time, three other groups have written poetry, made music, and constructed polyhedra from plastic shapes. Each activity was, in essence, creative. Each required a different amount of time for its consummation.

Secondly, the teacher should provide children with the opportunity to touch. Essentially, art in school is education through the senses, and, in young children, the pleasure gained through tactile experience is immense. In addition to displays of children's work, classrooms should also contain small ever-changing exhibitions of things which children can handle. These could contain man-made objects (carvings, ornaments of glass and clay), or leaves and stones, shells, pieces of bark, and feathers. An Indian's moccasin and a robin's egg provide the young child with essential visual and tactile experience, as well as material for a discussion on colour, pattern and texture. How might this work in practice?

2 A Museum Project

A group of eight-, nine- and ten-year-olds were involved in a museum project. They had spent, with their teacher, three days working in a folk museum. They arrived when the museum opened (at 10 a.m.), and left late in the afternoon, having taken a packed lunch so that no time was wasted on meal breaks. They were allowed to use all the museum facilities—the library, the studio and the galleries. The curators were also involved, giving short talks, where appropriate, on particular aspects of the museum's collection. During these three days children touched and talked, researched and read, drew, wrote, modelled, made tape-recordings, listened and looked. On return to school, they made illustrated booklets, models, and diagrams, relating to their particular study.

A few weeks later the teacher decided to try to re-create a similar learning situation in her classroom by bringing some 'museum pieces' into school. These consisted of all manner of 'by-gones' borrowed from all manner of places—from a museum, from her friends, from other members of staff, from parents of children in the school. The final collection was quite impressive: an eighteenth-century book, an Elizabethan shoe, a Georgian trinket box, some Victorian earthenware, fossils, large tropical shells, a gourd, an Indian footscraper, a small metal horse, a miner's lamp, a delicate Chinese bowl, an oil lamp and some modern blue-green glass.

The exhibits were discussed, handled, examined, and, of course, books were referred to for background information. What was a gourd? Where did it grow? Was it of value? Could it be put to practical use? What was the horse used for? The person who lent it (a museum curator) said it was a votive horse. What did that mean? How could we find out?

In the discussion, the teacher suggested ways of finding the answers to some of the questions, deliberately leaving the topic open-ended so that the children could follow up some of the suggested leads and make discoveries for themselves.

How would they set down their feelings? The objects could be described in words, drawn in whole or in part, studied through a microscope, or used as starting points for printing, painting, or model making. While each child worked on the object of his choice (cooperating with other children if need be), the teacher moved from child to child giving advice and help as required.

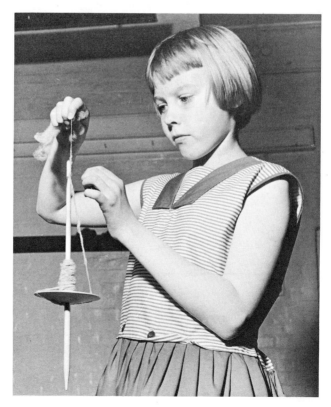

Spinning by hand—
a ten-year-old

Weaving on table looms—nine- and ten-year-olds

Girls enjoy using fabric, but their activities should not be restricted to sample sewing and stitchcraft. In an age when sewing machines can do almost everything required of the needlewoman, it is far better to give the children some idea of how fabrics are made and how they can be patterned.

As work was finished, it was displayed on tables, so that each piece could be discussed at the end of the session. When school closed for the day, not only had this been done but an attractive wall display had also been mounted in the classroom.

Work of the type described above places particular demands upon the teacher. He will suggest lines of enquiry and methods of approach, rather than dictate the content and format of the children's studies. The freedom which this method gives will be reflected in the opportunities it allows for children 'to select and reject and form first-hand judgements'.[1] The very act of selection (whether it

[1] HANDBOOK OF SUGGESTIONS FOR PRIMARY SCHOOL TEACHERS. HMSO 1959

be of materials or of work) seems to heighten children's sensitivity.

This is best illustrated through their writing. After handling the shell, Susan, a nine-year-old, wrote:

A Shell

Big and spiky
Spiral
Twisted
And rough outside
Inside so pink
A glorious pink
It goes lighter
And lighter
Till the pink turns to white
Shell
Oh, coral shell
How beautiful you are.

The votive horse was drawn and written about by a number of children. Graham, aged ten, spent much time cradling the horse in the palm of his hand. Then he wrote:

Horse

Horse made of metal
Horse with a twisted tail
Horse made for sacrifice
How many he has seen
I could not tell

Horse with a thin tummy
Horse with a long neck
Horse with a small head
How much his eyes have seen
I could not tell.

Madeleine, aged nine, was far more influenced by the 'magic' which lay at the root of its very existence:

The Horse

Horse made of metal . . .
Heavy
Twisted tail,
Sacrificial
Long ago they used a real horse.
Plunged the knife into its neck.
Kept the blood.
Hole in the altar
Through which the blood runs.

Horse made of metal . . .
Heavy.
Twisted tail,
Sacrificial.
Now
No blood,
No knife,
No death.
Just a votive horse.

'A Seaside Town', by a group of nine- and ten-year-olds. Forty-five children helped make this model which was constructed entirely of 'junk' material. The final layout was made the responsibility of a small committee—who had also to paint the ground plan and the backcloth.

3 Conclusion

It therefore becomes apparent that organization within the classroom may need rethinking. Is it necessary for all the children to paint at the same time? (If we remember that no child will take the same time over a piece of work, the question has something more than mere academic interest.) If each activity can be seen as a different method of communicating, the traditional methods of class organization become irrelevant. If tables full of art equipment are left out for continual use, and an 'art area' is made in the classroom, children will begin to regard painting and model making as something more than a weekly interlude between spelling and mathematics, and a reward for good behaviour.

Children learn by looking and touching, talking and listening, reading and research. Here a group of eight-, nine-, and ten-year-olds have been allowed to handle exhibits from a local museum. This experience triggers off reading, writing and picture making, each child using a variety of ways to express his feeling. Here art practice is used to consolidate experience rather than as the starting point for self expression (compare with photographs on pp. 334–8).

In schools where each room is divided into subject areas (for example an area for mathematics, an area for art, a library area, an imaginative-play area, a writing area) the problems of security—be it 'covering' the curriculum or organizing the teaching time meaningfully—are more easily overcome. The arrangement of the room makes for easier organization, and the physical structure within it (such as the furniture) imposes a discipline of its own.

'A Busy Port', by a group of seven- and eight-year-olds. Balsa wood was used for this model

Art and life

In addition to art practices which flow from drama, music, poetry, and local studies, some crafts will be undertaken simply for their own sake. What is the point, the cynic might ask, in letting an eight-year-old fashion a pot from green clay when he can buy one which holds water from the local store? Why bother to tie-dye fabric, or pattern it with lino blocks for a school display table, when the supermarket two streets away sells attractive material at a few pence per yard?

Hidden in the answer lies the basic reason for art practice. Man's progress towards civilization has been marked by his ability to discipline materials, to fashion clay, metal and wood, to spin, to weave, to carve, to construct, to build. In an age when individuality is being continually undermined by mass production ('soft sell', built-in obsolescence' and all), our children, born into a technological society, need to have some awareness of the basic processes of mankind, if they are to live fully.

Thus, the majority of British primary schools also include traditional crafts as part of their art programme. Weaving, spinning, cane and raffia work, sewing (embroidery and simple dressmaking), woodcraft, basketry, pottery, and bookcraft continue to be practised. Sometimes, crafts which are found in the local community (for example, corn-dolly making[1]) are also to be found in the neighbourhood schools. At this stage, girls and boys will be found following similar crafts—there is little specialization by sex. Often, boys sew or make collage pictures in fabric and braid, and girls use wood and cane.

In the best of British primary schools, art is not regarded as something unrelated to living and learning. It is seen as an integral part of the life of the school and of the community beyond, providing, as it does, an outlet for the young child's innate desire to explore with hands and eyes, and to express himself freely through an incredible range of materials, both unconventional and traditional.

The weaving of dolls from corn husks

365

Appendix

Paints: water-colour (tubes and blocks); poster-colour; powder-colour; oil-colour; polymer acrylic paint (eg: Margro's 'Marvin', 'Reeves' 'Polymer', Rowney's 'Cryla', 'Hyplar', 'Liquitex', 'Vanguard'); balsa wood paints; stains (eg, ebony stain).

Pastels: oil pastels and oil crayons; chalk; wax crayons.

Drawing materials: lead pencils; ink (black and white); charcoal—sticks and pencils; felt pens (eg, 'Color-sticks', 'Magic Markers', 'Permanent', 'Dry Mark'); coloured pencils; coloured inks.

Papers: sugar paper or pastel paper in a variety of colours; tissue paper; coloured sticky squares; brown sticky paper tape or 'Sellotape', 'Scotch tape'; kitchen paper; newspaper, glossy magazines, woman's weeklies; silver paper and metallic papers; transparent plastic papers; cartridge paper (drawing paper); cellophane; crêpe paper.

Card: strawboard (oak tag)—thick, medium, thin; manilla board in a variety of colours; cardboard boxes in all sizes; corrugated card.

Pins: dressmakers' pins; panel pins; tacks; nails (up to $\frac{1}{2}$ in).

Fastenings, glues, gums, paste: brass paper-clips; brown sticky papers; 'Sellotape', masking tape; cold water paste; quick drying cement (eg, balsa cement, aeroplane glue); wood glue (eg, 'Croid', 'Duco'); impact adhesives (eg, 'Bostik', 'Weldwood' contact cement); gum (eg, 'Cow Gum', 'Le Page's Gum');

acrylic resin, acrylic medium, (eg, 'Marvin Adhesive', 'Elmer's Glue').

Cloth and fabric scraps: felt; ric-rac; braid; thread; crash; imitation linen; cotton; Vilene; velvet; needlecord; net curtaining; towelling; ribbon; wool; tape.

Other materials: sandstone, chalk, local stone, for carving; sand, clay, cane, raffia, rushes; raw wool, raw cotton (if available); thistledown; fruits and seeds (eg, hips, haws, fir cones, ash, maple and sycamore keys, acorns, chestnuts).

Objects gathered from the sea-shore: eg, smooth, weathered stones; wood and pebbles; glass oddments; shells; twigs, bark, feathers.

Scrap and junk: raffia, packing straw, string, sweet-packing, cottons, rug wool, hair, wood shavings, newspaper and magazines, old cardboard boxes, card strips, wallpapers, sandpapers, fabric and leather scraps, cotton reels, matchboxes, card tubes, drinking straws, cotton-wool, feathers, silver paper, foil, corrugated card and papers, 18-gauge wire.

Booklist

Alexander, E. and Carter, B. ART FOR YOUNG PEOPLE Mills & Boon, London 1950

Ash, B. and Rapaport, B. CREATIVE WORK IN THE JUNIOR SCHOOL Methuen, London 1968; Barnes & Noble, New York 1968

Dean, J. ART AND CRAFT IN THE PRIMARY SCHOOL TODAY A. & C. Black, London 1970 (second edition); The Philosophical Library, New York 1969

Jordan, D. CHILDHOOD AND MOVEMENT Blackwell, Oxford 1966

Marshall, Sybil EXPERIMENT IN EDUCATION Cambridge University Press, London and New York 1963

Marshall, Sybil ASPECTS OF ART WORK Evans, London 1970; International Publications Service, New York

Melzi, M. ART IN THE PRIMARY SCHOOL Blackwell, Oxford 1967; Humanities Press, New York 1971

Pluckrose, H. A. CREATIVE ARTS AND CRAFTS Macdonald, London 1968

Pluckrose, H. A. LET'S MAKE PICTURES Mills & Boon, London 1965; Topinger Publishing Co., New York 1965

Pluckrose, H. A. CREATIVE THEMES Evans, London 1967; International Publications Service, New York 1970

Read, Sir Herbert EDUCATION THROUGH ART Faber & Faber, London 1958

Richardson, E. IN THE EARLY WORLD Pergamon Press, New York 1969

Stevani, M. ART AND EDUCATION Batsford, London 1968; Atherton Press, New York 1968

Tomlinson, R. R. and Mills, J. F. GROWTH OF CHILD ART University of London Press, London 1966

See also the INTRODUCING series published by B. T. Batsford (London) and Watson-Cupthill (New York). This series covers a whole range of basic art techniques. Other useful publications are SCHOOL ARTS (nine issues per year: Warren Davies, Baltimore, Maryland) and ART AND CRAFT IN EDUCATION (monthly: Evans, London)

See also AN INTRODUCTION, SPACE, TIME AND GROUPING, A RURAL SCHOOL, AN INFANT SCHOOL, A JUNIOR SCHOOL, ENVIRONMENTAL STUDIES, THE TEACHER'S ROLE, THE PUPIL'S DAY in this series.

Informal Reading and Writing

**Jean Johnson
and Joan Tamburrini**

The Authors

Jean Johnson After teaching in infant schools, Miss Johnson joined the staff of the Froebel Institute College of Education, and is now responsible for the training of nursery, infant and junior students. She is particularly interested in the developmental theory of learning, and its implementation in a school environment.

Joan Tamburrini Her teaching experience has been with children of all ages—infant, junior and secondary—and with slow learners. Mrs Tamburrini's major discipline is psychology of education, and her degree is a London BA in psychology. Her chief interest is in in-service training, and she is a tutor, to teachers taking an advanced diploma, at the Froebel Institute College of Education.

Mrs Tamburrini recently visited Boston, Massachusetts, as a consultant to the EDC Follow-Through Program.

Introduction

'Yesterday I couldn't read, today I can!' This six-year-old's recognition that she had mastered—suddenly, as it seemed to her—the visual word, is a common experience for teachers of young children. Learning to read depends on many factors in a child and his environment. However slowly these may interact to develop the skill, it seems to happen suddenly, 'as if by magic', as one teacher expressed it. Examination of the thought and effort with which most children build up their knowledge of the clues which lead to mastery suggests, however, no magical process. We do not know exactly how a child learns to read, but we do know that when teachers understand the psychological and environmental factors involved, practice improves in the classroom. It is the purpose here to describe and examine some examples of learning and teaching which have led to the development of successful reading and the associated skill of writing.

The examples have been collected from three schools; one in a 'good' residential area, another on a developing housing estate, and the last in a deprived area. All the schools were organized into 'vertical grouping' with an 'integrated day'.[1] In spite of wide differences in the children's backgrounds, the examples gathered were surprisingly similar in quality, as shown in the comments made, the questions asked, and the understanding demonstrated in illustrations and descriptions. It seems that the similarity in quality of the material collected is explained by the similarity of educational principles pursued by the schools. In general the ages of the children are not given, since the emphasis is on the development of reading which is

[1]There are other forms of organization, as discussed in this series, in SPACE, TIME AND GROUPING by Richard Palmer

taking place in the four to seven age range. The ways in which this is brought about, and the ages at which it occurs, vary with individual children; processes rather than ages are dealt with here. It should be stressed, at this point, that the incidents described arose in a wide context of varied activities in which learning was taking place. In all examples which follow, individual differences are valued rather than merely tolerated. For a large part of each day, children are engaged in a variety of activities which reflect their particular concerns and levels of development. The teachers foster language in general, and reading and writing in particular, in relation to these specific concerns and levels of development. Acknowledgement of individual differences is also reflected in the range and variety of reading books found in these classes; as one teacher said, 'I used to order thirty-five copies of a book—now I order thirty-five different books!' The children who participated did so from an interest in a particular topic and not at the direction of the teacher, although the manner in which she presented material and the developments she encouraged provoked children who might have been uninterested to become involved.

1 Four Case Studies

A study of autumn

In one class, some of the children had been discussing the changes taking place as autumn approached, and had brought in a varied collection of leaves, fruits and grasses, to which the teacher added a large marrow. She also brought a book she had made about autumn, a collection of poems, and some work cards of appropriate nouns and adjectives; for example, 'autumn', 'red', 'crinkled'. She told stories about autumn, such as THE ANT AND THE GRASSHOPPER, THE GIANT MARROW, and others she had made up herself.

The interest aroused by this material developed into a wide range of activities throughout the term:

Mathematics involved counting leaves and conkers (horse chestnuts), measuring and weighing the marrow and other fruit and vegetables, which led to an interest in cooking.

Science, arising from a study of hibernation and migration, included observations of animals and their different skeletons. From this, the children became interested in food, its taste and smell, and the ways in which it decayed and produced mould. The study of animals' habitats developed into an interest in trees and falling leaves, and in the effects of wind and other kinds of weather.

Music, and study of sounds made by different instruments, developed from listening to sounds associated with autumn, such as those produced by walking in fallen leaves.

Movement of the children's own bodies was explored after considering the different ways in which leaves fall from trees.

376

Children developed their interests in creative work in many materials such as paint, clay and fabrics, but above all in language. They discussed as they investigated the materials together, and the teacher followed this in further talk with individuals, small groups and the whole class. She provided books on foods, musical instruments, cooking, weather, mammals and fish, and also wall charts of poems and cooking recipes to further their interests. Some of the books were made to be read to the children, while others were made with the more specific aim of encouraging the children to read, by using large print and putting a folder in the back covers holding separate words which could be matched to the words in the script. The vocabulary included words from the published reading scheme used in the school, and particularly any with which the children had difficulty. The children were fascinated to discover the words in a new context, and they commented on the length and shape of each word, and the number of times it occurred. Other books resulted from the cooperative efforts of the children, and they contributed both pictures and writing to them. These were read by the children, and by the teacher to groups or to the whole class.

The intrinsic relation between reading and writing was acknowledged by the teacher, whose provision of these books and charts encouraged many children to make books of their own. At first these derived from current interests, but soon they took on the personal interests of the children, and covered a wide variety of topics.

Vocabulary introduced in cooking, science, movement, and other activities was written on cards for the children to see, read, and use in writing. The following are some of the words provided in this way:

autumn	apple	crack
leaf	carrot	crunch
leaves	fruit	curve

seeds	marrow	hard
stalk	orange	heavy
	pear	light
acorn	pomegranate	long
berries	tomatoes	round
chestnut	vegetable	rustle
conker		soft
		squash
salt		
smell	brown	
sour	green	bread
sugar	red	corn
sweet	stripes	flour
taste	yellow	wheat

The wide range of reading material aroused great interest in reading itself, and during the term the children became increasingly conscious of the function of reading and writing. Among the younger children, many, for the first time, directed their energy towards the acquisition of the necessary skills.

The concept of reading readiness has sometimes been misinterpreted to imply that the moment of readiness is purely maturational, and that the teacher should simply wait until that moment is reached before introducing a child to reading material. While some factors contributing to reading readiness are probably physiological and maturational, factors to do with language development will depend to a great extent on the experiences which adults, including teachers, have provided. Far from simply waiting for reading readiness to emerge, teachers can provide experiences which will make a child ready to learn to read.

The teacher of this class recognized the importance of the development of oral language, and the provision of written language relevant to the children's own experiences. There were frequent discussions with the class, with groups of children, and with individual children, in which she was concerned both with increasing their vocabulary and with the development and understanding of more complex sentence structures. Meaningfulness was ensured, because the material written for the children and read back to the teacher was basically the written expression of their own thoughts.

A study of wild animals In another school, a broken strip projector had been out of use for some time. When it was repaired, the children wanted to use it, and put through a number of film-strips simply for the pleasure of being able to use it again. One of the strips, about African wild animals, held their attention and led to the making of models, to painting pictures, and to drawing and making books. This interest was encouraged by a visit to the zoo, and the children took a tape-recorder and cine-camera with them. Photography and tape-recording were part of the normal activities in the school, and the children were themselves able to take photographs and record sounds of the animals. The photographs were made into books, and the tapes were listened to and discussed. The visit itself led to a wide range of creative work, modelling and painting, and to more drawings and books.

Language, both oral and visual, was constantly used and developed in all this work. The teachers made picture and reference books for the children to use, and dictionary cards for them to refer to when making their own books. In this school, the children are encouraged to make individual books, and the words given to them for this purpose included the following:

animals	giraffe
bright	hide
bird-of-paradise	lions
bull	parrot
cockatoo	sharp
colours	snake
crocodile	stripey
dinosaur	tigers
elephant	zebra

A number of children were particularly interested in snakes, and vocabulary written and read by them included:

camouflaged	round
climbing	sheds
coils	skin
crawling	stretching
curls	squiggling
fangs	twists
gliding	wriggling
poisonous	

Labelling of models or paintings was provided when the children concerned recognized it as a significant extension of the original work. The labels remained only for as long as the children referred to them. In appreciating the width and quality of this vocabulary, it is important to realize that these children lived in a very deprived area of London. The following examples, taken from their books, show their use of this vocabulary: 'the snake twists and curls through the trees in the jungle'; 'the bull is big and strong with sharp horns'; 'the snake coils like a rope' (see photographs on following pages).

The snake twists and curls through the trees in the jungle

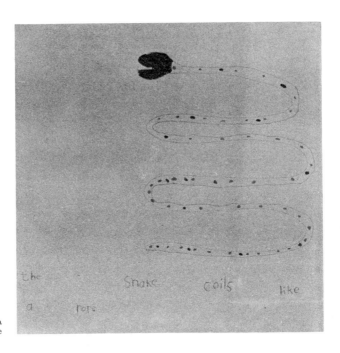

The snake coils like a rope

Making and reading individual books led the children to refer to library books provided by the teacher, and these in turn gave the children information, ideas, and language which extended and elaborated the expression of ideas in their own books. The constant interaction between first-hand experience, verbal expression, and reference books, built up the conditions for satisfying learning.

Acknowledgement of this close inter-relationship between language and thought underlies two aspects of the procedures which have been described. Firstly, the relating of reading material to the children's own experiences and concerns was continued by the teachers beyond pre-reading experiences. It was implicit in the group work which started with the children's explorations of the phenomena of autumn, and in that which centred around the wild animals. In both these

The snake sheds its skin

examples, the children's reading and writing developed as the teachers paid attention, on the one hand, to the elaboration of language—by making books for the children, by providing relevant library books, and by reading stories and poems connected with these concerns—and on the other hand to the provision of further experiences, such as cooking facilities and a visit to the zoo. This latter in turn gave rise to the need for further language.

Secondly, the development of children's specific understanding of written symbols also related to their conceptual development. The teachers ensured that vocabulary recurred frequently in different contexts. Many words were common to the books the teacher made on mammals, on the weather, and on cooking, and were deliberately chosen because they were part of the vocabulary of the books in the reading scheme. Questions put to the children like, 'Where have you seen that word before?' both help to establish for children that words have consistent meaning, and enable a teacher to find out whether a child has progressed from recognition of sentences as meaningful units, to identifying single words in different contexts.

A teacher often has to build up considerable knowledge about a child to decide on the most helpful procedures in teaching him to read. This may take quite a long time and include a variety of approaches, as the next example illustrates.

The bull is big and strong with sharp horns

The zebra has a stripey coat

Jean-Paul Jean-Paul was a French boy who had difficulty with the English language. He was a shy boy, and lacking in confidence when faced with any new situation. Although his elder brother, Pierre, was in the same class, Jean-Paul took quite a long time to settle into school, and relied on his brother for ideas and guidance. When Pierre started school he had even less English than Jean-Paul, but his family encouraged 'school learning' and within a year he was speaking good English and was ahead of most of the children in reading. The same pressures were applied to Jean-Paul, and he came to school eager to learn to read.

It was the custom in the school to give children a reading book as soon as possible after entry. This was delayed for a term in Jean-Paul's case, and although he was delighted when it was eventually given to him, he was unable to recognize any of the words. It was at this point that a new teacher took over this class. Because of Jean-Paul's desire to read and write, she decided to try to help him to make his own books, using as much as possible of the reading scheme vocabulary. He made books about aeroplanes and his home, and within a week he began to recognize such words as 'Look', 'Oh', 'See'—becoming increasingly enthusiastic and anxious to read. It was evident that his attention was directed towards mastering the mechanics of reading, since he was interested neither in the meanings of the phrases nor in the accompanying illustrations.

These first signs that he was learning to read were praised by his parents, and inspired even greater efforts on his part. The following week the teacher noted that, in addition to asking to read from the scheme, he voluntarily worked at his own books each day, eagerly tracing round the letters of words written for him, but not wanting to illustrate them. It was therefore impossible to know how much he understood, since he had difficulty in talking about what he had written. To try to extend his attention to meanings, the teacher provided a series of illustrations which she thought might interest him, and he was attracted to these. For example, he chose a picture of a sponge pudding, and traced the word 'pudding'. He quickly learned, and was able to remember, new words, but because these were restricted to his own limited vocabulary, he became bored with what he could write. He was encouraged to take part in such social activities as home corner play, so that he could develop his language.

At this time it became clear that, at home, he was being taught the names of letters, as he continually named them in words he was trying to read. To use this interest, the teacher isolated letters in words he knew, for example, 'p' in 'pudding', and began to teach the sounds to see if this would help his reading. On the contrary, however, he quickly lost interest in this, and it began to be evident that he was not retaining words apparently known during the preceding six weeks, unless these were accompanied by an illustration.

Careful observation and evaluation of Jean-Paul's behaviour in school indicated that the almost fanatical desire to read stimulated by the home, was not supported by his intellectual development. On the Goodenough Draw-a-Man test he scored 5.–M.A.,[1] approximately four years, and much of his activity was at this level. For example, when using scrap materials, his satisfaction was in performing the sensori-motor actions of cutting or sticking—he made no attempt to represent objects. His reluctance to illustrate also indicated his limited use of representational behaviour, and even at the end of term, writing, for him, involved the imitation of writing, not the use of writing to describe objects or ideas.

No doubt his inadequate language limited both the understanding and the expression of his environment. For example, on one occasion when he needed a hammer for woodwork, he attracted the teacher's attention by touching her, pointing to the cupboard and then to the woodwork bench, and making a 'bang, bang' sound. This was like the behaviour of a much younger child.

His social intercourse with other children was necessarily limited, and this aggravated his feelings of inadequacy and his lack of confidence. By the end of the term he was still keen to read, because the skill was highly valued by his parents,

[1]This test is described in MENTAL TESTING by F. L. Goodenough, Staples Press, London 1950. A revision and extension of this test is to be found in CHILDREN'S DRAWINGS AS MEASURES OF INTELLECTUAL MATURITY, Harcourt, Brace and World, NY 1963

but he had not developed the necessary mental skills. His visual and aural discrimination were poor: he was even unable to distinguish longer from shorter words, and was confused between the sounds in his two languages. Formal instruction in reading at this stage, therefore, would have been likely to lead to successive failures which, in view of the high status given to reading ability by his parents, could have been serious.

He needed a steady build-up of first-hand experiences associated with visual and aural language, to encourage a major shift in intellectual development from his predominantly sensori-motor interactions with his environment to the use and understanding of symbolic representations. The teacher used a variety of approaches to provoke this. She talked with him about the many real objects and events in the classroom and school in which he was interested, and encouraged him to represent these in painting, drawing, and attention to detail, and particularly to similarities and differences. For example, on one occasion when small cakes were cooked, iced, and decorated, he was asked to tell her how each was different from the rest. On another occasion, he and another child had together painted a traffic scene, and the teacher helped him to pick out the similarities and differences between the cars they had painted. To supplement this help in discrimination, the teacher also made some use of published material, designed to refine visual perception, in which series of pictures and symbols contain differences of position, angle, direction, and detail.

The refinement of his visual and auditory perception was further encouraged as she looked at and read books with him. At first, his attention was drawn predominantly to detail in the illustrations, but, gradually, significant words in the text were pointed out and, again, ways in which these were similar to and different from other words were discussed.

As, gradually, he began to make representations in paintings and drawings, his own verbal descriptions or stories were written for him, and sometimes, these were discussed with other children. This created social situations in which representations in pictorial symbols and verbal signs were seen to be a means of communication between persons. Social interaction was important for Jean-Paul, not only for his personal development, but also to bring about discussions in which he could elaborate and refine his comprehension and use of language. The teacher sometimes had to intervene to help the children to understand each other, but gradually he began to be more independent as his grasp of the English language increased.

By the end of the term, Jean-Paul had built up a small vocabulary of written words which he recognized out of context. These words were meaningful symbols to him, for they referred to objects and events related to his own interests and activities. In addition, he had begun to discriminate certain similarities and differences between these words. For example, he was interested to discover which words had the same initial letter. When he came across a new word, he paid attention not only to visual and auditory clues but also to contextual clues to meaning. His previous obsessional approach to mechanical reading skills, which had been over-anxious and lacking in understanding of meaning, was replaced with a growing understanding of symbolic representation, which is fundamental to a meaningful and successful approach to reading.

It is clear from Jean-Paul's case history that his first introduction to a reading primer was premature. He was certainly well motivated. The emphasis his home placed on learning to read, and his desire to emulate his older brother, led him to approach the acquisition of the skill with enthusiasm. However, although he showed a considerable desire to learn to read, in terms of his conceptual development and of his vocabulary, he was not yet ready for his first reading primer. Desire to learn to read is not an adequate criterion for readiness, and initial enthusiasm is soon dissipated if it is not followed by the feelings of achievement which accompany success. Jean-Paul's gradual loss of interest followed a downward spiral of boredom and the feelings of failure that can occur when other aspects of readiness are not taken into account.

Richard   An interesting comparison is the study of Richard. Richard was a happy and confident child who enjoyed taking part in any new activities which arose in the classroom. He was sensitive to other children, and was a leader who often initiated new ideas or enthusiastically participated in those started by other children. His parents were interested in everything that happened in school and cooperated whenever possible. He made easy relationships with adults, enjoyed talking with visitors, and when a special harvest festival was held, helped to look after the old people who were invited.

In all social interactions, his well-developed language skill was apparent, and he used it to clarify his own ideas in discussion with others. These discussions revealed the levels of thinking he had achieved. In Piagetian terms, he demonstrated 'conversation' in his choice of nails to make legs of equal length on a wooden table, and 'seriation' in a description of building a staircase. He showed an understanding of 'balance' in a model boat which had to have centrally placed cargo to prevent it sinking, and of 'energy' in relating the speed of barge-horses to the weight of a barge.

He clearly recognized visual verbal material, both in books and in his own writing, as a means of extending and elaborating his own experiences and thinking. He had made good progress in the reading books used by the school, and constantly referred to those made or provided by the teacher. He was interested in any new words, and when learning their meaning he paid attention to the visual representation. For example, when the word 'trembling' came up in discussion, the teacher explained what it meant, but some of the children were still puzzled. Richard demonstrated its meaning by making his body tremble, later in the day used it to describe the effect of wind on an old house, and then pointed to its use in a poem he read about the wind.

He was a confident reader, and quickly learned new words, although he had difficulty with some small words (for example, 'here', 'is', 'on'), but this only occurred when he was working with printed books. He was not confused in his own writing. He was beginning to use phonic analysis to work out new words. To do this, he used the first letters of words he already knew, to build up his knowledge of sounds. He sometimes confused 'p' with 'b', but again this did not arise when he was analysing his own writing.

The build-up of his reading vocabulary seemed to develop from discussion with adults, then from his own writing; and from this came recognition and the ability to read the words in printed material. The books he made, and the contributions he made to class books, were factual rather than imaginative. For example, he wrote about the members of his family, and about his violin, which he and a friend were learning to play.

For Richard, learning to read progressed satisfactorily because he was able to use language to organize and understand experiences, and was learning skills of reading which enabled him to use visual verbal material for this same purpose. Reading, therefore, was a normal and satisfying activity, to which he gave attention and effort.

In order to give Jean-Paul and Richard appropriate help, their teachers drew on their knowledge of the homes from which these children came. This was particularly important in the case of Jean-Paul for, without it, his apparently obsessive interest in reading, but lack of learning, would have been difficult to understand. With this knowledge, however, the teacher was able to understand the child's anxiety; in order to help allay it, she provided the reading material. At the same time, she encouraged his involvement in the other activities which would give him vocabulary and meanings to bring to the skills of reading.

The pressures exerted by Jean-Paul's parents were doubtless motivated by the best of intentions but, in practice, interfered with his learning, whereas the support given by Richard's parents (which extended to his total life in school, while not directed specifically to reading) helped his progress in this skill, because of the confidence he could bring to it. Parents need help in understanding the multiplicity of factors which influence children's learning. The demonstration of reading skills is often rated highly by parents as an indication of progress in school. Many want to help their children but do not know how to do this. Teachers can indirectly assist children to read by discussing with parents particular ways in which their own child can be helped. Such discussions can extend a teacher's expertise into the home, and a child's progress can be encouraged and not hindered.

2 Learning and Language

How children come to understand symbols

Jean-Paul and Richard's case studies exemplify the wide range of individual differences which will certainly be found in a 'vertically-grouped' class and which are likely to exist in classes grouped by age. These individual differences make it both undesirable and unrealistic to expect all children either to be ready to learn to read at the same time or to progress at the same rate. The examples which follow illustrate how children begin to understand the meanings and functions of visual verbal symbols. Some come to this understanding quite early, for others it is a much slower process:

Franco (five years) had been at school three weeks, had made a number of wooden models, and had asked for them to be displayed. He had observed that some children had written descriptions or stories by their models and paintings.

Franco: I think I would like some writing on this.

Debbie (five years) having seen the teacher write a story under a painting: I want some of those things under *my* picture.

Jimmy (six years) had made a building using large bricks, and took the teacher a flat board which he wanted to be put in front of his building.

Jimmy: I want to put a notice on this.

Teacher: What for?

Jimmy: Well, like a notice when children cross

the road and tells them they shouldn't.

Alan (six years) had made a model car out of wood:
Will you write on some paper that it's mine?

*A class had been making a collection of new words
which were written on a chart and accompanied by
illustrations. A story was told to the children in which
the word 'jerking' occurred, and its meaning was
explained.*

Ashley: That could be a new word to go in our
collection.

Sophie (seven years): I'm making a new word
collection at home, and *I* make pictures too.

Further examples showed how the children
gradually became aware of reading as a skill to be
learned.

*Sharon, in her first term in school, had made a very
creditable attempt at writing.*

Teacher: 'You'll soon be writing, Sharon.

Sharon: Yes, and then I'll be able to read!

The words of Tom, Tom the Piper's Son *were
written in large writing on the wall.*

Ashley (looking at these words): Will you learn
me to read the words of Tom, Tom?

The teacher was sorting some old books.

Lee: I think I could read this one—can I try?,
and, next day: I can remember what I read in that
book yesterday!

*Sophie (picking up a book and showing it to the
teacher):* You know this book? Well, I can read it!

**Words and
letters** Before children can learn specific reading skills,
they must be able to perceive words and letters as
separate units. There were many examples of their

attempts to do this, often in relation to their own writing:

Kerry (pointing to an isolated letter): What is that word?

Franco: I do writing at home, you know. I write 'Look, look see Sally!' (*looks at page in reading book*). I can do *that* number (*pointing to a letter*).

Carlo: Sophie's got a doll's house but it hasn't got a flat roof like this one on our class—it's sort of like this. (*He demonstrates a pointed shape with his hands.*)
Teacher: Is that like any letter you know?
Carlo (goes to display of alphabet in capital letters): Yes, this one, (*points to 'V'*) but it's upside down.

Kerry (looking for box belonging to a younger child, Rosalind, which had her name on it): I can't find it. What letter does 'Rosalind' begin with?

Jimmy (noticing a word that starts with 'a'): That letter starts with 'Alan' and 'apple', doesn't it?

Rosalind: Her name's 'Murphy' and mine's 'Murray'. It starts and ends the same—it's got the same number of letters. Oh! Only two letters are different!

Rachel had written: This is a rabbit hoel, the children have thrown sticks into the hoel. *When the teacher corrected 'hoel' to 'hole', Rachel remarked:* I used the same letters didn't I? But I put the 'e' and 'l' in the wrong place.

An investigation By writing in a child's presence what he dictates, reading it to him and having him read it back, teachers incidentally help children to understand the nature and function of the written symbol. The importance of this understanding is illustrated by

the results of Reid's[1] investigation of a group of
five-year-old children's notions about reading. In
the course of a year, the twelve children in the study
were given three individual interviews, which included questions to elicit the children's understanding of words like 'letter', 'word', and 'sentence', and
to explore their notions of the purpose of reading
and writing. The first interview took place when
none of the children could in fact read. To the
question, 'What is in books?', only one child replied
that books contained words, many referred to
pictures. There were many instances of confusions
between letters and numbers. Reid writes, 'It became obvious from the children's comments and
from what they later wrote that the term (numbers) was being used to mean "letters and numerals" or even just "letters".' Kerry and Franco were
in just this confusion. To the request, 'Can you
write something for me?', some of the children
were able to respond by writing a simple word or a
simple sentence obviously recalled from their reading primers. However, some of those who were able
to do so, clearly had no awareness that what they
had written conveyed meaning.

The confusions that children make between
words, letters and numbers, and the inadequate
notions they entertain of the function of written
language, are less likely when children's initial
reading material is written in their presence. Reid's
findings suggest developmental stages in children's
understanding of the inter-relationships of written
symbols and of their function. The children apparently moved from an initial confusion between
graphic symbols, numbers, letters, and words, to a
stage where they came to understand that language
and pictures are two kinds of symbol, that numbers
and letters are sub-classes of the class of written
symbols, that capital letters are a sub-class of the
class 'letters', and that 'names' are a sub-class of
the class 'words'. They only gradually became
aware of the relationship between oral and written
language. Reid implies that the development of

[1] Learning to think
about Reading by
J. F. Reid.
EDUCATIONAL
RESEARCH 1966, 9,
56–62

these increasingly refined categorizations of written language, is related to children's conceptual development generally. The case study of Richard certainly gave evidence of such a relationship. It will be remembered that he had quite advanced concepts, in, for example, 'seriation' and 'conversation'. (See page 389).

Sounds The realization that letters not only have names, but also sounds, is a further refinement required of children, and is more complex because of the range of sounds which can be related to any one letter. The following examples illustrate ways in which some of the children used varying strategies to analyse and synthesize letter sounds:

Kerry: I'm going to read the story under my picture. What does it say?

Teacher: Rosie the . . . what?

Kerry: I think it says 'Rosie the guinea big'—is that word 'big'? I don't *think* it is.

Kerry: Oh, that word says 'what' and that says 'want'!

Teacher: If I take the 'D' away, what does 'Dick' say?

Kerry: '-ick', and if you put a 'pu' on—no a 'up', then it's 'ick-up'!

Kerry was reading and came across the word 'tulip' which she was unable to read.

Teacher: Look (*covering up parts of the word*), there's 'tu' and there's 'lip'.

Kerry: Oh, if you can spell 'lip' *and* 'tu', then you can spell 'tulip' can't you?'

Edward: I know 'lorry' and that word ends the same way (*sounds c . . . a . . .*)—it must be 'carry'!

Sarah: That says 'Tim' not 'Time'. Oh, I add an 'e' on the end and it changes the sound!

Anthony: Isn't the English language stupid? 'ch' should say 'ch' but it doesn't in 'Christmas' or 'Charlotte'!

The teacher's observation (described on page 394) that Jimmy noticed that 'Alan' and 'apple' began with the same letter, and of Rosalind discovering that 'Murphy' and 'Murray' began and ended with the same letters, showed her awareness of the need to diagnose children's progress in phonic differentiation. The description of the teacher's questions to Kerry about the spelling of 'tulip' is an example of how she followed her diagnosis with specific help in phonic analysis. The importance of a developing awareness of differences, as well as similarities, is illustrated in Anthony's discovery that 'ch' could have different sounds.

Different processes
Initially, the unit of measuring is the sentence. From this children progress to discriminating single words, in different contexts and out of context. A further step in analysis is made when children recognize and discriminate phonic constituents, at first, normally, the initial sounds of words, and, later, more complex phonic elements and those coming in the middle or at the ends of words. The examples which have been detailed demonstrate this development, and it has been shown how teachers gave individual children instruction in phonic analysis when they indicated by their spontaneous comments or by replies to questions, that they were able to make the relevant discriminations.

Reading includes a number of different processes. Motivation is clearly necessary, but so also are language development, intellectual development generally and perceptual discrimination. All these processes need to be present and inter-related if a child is to progress. The importance of this inter-relatedness is indicated in a study by Clay[1] in which she investigated the progress in learning to read of a hundred children aged 5.0 to 5.2 on entry to school. Samples of their reading behaviour were taken once a week during their first year at school, and these records were analysed at the end of the year. The children who made most satisfactory progress in learning to read were those who became aware of dissonance between what they read and one of several 'messages' from the text. It might be that what the child said did not make grammatical sense. It might be that what was read was meaningless, or that there was a clear conflict between the meaning of what was read and the context or the illustration. The records of the children who made most progress showed that they were aware of such dissonances and corrected their own errors (like Kerry, see page 396).

Self-corrective behaviour is, of course, only possible if children's development in each of the processes of perceptual discrimination and of the syntactic and semantic aspects of language, is sufficient for these to be inter-related. Jean-Paul's initial failures occurred partly because his language was insufficiently developed for this complex thinking which self-correction of reading errors implies. His attention was confined to the perceptual mechanics of reading, and he could not pay attention to the meaning of what he read.

Many teachers of young children have experienced the disappointment either of finding children, returning after a vacation, unable to read a great many of the words they had apparently mastered before, or of seeing children progress to a limited point in reading, and then coming to a standstill. In both cases it is likely that such children, like Jean-Paul, were relying only on a single process, probably perceptual imagery, instead of on the multiple inter-related processes which Clay's study suggests are more desirable. If children can call only on visual imagery in reading, what is memorized on this level is likely to be forgotten

[1] *Reading Errors and Self-Correction Behaviour* by M. Clay. BRITISH JOURNAL OF EDUCATIONAL PSYCHOLOGY. 1969, 39, 47–56

after a vacation. There is also likely to be an upper limit to the memory load, and a child then ceases to make further progress.

3 The Teacher's Role

Jean-Paul came to school well motivated, but immature in respect of other factors necessary for learning to read. Sometimes teachers are worried by children who present the converse problem: having reached an adequate level in respect of language and conceptual development, they yet lack motivation. For such children, experiences have to be devised which will make them want to read. Most children have had such experiences as a normal part of their home life, and, even if not already able to read before coming to school, they pay attention to print, and are eager to master the skills which will enable them to interpret it. Other children, however, have not built up such anticipations, and all will need both opportunities and help if their use of written and printed language is to develop. The teacher is central to this development; the examples given earlier demonstrate the importance of other children (for discussion, help, and so on), but their contribution is secondary to that of the teacher.

In the early stages of reading, children seem to need physical contact with an adult, and every teacher of five-year-olds is familiar with the way in which a child leans against her, or maybe holds her hand or finger, while constantly looking into her face for reassurance as he attempts to read. The printed page only slowly becomes a source of information separate from the teacher—and, even as adults, most of us need to discuss with others a book we have enjoyed. Certainly, in classrooms where it is possible, children constantly take books to the teacher, to ask questions or to share information.

Teaching children to read is a skilled undertaking. Emphasis has been placed on establishing satisfying relationships between individual children and the teacher, in an environment which provides stimulus and opportunities to read, but more is necessary. Examples have been given of children developing perception of details and relationships in verbal material. The significance of these comments and questions was recognized by the teachers because they themselves had knowledge of the analytic and synthetic processes required in reading. Many children need more help than simply reading to an adult. A teacher's contribution to this is partly a diagnostic one, that is: to recognize a child's skills in reading, and the strategies he employs when confronted with an unknown word. It was discussed earlier how these strategies become refined as a result of developing mental ability and increasing experiences of reading material. A teacher, therefore, encourages efficient strategies, and gives clues appropriate to a child's stage of development. This involves the recognition of inaccuracies or confusions which are a normal outcome of a child's learning. Such inaccuracies were treated by the teacher described earlier, not as unfortunate mistakes which should never occur, but rather as diagnostic clues which could be used to help the children. Reid's research (described on page 395) showed that children confused numbers and letters. The examples of Kerry and Franco (see page 394) demonstrate this, and it seems clear that this particular error results from a child's own attempts to organize and refine graphic symbols. Compare this with the case of a five-year-old who had been given a primer when starting school, and had been trying for several weeks to read it. When presented with the phrase 'Here is Dick', he correctly read 'Here is—' and then guessed 'a ball? . . . a boy?'. In this instance the confusion arose from an attempt to recall a piece of rote learning imprinted by a teacher who had not recognized the child's inability to differentiate separate words. Richard's teacher had noted that his approach to new visual vocabulary was first through discussion, then through writing it himself, and finally through recognizing it in print (see page 389). This observation enabled her to use the child's own progression when introducing new words, which not only ensured that meanings were built into his reading skills, but also that, when writing, he paid attention to the particular arrangement of letters which made up the words he learned.

When classes may contain forty or more children, it might seem almost impossible for a teacher to encompass satisfactorily both the meaningful and diagnostic aspects of learning to read. Overlarge classes inevitably militate against efficient learning, but in the classes described earlier, this possibility was greatly reduced because the children were offered so many learning opportunities, both in the materials provided and in the time available for their use. The children were highly motivated to learn, had a variety of skills at their disposal, and were accustomed to working, and to helping each other. As a result, the teachers could be available to individual children, and could give the particular help needed by those who were learning to read and to write.

Reading and writing are often called 'skills' and sometimes 'basic skills'. Perhaps the term 'skills' is unfortunate, for it may imply that reading and writing are in the same category as perceptual-motor skills like learning to skate or ride a bicycle. We have tried to emphasize that satisfactory progress in reading requires more than a perceptual response: it requires also that meanings should be decoded. A level of language development which will ensure decoding for meanings is therefore a vital element in reading-readiness. Goodacre[1] investigated the characteristics of development named by headteachers and class teachers as signs of reading-readiness. Characteristics concerned with interest in books and the printed word, and keenness to learn to read, accounted for 48.5 per

[1] READING TO INFANT CLASSES by E. J. Goodacre, NFER 1969

cent of the items, and characteristics concerned with perceptual abilities for 13.2 per cent, while language development scored only 6.3 per cent, and intellectual ability 3.4 per cent. It has become clear, in the light of evidence like that of Clay's and Reid's studies, that, although perceptual-motor abilities are essential to the acquisition of these skills, there are also conceptual elements. Children may learn to read and to write in ways which ignore these conceptual aspects and rely on associate types of learning, but these are likely to lead to skills which are not basic in the sense that children will use them to read for information and enjoyment and to write in order to communicate, but are, on the contrary, divorced from these ends. In the work described, the conceptual elements of these skills are taken into account, and reading for meaning, and writing to communicate meaningfully are essential characteristics. What is more, these children were discovering that books could not only give them information and extend their understanding of the world, but were also a source of aesthetic satisfaction and enjoyment. Similarly, writing was not only a useful means of communication but also a satisfying medium of expression. To be able to read and to write, therefore, were highly valued because each could add a new dimension to the child's world.

Further Reading

Lovell, K. AN INTRODUCTION TO HUMAN DEVELOPMENT (Chapter four) Macmillan (second edition) 1969

Luria, A. R. THE ROLE OF SPEECH IN THE REGULATION OF NORMAL AND ABNORMAL BEHAVIOUR Pergamon Press 1961; Liveright, New York 1961

See also AN INTRODUCTION, FROM HOME TO SCHOOL, RECORDING CHILDREN'S PROGRESS, SPACE, TIME AND GROUPING, AN INFANT SCHOOL, EDUCATING TEACHERS, A JUNIOR SCHOOL, A RURAL SCHOOL, ENVIRONMENTAL STUDIES in this series.

Music

John Horton

The Author

John Horton taught for five years in elementary schools, after which he taught English and music in secondary schools, and took degrees in these subjects. In 1937 he was appointed to the BBC to take charge of music broadcasts for schools. In 1947 he was appointed His Majesty's Inspector of Schools, and in 1959 became Staff Inspector of Music. Since his retirement in 1967 he has acted as part-time teacher of music in a technical college and in a teacher-training institution, as external examiner to institutes of education, and as secretary to the Music Committee of the Schools Council.

He has published numerous books and articles on the history of music and music education. In 1968 he compiled, on behalf of UNESCO, a world bibliography of music education.

The references on page 432–5 refer to the record which accompanies the paperback booklet of this section.

Acknowledgements

The author acknowledges with gratitude the help received from members of the teaching profession who supplied recordings and photographs, answered questions and arranged visits to their schools; from advisers and inspectors who discussed the project at various stages, orally and in writing, and also supplied illustrative material; and from the BBC and publishing organizations who gave similar assistance. Particular thanks are due to the following:

Mr K. A. Antcliffe, Director of Education, County Borough of Brighton, and the Headmaster and staff of Patcham Junior School, Brighton.

Mr. J. Gavall, Music Adviser, West Riding of Yorkshire Education Committee.

Mr J. Hollingworth, Senior Music Adviser, Devon Education Committee.

Mr P. N. Davies, Music Adviser, City of Southampton Education Committee.

Mr K. L. Shaw, Music Adviser, West Suffolk Education Committee.

Mr D. J. Wells, Music Adviser, Hertfordshire Education Committee.

Miss M. Pape, Headmistress, Ivydale Infant School, Nunhead, London SE15.

Mr J. Enticknap, Headmaster, and Mr P. Morris, Hookstone Chase Junior Mixed and Infant School, Harrogate, Yorks.

Mr J. D. Colleer, Headmaster, Potkiln Junior School, West Suffolk.

Mr M. L. T. Williams, Headmaster, and Mrs S. Jackson-Smith, Christchurch Junior School, Christchurch, Hants.

Mr F. G. Smith, Headmaster, and Mr H. Hersom, Ambler Junior School, London N4.

Mr Bennett, Headmaster, and members of the staff of Teague's Bridge Junior School, Salop.

Miss C. Hudson, Drew Street Primary School, Brixham, Devon.

Miss V. A. P. Jones, Organizing Teacher, Salop Education Committee.

Miss V. Gray, Mr A. Chatterley, and other members of the staff of School Broadcasting Department, British Broadcasting Corporation.

Mr R. R. Roberts (Staff Inspector of Music at the Department of Education and Science) and the following other members of HM Inspectorate: Miss J. M. Sykes, Mr W. Drabble, Mr W. H. Parry, Mr I. P. Salisbury, Mr J. W. Stephens, Dr E. F. A. Suttle, Mr G. E. Trodd, Miss Warner.

Material for the accompanying record has been selected with the help of members of HM Inspectorate, and recorded in co-operation with the teaching staff and pupils of the following schools:

Ivydale Infants   Christchurch Junior
Teague's Bridge Junior   Hookstone Chase Junior

The extract from R. M. Thackray's CREATIVE MUSIC IN EDUCATION is reproduced here with the permission of the publishers, Novello & Company Ltd. The extracts from the Teachers' Notes which accompanied the Spring 1971 BBC Series of MUSIC CLUB and the Autumn 1969 BBC Series of MOVEMENT, MIME AND MUSIC, Stage 2 are reproduced with the permission of BBC Publications Ltd.

1 Music and the Curriculum

Although on historical grounds music can claim to be one of the foundation subjects of the English primary school curriculum, it is still in the process of revealing its educational possibilities to the full. Whereas in some older cultures, both primitive and sophisticated, the creative and performing arts have occupied a central position in community life, the tendency in more recent Western societies has been to relegate them to the periphery and to treat them as luxuries, as pastimes and diversions, as means of recreation after physical and intellectual effort, and even—to use the word sometimes applied to the arts, including music, by responsible educationists within living memory—as little more than frills, elegantly but unnecessarily adorning the fabric of learning.

New place in the curriculum

Now at last, music is beginning to come into its own as an essential part of that fabric, with unique educative functions for which no other subject or discipline can be a substitute. It has its own role to play within the philosophy of learning by discovery, since the universe of sound invites exploration no less than those of sight and the other senses. The production and selection of sounds, and their arrangement in significant patterns and structures, call both for instinctive response and for rational decisions, and entail the development of a variety of skills, many of which are acquired most rapidly and permanently in childhood.

Music can be one of the most subjective and intimate expressions of the individual personality, and as such has been valued from time immemorial as a life-enhancing medium, and not seldom as a therapeutic agent. But it is also an art of communication and social coherence, enabling members of a group to establish sympathetic contact with one another with minimal need for the intervention of verbal language. This process can be observed, as it were under laboratory conditions, in the music corners of the modern infant school and in the kind of group music activities that develop in some open-plan junior schools.

It would be wrong, however, to regard music as merely a self-sufficient medium of personal and social expression and communication. Its present position in the curriculum owes much to a growing appreciation of its relationships with other vital areas of human experience, including verbal language and the sister arts of movement, dance and drama.

Up to the end of the nineteenth century, music in the English elementary school almost invariably meant choral singing. The concept of the music lesson as a full-class activity not only accorded with the teaching methods used in other subjects at that time, but also reproduced in miniature the nation-wide institution of the choral society. Some of the more privileged children, it is true, received individual instruction—usually in piano playing— but the school had little to do with this; it was arranged and paid for by parents and went on mainly in the front parlours of private teachers. One of the interesting aspects of contemporary music-teaching is the tendency for the school and private sectors to overlap and often merge with each other. The breaking down of the large class unit into small working groups allows for a considerable measure of individual teaching, some of which may be given by a visiting teacher employed by the education authority. At the same time the growth of the so-called junior music schools, usually meeting on school premises but outside official class hours, provides extra voluntary teaching for children with special talent or interest. In most cases the visiting or 'peripatetic' teachers and those who staff the junior music schools are drawn from the kind of specialists who in former days would have been carrying on their work privately and in isolation from the schools where their pupils were in full-time education.

Such welcome developments have helped to give a period quaintness to well-authenticated stories of children asking permission to leave the singing class in order to attend their 'music lesson'. But it would be true to say that the choral tradition of the elementary school[1] has by no means been discarded in the primary school of today. In fact most teachers, including those with wide experience in the new media that became available from the turn of the century onwards, remain convinced that music education, at the primary stage at least, should have singing as its basis. Many would go further and say that some of the old-established class-singing techniques, such as those evolved by John Curwen, can still be made relevant to modern needs. This belief has been strengthened by the systems of training in basic musicianship and the creative use of voice and instruments which have emanated from other countries during the past few decades. The widely-studied Carl Orff method, for example, is fundamentally vocal; instruments figure prominently in it, but their real function is to imitate and enrich the rhythms and intonations of speech and song. The Kodaly method has an even firmer vocal foundation, and is closely related to the English tradition, being a brilliant synthesis of John Curwen's class-singing principles, continental solfège, and Hungarian folk music. The Ward method draws most of its study material from pure unaccompanied song in the forms of Gregorian chant and folk song.

All these methods are presented through their literature in ways that make it feasible for the all-round, non-specialist classroom teacher to follow them confidently and effectively. For this reason they appeal to many reared in the class-singing

[1]Before the 1944 Education Act came into operation the majority of children were educated in elementary schools catering for children between the ages of five and eleven, eleven and fourteen, or, in many cases, five and fourteen

411

tradition, since that too was largely carried on by non-specialists with musical interests. It must be remembered also that the subject specialist is almost as much of an anomaly in the modern primary setting as he was in the older elementary school. Even when a musician is a full-time member of a primary school staff, he is, more often than not, active in other areas of the curriculum.

The non-specialist character of most primary music teaching is one of the factors that has to be borne in mind in any scheme of professional training, and if, as we have suggested, the principal medium for musical experience at the primary stage will continue to be the voice, everything possible must be done to encourage teachers of young children to sing in an easy, natural way and to build up their own repertoire of nursery and folk songs which will form the basis of musical communication and creation in the infant and junior school. In the accounts and examples that follow, the central position of singing will be taken for granted, though we shall pay attention to ways in which it may be combined with other forms of expression.

Music and movement

With this proviso, we may now turn to some of the directions in which the scope of primary school music has been extended beyond the limited though valuable class singing lesson. One of the earliest advances, and also one of the first steps in breaking down the barriers between school subjects, was the combination of music with bodily movement. Just after the beginning of the present century, Cecil Sharp's revival of the traditional English dances helped to reveal the connexion between rhythmic physical movement and musical phrasing and form. Soon afterwards the eurhythmics of Jaques-Dalcroze provided a detailed and progressive scheme of music education founded on gesture and movement. In the middle years of the century the school broadcasts of Ann Driver, who applied

Dalcroze principles to a wider range of imaginative ideas in both movement and music, had considerable influence, while other systems like the modern educational dance developed by Laban and his followers laid rather more emphasis on movement techniques. In the primary school today, the English tendency towards synthesis and eclecticism can be nowhere observed better than in the flexibility of the music-and-movement partnership; not only are elements taken from different systems including those already mentioned, but other sectors of the curriculum are becoming involved. Drama is particularly liable to overlap with movement; language and the visual arts and crafts are frequently laid under contribution; and ideas for creative music are found in the areas of traditional subject divisions like history, nature study, and religious education. It is, in fact, a leading principle of the contemporary primary school that the performing and creative arts derive inspiration and momentum from the rest of the curriculum and, in their turn, fertilize and invigorate all other areas of education.

Since BBC school broadcasts not only give a nation-wide lead to the exploration of fresh approaches to learning but also act as a barometer of current trends in educational thinking, it may be instructive to glance at the illustrated leaflet of Teachers' Notes supplied, in connexion with a junior series (ages nine to eleven) for autumn 1969. The title of the series, MOVEMENT, MIME AND MUSIC, Stage 2, has a special significance. The first and third of these Ms have been linked in school broadcasting for more than thirty years, and the BBC still runs two MUSIC AND MOVEMENT series catering for the youngest children of school age, and having a registered audience of over ninety per cent of all the infant schools in the country. The addition of the middle term MIME in the junior title points to a still wider field of reference; in the actual series here described the programmes are placed in a setting of archaeological discovery, and involve associated follow-up work in art and craft, history and science, and verbal composition. These broadcasts, the notes explain, are designed to:

(a) *provide twenty minutes during which children are stimulated physically and mentally by a wide variety of musical and dramatic movement;*

(b) *stimulate a wide range of activities in art, craft, library research, English, science, and so on;*

(c) *act as a confidence builder—especially for children unable to shine during more formal lessons.*

The musical material used in these broadcasts includes African drums, radiophonic sound-patterns, and works by Bizet, Mussorgsky, and Villa-Lobos. And here it may be noted parenthetically that one of the most beneficial effects of the development of the movement-music partnership has been the greatly increased range of good music, and especially good twentieth-century music (both serious and light), provided for children to move to, and hence to listen to repeatedly until its style and structure are familiar. It is becoming less and less surprising to find a record of such a work as Milhaud's LA CREATION DU MONDE (to quote an example from recent observation) on a primary school record player.

Musical appreciation In this way movement has introduced a new dimension to what was formerly called 'musical appreciation', though the term seems to be falling out of use and there must be a growing number of young teachers who have hardly known it. The appreciation movement began during the inter-war period when educationists like Percy Scholes and Walford Davies urged the need for training in listening as an essential component in a well-balanced scheme of school music. Its progress was hastened by the increased accessibility of both light and serious music, brought about by the mechanical media, and partic-

An infant group singing, with some help from one of their number at a small electronic organ

ularly radio and gramophone. It has not always been easy to avoid too academic and formal an approach to musical appreciation in the classroom. Presentation has often become either too analytical or too subjective, with over-much reliance on narrative or pictorial aspects. There has not always been a strong enough thread of connexion between the appreciation lesson and the performing and creative aspects. The capacity of most young children, and indeed of many older children, to listen passively for more than a minute or so at a stretch has sometimes been over-estimated. The range of material thought suitable has been unduly restricted in period and style, and has too often excluded the best popular and 'entertainment' music of the present day.

Variety of material

Here we may again digress to observe that one of the healthiest aspects of our primary music teaching at its best is its catholic but critical attitude towards the choice of material for singing, playing and listening. The sheer quantity available can itself be stimulating; teachers in one infant school were able to draw upon no fewer than seventy different collections of songs for young children. Nor is the repertory restricted to the contents of publications designed expressly for school use. Younger teachers especially, many of whom have themselves grown up in a musical environment of popular song, guitar, and a small supporting group of voices or instruments (rather than in the choral and keyboard environment of their predecessors), are prepared to use any song or instrumental piece, recorded or live, that seems to them vital and appropriate, regardless, or in some cases because of, its freedom from educational intention or association.

Folk music, as already noted, made its entry into English elementary education at the turn of the century, though on a comparatively narrow front, almost entirely restricted, as it then was, to the traditional songs of the British islands. Since that time the folk revival has undergone a dramatic transformation. It has become in every sense popular, with its leading exponents ranking high in the world of commercially-sponsored entertainment; it is no longer backward-looking but is genuinely part of the contemporary scene; and above all it is international and inter-racial. The spring 1971 BBC schools radio series MUSIC SESSION, intended for ages 11–13, included the traditional Australian round, *Kookaburra,* the African *Asikatali* from the repertory of the Spinners, the West Indian *Adam in the Garden* from the same source, the Israeli *Donna Donna* popularized by Joan Baez, the African round *Wimoweh* associated with Pete Seeger, and Tom Paxton's song in folk idiom, *This world goes round and round.*

Another aspect of popular music which the modern teacher is tending more and more to take in his stride is the chordal but non-academic harmony of the vocal and instrumental 'group', conditioned, as much of it is, by the tunings and frets of the guitar family. Harmony, formerly treated as an esoteric mystery to be understood and practised only by a gifted minority, and seldom making an appearance on the educational scene until most children were about to leave it, is now brought into the junior classroom, where it is taught not as a specialized discipline but as one of the normal dimensions of music, with the aid of such instruments as chime bars, sorted into chord-formations and played by teams of children; the ingenious and inexpensive 'Roberts' instruments (to be referred to later); and various combinations of 'Orff' type instruments which lend themselves particularly well to the sort of rhythmic *ostinato* that is a common feature of folk and pop settings in commercial entertainment music.

Familiarity with a wide range of styles, both popular and sophisticated, is enabling the teacher to infuse much greater rhythmic interest into classroom music. To give but one example, a very mild syncopation introduced into one bar of a school song by a staid English composer in the early decades of this century was discreetly removed by teachers who feared it might confuse the children. A similar rhythm occurs not once but continuously throughout an enjoyable and successful piece of modern classroom music, Brian Bonsor's *Beguine*. Latin-American and Afro-American rhythms, in fact, are assured of success in the junior school, while among other sources of rhythmic renewal that may be mentioned is the growing western interest, which of course many teachers share, in the musical idioms and styles of Indian and Indonesian cultures.

The use in an educational context of any music merely because it happens to be labelled 'popular' may, however, amount to an over-simplification that is no more to be defended than would be an adherence to a conventional school music repertory. Much commercially-backed popular music, and particularly the species known universally as 'pop', is so closely bound up with teenage culture and social communication, and by its nature has so brief a life-span, that it may actually prove

A

irrelevant to the primary school, even if not out-
moded by the time it reaches the classroom. The
teenage world, classless and international though
it is, does not always welcome the intrusion either
of the adult or of the pre-adolescent child. Against
this, it has to be remembered that the age of puberty
is tending to fall, and already includes many children in the upper end of the primary school, though
even these may not necessarily want to wear in the
primary classroom the musical badge of their
initiation. Nor can it be assumed that children will
want to sing, play, and hear in school the selfsame
tunes that come to them by way of the domestic
radio, television, and record player. An exclusive
pop approach, therefore, can be as dogmatic and
unimaginative as the most slavish adherence to
educational tradition. The situation has been
admirably summed up in the Spring 1971 set of
Teachers' Notes for the BBC radio series MUSIC
CLUB. (These broadcasts are intended for the age-
range thirteen to sixteen, but the same considera-
tions can be applied to the junior school):

*One thing which always seems to bother teachers
is how much one can, or ought to, introduce pop music
into the field (of musical activity). The trouble is that
our cultural situation tends towards the presentation
of music in watertight compartments—classical or
serious, pop, jazz, light, and so on—and that not only
does this encourage sectarian attitudes, but it makes
cross fertilization difficult and is a very unserviceable
method of working in a classroom situation. It is nearer
the mark, surely, to say that there are as many cate-
gories as there are pieces of music, and no music should
be excluded from a teaching situation on the grounds
that its category is unsuitable, but only on the grounds
that it is unsuitable material.*

It is largely due to the influence of broadcasting
and the other mechanical media of communication
that, while there is now more listening to music in
the primary school than ever before, this is no

longer contained within the artificial boundaries of the 'appreciation' lesson. At the same time, the mechanical aids are extending the range of their contribution to music teaching. The gramophone record, for example, can be an effective and enjoyable means of learning a song, especially in the infant school, where recordings of nursery songs are a boon to the classroom teacher with modest performing abilities. The tape recorder has proved indispensable in the primary school, not only for taping broadcast programmes for use at any convenient time during the week, but also in connexion with the creative approaches to be described later. It is not too much to say that work along creative lines would be stifled and frustrated without the help that tape recording can give both teacher and children. Some of our recorded examples of children's original composition illustrate musical ideas of a rhythmic subtlety which few teachers, and only the very exceptional child, could have written down on paper in conventional notation.

2 Instrumental Music

Development of instrumental music

Another major development during the inter-war period was the introduction of instrumental music both as a part of general classroom music teaching and also in the form of extra-curricular group instruction. Paradoxically this movement started with the violin, an instrument that sets more technical problems for pupil and teacher than perhaps any other. Yet the reasons for its priority are not difficult to account for. The string family was, at least up to the middle of this century, the basic ensemble and the mainstay of the orchestra; the violin was in demand for amateur music-making; adult string instructors were relatively easy to come by, and a serviceable violin could be bought more cheaply than most other serious instruments. There was also the advantage that the techniques of string playing had been minutely studied for generations and that some able teachers believed it possible to devise step-by-step systems for imparting the skills of bowing and fingering through group instruction. A few even attempted to carry out this process in the full-sized singing class with its wide spread of ability and aptitude. Such experiments were usually short-lived, and the teaching group of six to eight pupils became the normal unit for beginners, the group being withdrawn from the main class or taken separately during the lunch hour or other out-of-class period. String teaching is nowadays usually given by a peripatetic teacher who has studied his instrument professionally and is employed on a full-time basis by the local education authority. It must also be said, however, that some of the best results in primary string playing have been achieved under established members of the school staff, who while not being themselves advanced performers are sensitive to musical values and have learnt, probably by attending part-time courses, to apply their general teaching experience to the special problems of instrumental tuition.

In any case, the closest cooperation between full-time school staff, peripatetic specialists, and local authority advisory services is essential if the group teaching of instruments is to justify the time and effort spent on it. One important question is the age at which tuition should begin. The first year of the junior school (average age: about eight years old) is generally considered ideal, though there have been instances of a successful start in the last year of the infant school.[1] Another point to decide is at what stage group instruction passes the peak of its usefulness, and needs to give place to individual methods—a problem involving administrative issues too complex to discuss here.

The importance of singing, and ear-training through the use of the voice, as a background to learning instruments, has not always been given enough attention by string teachers. Another factor contributing to ease and effectiveness in junior ensemble playing is the choice of suitable material. It is necessary for elementary string parts to be not only technically acceptable but also musically interesting.

Of recent years the universal popularity of the guitar in serious and light music has extended into the school. Some primary teachers use it in preference to the piano for accompanying singing groups, not the least of its merits from this point of view being the greater mobility of the teacher in the classroom, the closer contact obtainable with the children, and the more informal atmosphere produced. Furthermore, the possibilities of the guitar, as an instrument for junior children to play, are being recognized and some local authorities are appointing guitar teachers (at present in regrettably short supply in England) to give group instruction.

[1] The Suzuki method of violin teaching, which involves starting in early infancy is currently being investigated in England by the Rural Music Schools Association

421

Although the bowed and plucked stringed instruments are not, in the accepted sense, class instruments, they lend themselves to absorption into the kind of mixed classroom ensemble that is often found in the primary school. But before describing this characteristic development, two more types of instrument should be mentioned, which from their first introduction have proved their value in a variety of class situations, though they yield even better results when used with smaller groupings. These are the recorders and the percussion ensemble.

The recorder One can write with almost unqualified enthusiasm about the revival of the recorder or 'English flute' during the period following the 1944 reorganization. As a musical instrument the recorder already had a long life-history behind it, and had acquired its own repertory. It was really a whole family of instruments, of which the descant member was found the most convenient for the fingers of junior children, though later experience showed that the larger sizes were not beyond some pupils still in the primary school. Other advantages were that the descant and treble instruments could be manufactured cheaply but accurately in plastics; the sounds were formed and controlled in ways that could be related to the principles of tone production, intonation, and phrasing, learned in the singing class; the recorder combined admirably with string and percussion ensembles; it not only provided a ready means of learning to read notation but also, because of its versatility in part-playing, gave strong motivation towards acquiring musical literacy. Once again, as in the case of the strings, step-by-step teaching methods were devised, some of them so clearly set out with photographic illustrations that many junior children virtually taught themselves in their spare time at home, thereby incidentally interesting their parents, some of whom acquired and practised recorders themselves. For teachers, the success of the recorder brought a

Younger juniors experimenting with recorder and soprano xylophone, while the tambourine player considers further possibilities

fuller realization of how much a young child might achieve in the way of exploring sounds and acquiring performing and reading skills.

The percussion ensemble

The percussion ensemble has a somewhat longer history in primary education than the recorder, making its first appearance at a time when, even in infant schools, the large class was still the normal teaching unit. The intention was to give every member of the class a means of taking part in an instrumental performance, while at the same time developing his ability to hear what was going on in a musical texture, and to relate both what he heard and what he himself played to scores and parts displayed on charts or, at a more advanced stage, in individual printed parts. The instruments were miniature reproductions of the percussion of the classical symphony orchestra—triangle, cymbals, small and large drum (but not timpani)—plus one or two extras like castanets. As none of these were pitched instruments, a musical basis had to be provided by the teacher playing the piano, or from a gramophone disc. In either case it was the adult performer—pianist or conductor—who dictated tempo, volume, and style of interpretation. The percussion band, as it was called, laboured under other disadvantages. The instruments were not only unpitched but also restricted in tone-colour, any subtler qualities of timbre they possessed being obscured by the multiplication of instruments of the same kind in a large class. Nor was the combination of percussion, often with instruments of indifferent workmanship, and piano or recorded orchestra, always aesthetically satisfying. Moreover the rhythmic vocabulary used in the prepared scores was arbitrarily restricted and was seldom related to the children's experience of singing and movement. Unfortunately also, 'the band' was most commonly prescribed as an activity for infant classes, where the children were too young to take part in this type of disciplined team-work under adult direction, thinly disguised though this direction might be by the appointment of a juvenile 'conductor'.

Used with junior classes, especially if larger instruments of superior quality could be obtained, the percussion movement was more fruitful, and in time the addition of pitched or melodic percussion made it possible to bring about a transition to the more flexible and satisfying ensemble-playing now general in the primary school. The standard instruments of the old percussion band, instead of being employed for massed performance, were now shared out among the various music corners and activity groups as required. To them were added pitched percussion—glockenspiels, tubular bells, xylophones and so on—whose advent amounted to another breakthrough in music education, not only because the new instruments greatly enriched the performing resources but also because they were accompanied by, and indeed partly arose from, important discoveries about learning processes in general.

This development began with experimentation in the infant school with all kinds of materials, not excepting those related to the sense of hearing. Thus pitch and tone-quality of wooden and metal objects of different sizes and densities were compared, water was poured to different levels in bottles or jam jars and pitch changes noted, bars or rods of metal and wood were arranged in series to form musical scales. The chime-bar, really a single glockenspiel note mounted on its own resonator, appeared on the market and could be collected note by note until a complete pentatonic, diatonic or chromatic range was available. Sets of chime-bars could be used by one child or shared out among several, and were found to lend themselves not only to melodic playing but also to the improvisation of *ostinato* figures and to the building up of chords. A college of education lecturer, combining the skills of craftsman and musician, devised a whole series of stringed and percussion instruments based on folk and medieval prototypes. These can be constructed cheaply, but up to a high standard of workmanship, by an adult or by secondary school pupils, using published working drawings. The 'Roberts' instruments, as they are familiarly called, have opened up new paths in group instrumental improvisation in the primary school, not least through their harmonic possibilities. The inventor, describing the construction and purpose of these instruments, makes the good point that musical instruments have always been treasured possessions, especially if they are visually as well as aurally attractive. He mentions instances of primary children gaining so much affection for an instrument that they refuse to part with it when they transfer to the secondary school.

Another important range of percussion instruments, both pitched and unpitched is that associated with the Carl Orff method of music education. The principles, as well as the extensive literature and the characteristic instrumentarium of the Orff SCHULWERK are so well known throughout the world that there is no need to describe them in detail. Their impact on the English primary school has been both direct and indirect. Some teachers have gone to the fountainhead and have made Orff's

teachings and those of his disciples the focus of
their class work. Others are adding Orff-type instruments to their other resources but are applying the
method more freely, to musical material of their
own choice. The Orff method in fact finds many
echoes in tendencies that have been at work in
English primary music during the last two decades,
if not longer. Among these are a wider concept of
rhythm, involving bodily movement and speech as
well as metrical time, the liberation of melody from
the nineteenth-century confines of major and
minor, the use of pentatonic, modal and other types
of scale occurring in folk and non-European music,
harmonization by means of *ostinati*, pedals, and
parallel block chords rather than by orthodox
classical procedures, and a heightened interest in
the timbres and dynamics of sounds for their own
sake. This enlargement of musical perceptiveness is

not only enriching the scope of music for children in school, but also bringing music education into a closer relationship with aspects of contemporary music in the world outside. Above all, the Orff method underlines the importance of the creative as well as the performing element in music education, at all stages from the nursery and infant school onwards, and it is in this field that some of the most revolutionary advances have been taking place.

3 Creative work in music

Until fairly recently, school education, in dealing with the arts, concentrated chiefly on analytical study, on imitation, and, in the case of drama and music, on performance. Just as objects were drawn with pencil or brush, poems memorized and recited, and plays read and acted, so music was sung or played according to the composer's written directions, plus such interpretative insight as the conductor or teacher might bring to bear on it. The arts of movement, dance and drama were the first to break away from the domination of performance and to assert the claims of the individual imagination to find direct expression through the media. The visual arts followed, largely through the pioneer work of Marion Richardson in the 1920s. By this time, it was already beginning to be asked, though among educationists at large rather than among teacher-musicians, if some comparable road to musical expression could be found, by-passing if necessary some of the more difficult techniques of performance, composition, and the handling of notational complexities, which appeared to rule out creativeness in the art of music except for a gifted few.

The answer usually given—and it was one that contained a measure of reason—was that music differed from most of the other arts in having already two modes of creativity. There was that of the composer, which by its nature could be shared by only a very small minority; while the other arose from the necessity of renewing the existence of a musical work, as it were, on every separate occasion (unless mechanically reproduced); this process of performance and interpretation was in itself an act of re-creation, giving deep satisfaction to those who took part in it with voices or instruments. Such a rationalization did not, however, always convince even musicians, many of whom would subscribe to the opinion expressed by R. M. Thackray in his CREATIVE MUSIC IN EDUCATION:

Music in education has for too long been regarded as mainly an interpretative act; the creative aspects of the subject have been either merely dabbled with, or left to the exceptionally gifted.

Creativeness in this more radical sense now having won general (though by no means universal) acceptance as an indispensable part of a sound musical education, it is being explored with enthusiasm in various directions, some purely musical, others leading to a closer association between music and other parts of the curriculum.

Controlled improvisation Most teachers take as their starting-point the kind of controlled improvisation with percussion which is explained and illustrated in the Orff manuals or in material derived from them. Improvisation can range from the imitation of verbal rhythms or a

Partnership in improvisation with restricted note series

Older Juniors engaged in group improvisation, using soprano, alto and bass xylophones, cello, and tabor

single note repeated as an *ostinato* to the elaboration of chord series and the building of larger musical structures by the introduction of contrasting ideas. Pre-existing melodic material, such as folk-song, may be taken as a basis, and some find it helpful to follow both Orff and Kodály in restricting the range of sounds, in the earlier stages, to the pentatonic scales—as can readily be done by removing some of the bars of the pitched percussion instruments and eliminating semitones. Others encourage the freer exploration of sounds of every kind, whether 'musical', in the older sense, or otherwise, thus representing as it were the avant-garde movement in music education. Whispers, shouts, conventional instruments used in unorthodox ways, note-clusters, and electronic manipulations are but a few examples of the material that may thus be extracted from the total universe of sound.

An interesting example of the kind of discovery that may come about through the use of Orff-type instruments was observed in a fourth-year junior class. These children had been accustomed to improvising mainly on a pentatonic basis, and sometimes laid out their instruments to produce the scale of D pentatonic:

But they wanted to invent a piece of 'Chinese' music to fit into a project, and after experiment among themselves agreed to substitute B flat bars for B naturals, giving a scale which they described as 'spooky' (their vocabulary did not extend to 'exotic') and which, unlike the normal pentatonic scales, contains a semitone:

The class was intrigued and stimulated by this novel pattern of intervals, and evolved an exciting piece from their discovery. Experienced adult musicians would be unlikely to arrive at such a scale except, like Bartók, by way of folk-music study, like Busoni by theoretical formulation, or by imitation of non-European melodic patterns such as the Indian *ragas*.

What may be termed the functional and impressionistic approaches to creative work make use of external stimuli to the musical imagination. An evocative subject is chosen—the sea, night, fire, witchcraft—or a poem or prose extract is read, or a picture is shown, and a responsive study in sound is built up from the children's experiments and from suggestions derived from the sound-producing media they have available. Not only the various branches of literature—poems, stories, descriptions, dramatizations—are thus laid under contribution, but also historical and legendary matter taken from other subject areas. Religious education has been particularly fertile in providing stories and situations which evoke, as they have throughout the Christian era, expressive response through vocal and instrumental music. It is therefore not surprising that some of our recorded examples of children's work are taken from this source.

One lesson to be learnt from the specimens given is that no two primary schools are exactly alike in the materials they use for creative music-making, in the ways in which they start and continue it, and in the relative proportions of time they give to creative and to more formal or traditional music education through performance—a matter to which it will be necessary to return later.

Side 1, band 1 of the record demonstrates a purely musical approach, and is instructive as showing what kind of result may be expected in a comparatively short time. This school, in a new housing area on the edge of a northern town, already had quite a rich background of choral singing and listening, but had embarked on creative methods only after the arrival of a new member of staff some three months before the recording was made. The teacher referred to, though not a specialist musician, had become interested in improvisation through his enthusiasm for jazz, and in compositional techniques through the pieces of Bartók's MIKROKOSMOS, each of which is based on some technical or impressionistic idea. The influence of Bartók is reflected in some of the children's work: the first two pieces are entitled respectively 'in the dorian mode' and 'in the mixolydian mode', the children having been introduced to these types of scale and encouraged to improvise freely within their framework. The two pieces that follow, *Soldiers* and *Runaway Horse*, show rhythmic features of considerable subtlety and would be difficult for an adult musician to write down. These children in fact make no use of notation, but their musical imagery and memory appear to develop rapidly and they are able to reproduce, individually or in groups

432

of two to six, lengthy improvised pieces as often as required. Their grasp of musical form is well developed, and they also show a facility, observable in junior children elsewhere, in transferring the technique of one instrument to another; thus two children accustomed to improvising duets on a single xylophone will effectively do the same thing on a piano keyboard, though neither child has had any formal piano tuition.

The second group of examples (side 2, band 1) was recorded in another junior school, situated in a rural area with some urban development. The work was carried out under the guidance of a class teacher who disclaimed any specialist musical qualifications, though she had taken a year's course in creative music-making at an Institute of Education. These children had been working on creative lines for about two years, a longer period than those in the previous examples, and non-musical impressionistic stimuli play a greater part in their improvisations. The main reason for this is that the school curriculum is fully integrated, with environmental studies as the main source of material and motivation for writing, art and craft, drama, movement, and music.[1] All the expressive and creative arts are closely inter-related, a favourite pattern of expression being the mosaic or sequence in which passages of the children's own verse or prose are interspersed with movement and improvised music. In this school also, improvisation is carried on without the aid of notation (though notation is taught in connexion with other musical activities), and as many as thirty children are able to reproduce an elaborate improvised piece lasting up to two minutes, without a conductor, without notes, and with scarcely a glance at one another, making their entries and dropping out of the ensemble with the split-second timing of expert orchestral musicians. This result is achieved through the growth of an instinctive sense of form which owes nothing to a knowledge of note-durations, rests, phrase-marks, staves and other sup-

[1] See, in this series, ENVIRONMENTAL STUDIES by Melville Harris

433

posed essentials of accurate ensemble performance, nor to the kind of analytical approach to musical form that is normally considered to belong to comparatively advanced stages of executant musicianship. To an adult observer both the appearance and the sound of one of these improvising groups in action is strongly reminiscent of the Indonesian *gamelan*, although enquiry reveals that the comparison would be meaningless to the children and has certainly not occurred to the teaching staff. There seems no doubt, however, that one of the major discoveries arising from the development of creative music in the primary school is that most children have this innate capacity to apprehend rhythmic shape, shown not only in a feeling for underlying pulsation and the perception of rhythmical groupings, but also in the ability to hold in the memory, and reproduce, long and complex structures existing only in time. This revelation alone should revolutionize much traditional thinking about musical appreciation, performance, and creativeness, and lead to further and deeper studies of such subjects as musical memory.

The three examples of work contributed by this school are imaginatively titled movements: *Summer Gaiety*, which is pentatonic and presents interesting structural features, *The Beach*, which combines most attractively a slow melody on individual glockenspiels with wave-like xylophone glissandi and other water-effects produced by maracas, and *The Witch Doctor*, an experiment in the macabre, based on arpeggio figures with *ostinato* rhythms for cymbals, glockenspiels and xylophones.

Two more elaborate examples of group work, one from an infant school and the other from a junior school, illustrates the use of Old Testament stories. The Noah's Ark story (side 1, band 2) is treated by infants aged six and seven.[1] The children knew nothing of Britten's NOYES FLUDDE, but they had among their books the vigorous paraphrase in verse and coloured drawings, NOAH'S JOURNEY, by George Macbeth and Margaret Gordon. With this as

[1] A fuller account of the origin and development of this project is given in GROWING UP WITH MUSIC by Mary Pape

a point of departure they worked out their own ideas in spoken and written language, in movement, and in music and sound effects. Different groups undertook various stages of the drama, and the final sequence was put together with the teacher's help where necessary. The children set the scene by reading from their own versions of the story, and the ark-building team then goes into operation. In this industrial area, the children know there has to be a tea-break, which is duly signalled by a hooter. When the ark is finished the people and animals go aboard. Here the range of material and style drawn upon is interesting: Mr and Mrs Noah enter to an improvised cannon,[1] the rabbits to an American folk song that happened to be in the children's repertory, the birds to an ensemble of tuned percussion, whistles and chirps, and the dinosaur (a creature with which the children were fascinated at this time) to a chanted prose-poem of their own: 'Dinosaur, dinosaur, Bront(i)osaurus, You are too big to go into the ark, You must swim behind: Take hold of the rope.' The storm begins—like Britten's—with drops of rain and swells up with the full volume of xylophones, glockenspiels, metallophones and other percussion. It breaks off suddenly, and one child reads her account of the end of the episode.

Children in a junior school in a mixed residential and commercial area produced a composite version of the story of David and Goliath (record side 2, band 2). Compared with the preceding example a more elaborate technical treatment is to be expected, not only because the children are older but also because their school is outstanding in giving them many forms of musical experience, including choral singing, opportunities for learning orchestral instruments, abundant scope for experiment with classroom instruments, and a great deal of music in conjunction with movement, speech and drama. About eighty of the children, representing one-fifth of the school, study violin, viola, cello, piano and brass under group tuition, and, with the help of the local education authority and the

[1] The excerpt on the record ends at this point

435

Communication of
ideas within an
infant group
parent-teacher association, a remarkable stock of
instruments has been built up. It includes recorders,
violins, cellos, glockenspiels, metallophones, xylophones, chordal dulcimers, melodicas, miniature
timpani, other drums of various sizes, tambourines,
triangles and maracas. The children develop a
notably mature attitude of responsibility and co-
operation in marshalling and using this complex
material. Their command of performing techniques
and their general musical knowledge are also impressive. They can readily name the notes of primary chords in several keys before playing them on
pitched percussion, they can strike sequences of
triads with two beaters held in the right hand and
one in the left, they can improvise spontaneously
and accurately in asymmetrical rhythms like
3+3+2. Their resources, as illustrated in the DAVID
AND GOLIATH example, include dramatic speech and
movement as well as invented choral and instrumental passages. Notation is used more extensively
in this school than in the other junior schools already described, some of the most useful rhythmic
groupings being available on flashcards during the
early stages of building up an improvised piece.

The role of the teacher, clearly defined as director of operations in the traditional choral singing and class-lesson situation, must obviously be very different in relation to creative activities of the kinds described and illustrated. His first task must be to provide the environment, opportunities, and materials which will make such work possible. A good example of such provision is the music corner, now increasingly common in infant schools. Sound-producing media of various kinds, including pitched and unpitched percussion instruments, are placed in the corner, and some schools display simple music-books, or tunes copied out on large sheets of paper. The tape recorder, with special short programmes taken from BBC series, which the children can switch on for themselves, is among the more recent additions to the music corner. An important stage occurs when very young children pass from concentration on their individual experiments, and begin to communicate their musical discoveries to one another. Still later arises the concept of several children working together as a team, as in the Noah episode described above.

The more varied the instruments, the more active and progressive the children's work is likely to be. Musical ideas often arise spontaneously from the nature of the sound-producing media, just as constructive and expressive ideas in the arts and crafts spring from the textures, shapes and colours of materials. But the children need help and advice in obtaining the best results from those materials, and much of the teacher's attention will be directed to demonstrating elementary technical points in the handling of instruments. Correct ways of holding xylophone beaters, of striking a drum in different places, of breathing into a recorder, all have to be demonstrated and practised. Gradual extensions of technique must also be introduced when the teacher sees that the right moment has arrived for the child to make the step forward. Equally important is the teacher's part in building musical vocabulary, by suggesting verbal rhythms that may be translated into musical patterns, by seizing on a child's accidental discovery of a promising melodic progression and showing how it can be carried further, or simply by going round and discussing with the children the work they are engaged on. Another way in which the teacher can help is by constructive criticism bearing upon formal organization in larger musical structures. Thus he may suggest that a musical theme or idea should return later in the piece, that a contrasting theme might be welcome at a particular stage, or that an instrument might drop out for a brief period or another be introduced.

Teachers who have worked on these lines say that one of their greatest difficulties is to know when to offer advice and when to stand back and leave the children to continue without interference. One headmaster confessed that there was sometimes an almost irresistible temptation to grasp the instrument and show the child what he *ought* to do, but he was fully aware that such an action would inhibit any genuinely creative impulse on the child's part. The teacher also has the responsibility of deciding what proportion of the available time should be spent on free work, and what proportion on traditional forms of musical experience

The teacher drops in on an improvising group and offers some technical guidance

like performing and listening to music already in existence. Few would wish to throw overboard the entire legacy of the past and the mature and inspired work of professional composers, in order to confine the children within the limits of their own ideas, however fruitful, and their own technical powers, however rapidly these may be unfolding.

Achieving a balance The view taken by those who have faced this dilemma is that a balance can and should be found between performance and listening on the one hand, and invention and discovery on the other, and that these two aspects are educationally and artistically complementary, each helping and enriching the other. It may be remembered that Carl Orff originally formulated his method of creative improvisation on the assumption that it would be used in the teaching of young people who were already learning instrumental and vocal music in traditional ways and who would continue to do so—with their perceptions and reactions made more alert and vigorous through the kinds of additional experience the SCHULWERK provides. As far as English schools are concerned, there seems little question that the creative approach is most successful where performance and listening are well-established and are continued side by side with improvisatory methods. There is certainly no reason why one aspect of music education should preclude the other.

Children who have been encouraged to experiment with sounds and to exercise their own powers of invention are naturally more likely to take an interest in the aims and work-processes of professional composers, just as the learning of an instrument leads to deeper appreciation of the achievements of the concert artist. Understanding between adult composers and school children has never been stronger in this country than it is at present; not only have works involving the participation of children been produced by almost every composer of note, with Britten and Tippett heading the list, but the amount of music commissioned for schools by local authorities, the broadcasting and television organizations, and other forms of patronage, increases from year to year. One of the happiest features of this trend is the willingness of composers to study their young performers by going into the schools before and during the process of composition, and by attending and sometimes conducting rehearsals and performances. On such occasions the children are able to share with adults an experience of the creative process at its height, and yet to accept it as an extension of their own exploratory and inventive efforts. The reciprocity between classroom creativeness and the work of the professional composer also has the effect of enabling children to assimilate styles and techniques that go far beyond the timid conservatism that was formerly a characteristic of most 'educational music'. No longer need children's music performance be hedged in by safe but dull diatonic melody, protected from all but the mildest dissonances, and guarded by regular time-measures and uniform phrase-lengths. The pioneers of modern music for young people—Bartók and Kodály, Hindemith and Orff, Holst and Britten—have led the way to an emancipation of school music which the younger generations of composers are completing.

Broadcasts and festivals Two valuable agencies for the dissemination of new works may be mentioned at this point. Some reference has already been made to radio and television programmes as sources of fresh materials and ideas for presentation. An outstandingly successful venture of this kind was the miniature television opera, THE MIDNIGHT THIEF, based on a Mexican folk tale. The BBC commissioned Richard Rodney Bennett to write simple but memorable tunes which could be quickly taught by way of the classroom television set and accompanied by the children with home-made percussion. The series culminated in a studio performance combining the basic material with a children's percussion group, and with extra orchestral parts for a small professional ensemble, but many less ambitious performances also took place in schools up and down the country, each with its local individuality. THE MIDNIGHT THIEF has had several successors on radio and television, and the BBC has done further service to the schools by arranging series of television programmes to demonstrate actual classroom practice in teaching music by new methods.

Another means of bringing fresh ideas into the schools is the area festival, which has a history going back to the early years of the century but is now undergoing a transformation. From being an occasion when schools met to sing—or less often play—short items before an adjudicator or director who gave his comments on the performance orally or in writing, the schools music festival is now tending to become a forum for large-scale enterprises (often again concerned with a commissioned work) in which many children can take part, involving music, drama and dancing, and with decor produced from the schools' own resources in art and craft. In this way, also, a challenge can be given to the schools of a wide area in an atmosphere of exciting adventure.

4 Future developments

The future development of music education in England depends, as doubtless it does in all other countries, on continuity of skilful, sympathetic and imaginative leadership. While assuming, as we have throughout this account, that most teachers are, like most children, potentially responsive to music, we must accept also that only a minority overflow naturally with music to an extent that communicates itself irresistibly to others. Nor can the teaching of music be learned by reading or by attending lectures. Only by engaging actively and pleasurably in musical activities, whether 'performing' or 'creative', can the teacher become equipped with an understanding of the art and with confidence in sharing it with children. This inescapable fact was well expressed a century ago by John Hullah, at that time chief inspector of music in schools. In one of his official reports he wrote:

A skilful teacher may, and often does, give a clever and useful lesson on something with which yesterday he was comparatively unacquainted. . . But the most elementary singing lesson involves, on the part of him who gives it, a sympathy of eye and ear that can be attained only by long cultivation, can be made available only when it has become part of his being; and when thus attained and made available, can no more be lost or forgotten, than the power of speaking or understanding his native tongue.

Hullah's advice to the teacher of class-singing was to become a member of one of the choral societies that then abounded in every town and village; very many followed his advice, and passed on to their classes the experience they had themselves enjoyed as practising amateur musicians. Modern methods of teaching music similarly call for modes of initial and in-service training through which teachers can become personally involved not only in the performance of music but also in its invention, discovery and creation, using as far as possible the kind of instruments and other material which will form the basis of their teaching.

The colleges of education are laying particular emphasis both on performing skills and on creative enterprise in the music courses they provide at various levels during the three-year initial training. Not only do students offering music as a main subject in these institutions receive every encouragement to extemporize, compose on paper, and try out their original work with the aid of their fellow-students, but in most colleges a 'basic' or 'curriculum' course in music is available to any prospective infant or junior teacher, and the necessarily simple and compressed syllabus usually includes the use of classroom instruments, the invention of rhythmic patterns derived from words, and other means of approach to active music-making. No one imagines, however, that any initial course can of itself equip the teacher with all the knowledge and dynamic needed to carry him through his professional career, especially in a subject like music which requires not only keeping up to date with methods and materials but also the periodic recharging of the teacher's own batteries through direct personal contact with musical performance and creation. This is where the in-service course[1] has an essential part to play. It may take many different forms. It may last only a day or two, perhaps at the weekend, or it may be spread over an entire school year with an evening meeting once a week. It may be organized by an institute of education, by a local authority, by a publishing house—to mention but a few of the possible sources from which help may be forthcoming. It will generally include lectures and demonstrations and—which are even more valued—opportunities for the

[1]See, in this series, EDUCATING TEACHERS by Molly Brearley and Nora Goddard, Bill Browse and Tony Kallet

443

practising teachers attending to sample new material through active participation. In such a setting, ideas for creative group-work can be tried out first by the teachers themselves, then taken back to their schools for testing under classroom conditions, and reassessed in the light of this experience at a subsequent stage of the in-service course. This process is one that teachers, particularly those without specialist musical knowledge, appear to find personally reassuring and professionally stimulating. It also has the advantage that it can be renewed from time to time throughout the teacher's career, so that he can keep abreast both of educational developments and of stylistic changes in the art of music itself.

Booklist

Addison, Richard CHILDREN MAKE MUSIC (with record in pocket) Holmes McDougall, Edinburgh 1967; Available in the USA through Marlin Brinser, New Jersey

ANNUAL PROGRAMME FOR PRIMARY SCHOOLS Radio and Television for Children of 5–13, BBC, London (published annually)

Bentley, Arnold AURAL FOUNDATIONS OF MUSIC READING Novello, London 1966; Available in the USA through Belwin Mills Publishing Corp., New York

Blocksidge, Kathleen MAKING MUSICAL APPARATUS AND INSTRUMENTS Nursery School Association of Great Britain and Northern Ireland, 89 Stamford Street, London S.E.1

Collins, Gertrude VIOLIN TEACHING IN CLASS OUP, London and New York 1962

CREATIVE MUSIC IN SCHOOLS Reports on Education No. 63 April 1970. Free, from Department of Education and Science, London

Dinn, Freda THE RECORDER IN SCHOOL Schott, London 1965; Available in the USA through Belwin Mills Publishing Corp., New York

Dobbs, J. P. B. THE SLOW LEARNER AND MUSIC OUP, London and New York 1966

Driver, Ann MUSIC AND MOVEMENT OUP, London and New York 1936

Hall, Doreen ORFF-SCHULWERK: TEACHER'S MANUAL Schott, Mainz 1960; Available in the USA through Belwin Mills Publishing Corp., New York

Keller, Wilhelm EINFÜHRUNG IN 'MUSIK FÜR KINDER' (Orff-Schulwerk) Schott, Mainz 1963; Available in the USA through Belwin Mills Publishing Corp., New York

Mellers, Wilfrid THE RESOURCES OF MUSIC Cambridge University Press, London and New York 1969

MONOTONES Music Education Research Papers Number 1; Novello, London 1968; Available in the USA through Belwin Mills Publishing Corp., New York

MUSIC IN SCHOOLS (Department of Education and Science) HMSO, London 1969; Available in the USA from HMSO, Pendragon House Inc., 899 Broadway Avenue, Redwood City, California 94063.

Pape, Mary GROWING UP WITH MUSIC (Musical Experiences in the Infant School) OUP, London and New York 1970

Paynter, John & Aston, Peter SOUND AND SILENCE Classroom Projects in Creative Music (Illustrative record available) Cambridge University Press, London and New York 1970

Rainbow Bernarr THE LAND WITHOUT MUSIC (Musical Education in England 1800–1860 and its Continental Antecedents) Novello, London 1967 · Available in the USA through Belwin Mills Publishing Corp., New York

Rainbow, Bernarr (Ed.) HANDBOOK FOR MUSIC TEACHERS Novello, London 1968; Available in the USA through Belwin Mills Publishing Corp., New York

Roberts, Ronald MUSICAL INSTRUMENTS MADE TO BE PLAYED Dryad Press, Leicester 1965; Available in the USA through Dryad Press, New Jersey.

Sándor, Frigyes (Ed.) MUSICAL EDUCATION IN HUNGARY Barrie and Rockliffe, London 1966; Boosey & Hawkes, New York

Szabó, Helga THE KODALY CONCEPT OF MUSIC EDUCATION (Textbook with three LP records); Boosey & Hawkes, London and New York 1969

Thackray, R. M. CREATIVE MUSIC IN EDUCATION Novello, London 1965; Available in the USA through Belwin Mills Publishing Corp., New York

Winters, Geoffrey MUSICAL INSTRUMENTS IN THE CLASSROOM Longman, London 1967

See also AN INTRODUCTION, DRAMA, ENVIRONMENTAL STUDIES, SPACE, TIME AND GROUPING, THE TEACHER'S ROLE, THE PUPIL'S DAY, AN INFANT SCHOOL in this series.

Glossary

For a fuller understanding of some terms that are briefly defined in the following list, the reader is referred to one or more books in this series.

Cooperative teaching
Team teaching. An example of cooperative teaching is described in detail in A RURAL SCHOOL.

Eleven plus (11+)
Term used to cover the procedures and techniques (eg, attainment and/or intelligence tests, and teachers' reports) used by local education authorities mainly to select pupils for grammar schools at the age of 11; formerly in universal use, now decreasingly, and only in areas where selection continues. A view of the eleven plus is given in AN INTRODUCTION by Joseph Featherstone.

Family grouping
See **Vertical grouping**.

Grammar school
Academic High School.

Half-term
Mid-semester (see also **Term**).

Hall
Multi-purpose space, large enough to hold the whole school (staff and pupils). Usually a large room, often combining the functions of dining hall, auditorium and gymnasium.

Headteacher
Principal. For an examination of the headteacher's work, and the differences between headteachers and US principals, see THE HEADTEACHER'S ROLE and THE GOVERNMENT OF EDUCATION.

Health visitor
Qualified nurse with special training who is employed by the local education authority to visit schools to check on the children's health.

Her Majesty's Inspector (HMI)
Her Majesty's Inspector of Schools. Appointed formally by the Privy Council to advise the Department of Education and Science, and schools, on the practices and standards of education; and to maintain liaison between the DES and local education authorities. See also THE GOVERNMENT OF EDUCATION.

Infant school	School or department for children from five to seven or eight years old.
Integrated day	A school day in which children may pursue various interests or themes, without regard to artificial divisions into time periods. The workings of an integrated day are fully described in A RURAL SCHOOL.
Junior school	School for seven- to eleven- or twelve-year olds.
Local education authority (LEA)	County or county borough council with responsibility for public education in its area. See THE GOVERNMENT OF EDUCATION.
Movement	An activity where the children explore expressive, agile, and games-like situations. This is done through the dynamic use of the body, with spatial orientation as it comes into contact with people and objects.
Primary school	School for children under twelve. It may be an **Infant school** or **Junior school** (*qq.v.*) or a combination of both.
School managers	Members of an appointed managing body of not fewer than six members who are representative of various interests concerned with the school. For a fuller explanation, and information on the powers and responsibilities of school managers, see THE GOVERNMENT OF EDUCATION.
School year	This begins in September and consists of three terms (see **Terms**).
Special classes	Remedial classes.
Standards I-VIII	Grades in the former Elementary Schools (for children from five to fourteen years).
Streaming	Tracking.
Teachers' centre	A centre set up by a local education authority to provide opportunities for curriculum development and associated in-service training for teachers. See EDUCATING TEACHERS.
Term	The English school year is divided into three terms (cf semesters): Autumn (Fall), Spring, and Summer.
Timetable	Schedule.
Tuition	Teaching. (In Britain, the word 'tuition' never has the meaning, 'fees'.)
Vertical grouping	(also called **Family grouping**): Form of grouping, found mainly in infant schools, in which the full age range for which the school provides may be represented in each class. See also SPACE, TIME AND GROUPING.